Scream Queens & Girl Ghouls
VS 5408

Madmen & Gore Gimmicks
VS 5409

Aliens & Sorcerers
VS 5410

The Walking Dead
VS 5411

Mad Scientists & Mad Monsters
VS 5412

Giants & Dinosaurs
VS 5413

VIDEOTAPES FROM HELL

A VISUAL HISTORY OF CULT, COLLECTIBLE, AND CRAZY VIDEO COVERS

VIDEOTAPES FROM HELL

EDITED BY STEPHEN JONES

FOREWORD BY JOE DANTE

APPLAUSE
THEATRE & CINEMA BOOKS

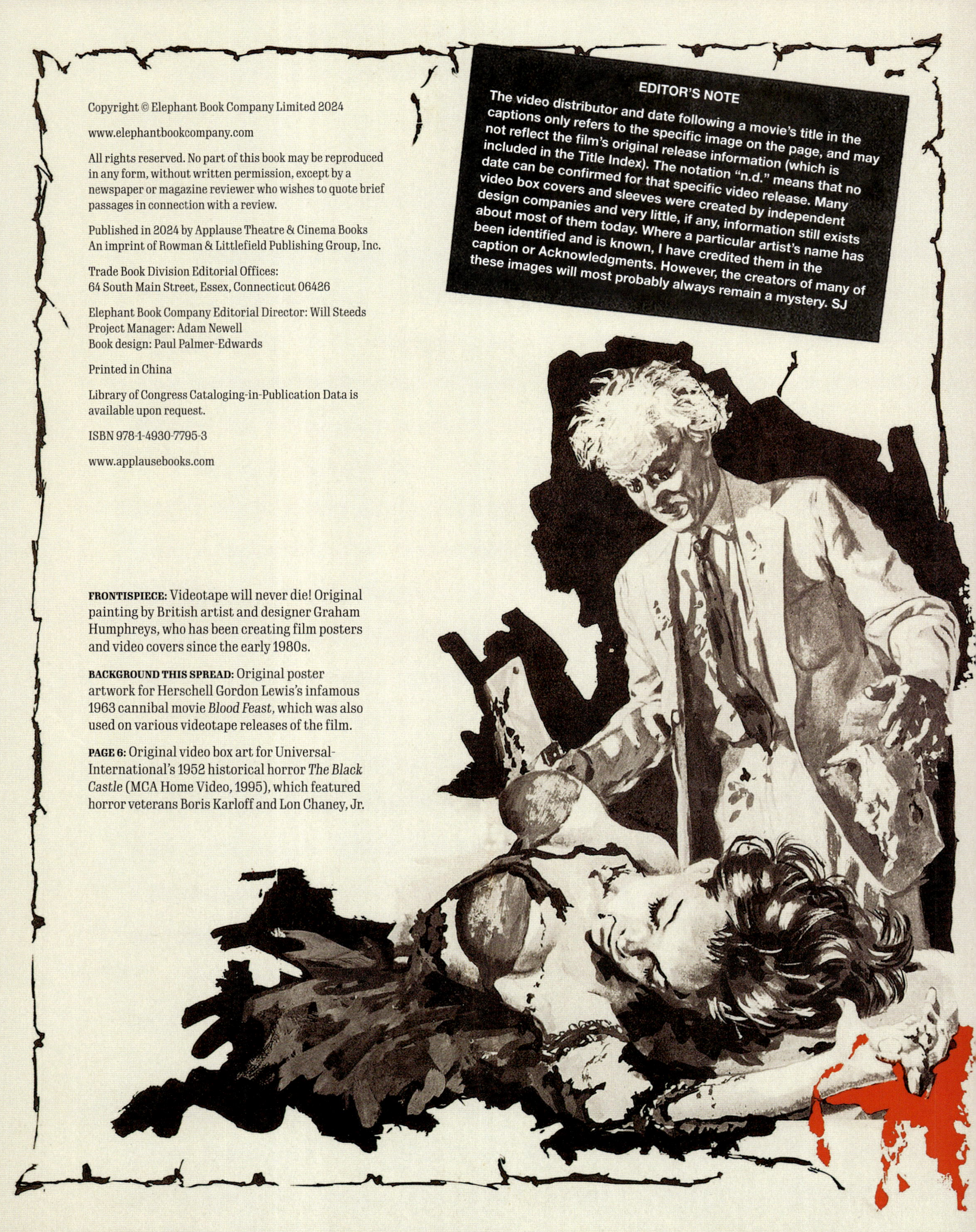

www.elephantbookcompany.com

Published in 2024 by Applause Theatre & Cinema Books
An imprint of Rowman & Littlefield Publishing Group, Inc.

Trade Book Division Editorial Offices:
64 South Main Street, Essex, Connecticut 06426

Elephant Book Company Editorial Director: Will Steeds
Project Manager: Adam Newell
Book design: Paul Palmer-Edwards

Printed in China

Library of Congress Cataloging-in-Publication Data is available upon request.

ISBN 978-1-4930-7795-3

www.applausebooks.com

EDITOR'S NOTE

The video distributor and date following a movie's title in the captions only refers to the specific image on the page, and may not reflect the film's original release information (which is included in the Title Index). The notation "n.d." means that no date can be confirmed for that specific video release. Many video box covers and sleeves were created by independent design companies and very little, if any, information still exists about most of them today. Where a particular artist's name has been identified and is known, I have credited them in the caption or Acknowledgments. However, the creators of many of these images will most probably always remain a mystery. SJ

FRONTISPIECE: Videotape will never die! Original painting by British artist and designer Graham Humphreys, who has been creating film posters and video covers since the early 1980s.

BACKGROUND THIS SPREAD: Original poster artwork for Herschell Gordon Lewis's infamous 1963 cannibal movie *Blood Feast*, which was also used on various videotape releases of the film.

PAGE 6: Original video box art for Universal-International's 1952 historical horror *The Black Castle* (MCA Home Video, 1995), which featured horror veterans Boris Karloff and Lon Chaney, Jr.

CONTENTS

VIDEO MEMORIES CONTRIBUTORS

WRITERS, ARTISTS, ACTORS, AND FILMMAKERS SHARE SOME PERSONAL MEMORIES AND STORIES OF THE GOLDEN AGE OF HOME VIDEO, FROM THE LATE 1970s THROUGH TO THE END OF THE 1990s . . .

PETER ATKINS

STEPHEN R. BISSETTE

RAMSEY CAMPBELL

LUIGI COZZI

BARRY FORSHAW

SIR CHRISTOPHER FRAYLING

MICK GARRIS

GRAHAM HUMPHREYS

C. COURTNEY JOYNER

STEPHEN KING

TIM LUCAS

R.C. MATHESON

DAVID McGILLIVRAY

LISA MORTON

KIM NEWMAN

DAVID J. SCHOW

ADAM SIMON

BRINKE STEVENS

FOREWORD

MOVIES IN YOUR LIVING ROOM!

JOE DANTE

I'VE BEEN HOSTING a podcast with screenwriter Josh Olson for the past few years called *The Movies That Made Me*, where we ask guests which films influenced their decision to get into the movie business, and I've been surprised how many of them point to their first exposure to their favorites not in a theater, or even broadcast television, but on VHS! (Video Home System, for those who've forgotten.)

People tend to forget how basically inaccessible most films were before the advent of home video. Waiting for your favorites to show up on your local TV stations, cut-up and sandwiched between commercials, was pretty frustrating. My own solution was to start collecting black market 16mm prints, mostly discarded by TV stations, prisons, and rental houses, but the powers-that-were looked askance at that practice, which they considered piracy, and many collectors were forced underground.

The tune changed once the studios realized they could monetize the public's need for old and recent movies in their own homes and began licensing their product for home rental on videotape. You could even buy your own cassette for a hundred bucks or so, which was what they were charging the mom-and-pop rental stores. But as demand surged, the prices came down and home video really took off—enterprising producers began actually making films for the video market. Eventually a trip to the video store became part of every family's routine, and once it became possible to record off the TV (those cheapo Extended Play and Super Long Play tapes could hold up to eight hours of programming) people started their own movie collections. Of course the quality suffered and the noisy tracking was all over the place, but hey—you had Movies in Your Living Room!

Films from the pre-1954 era looked okay on the boxy 4 x 3 TV screens of the day, but when CinemaScope and other wide-screen processes came along they had to be severely cropped to fit the small screen, which led to the dreaded pan and scan. An anonymous technician with no connection to the material made visual editing decisions that really belonged with the director of photography and director. The dictum seemed to be, whoever's talking should be onscreen, even if they're just an out-of-focus foreground head. Add to this the lack of resolution that came with blowing up the image and you've got a very unsatisfactory impression of what was intended. So for decades TV viewers who saw

ABOVE: After cutting trailers for Roger Corman's New World Pictures, Joe Dante made his solo directing debut in 1978 with *Piranha* (Concorde-New Horizons, 2000). Scripted by John Sayles, it was Corman's low-budget answer to Steven Spielberg's *Jaws* (1975). When Universal Pictures considered blocking the release of the movie, Spielberg stepped in and convinced them not to.

"IF YOU SAW *THE HOWLING* OR THE HIGHLY RATED 'IT'S A GOOD LIFE' CHAPTER OF *TWILIGHT ZONE—THE MOVIE*, YOU ALREADY HAVE A GOOD IDEA OF DIRECTOR JOE DANTE'S DELIRIOUS VISUAL MAGIC. IN A DANTE MOVIE, THINGS GO WRONG."

GREMLINS **VIDEO BOX BLURB (1985)**

wide-screen epics like *Chinatown* (1974) and *Jaws* (1975) on videotape thought they'd seen the movie!

Personally, although I love the format, I resisted shooting any of my own projects in 'Scope for years simply because I knew they'd be seen by many more people on TV than in theaters. When *Innerspace* (1987) came out on VHS, I was proud to be able to say that I talked the distributor into releasing it in letterbox format, showing the whole 1:85 picture area. Around this time the Directors Guild of America and Turner Classic Movies began an educational campaign to explain to viewers that they were getting more picture, not less, with black bars on the top and bottom of the screen. The welcome advent of wide-screen 16 x 9 TV monitors eventually obviated this issue.

But another aspect of video that gets overlooked is how home exposure transformed box-office disappointments into popular, even beloved successes, and made the 1980s as iconic to a new generation as the '50s was to mine. Movies that stayed only a week or so at the local theater had no such limits on the video store shelf. And these cassettes were passed on from viewer to viewer, raising the number of eyeballs for any given title exponentially. Any number of filmmakers whose careers were limited by the grosses of their more unappreciated subjects were suddenly deemed bankable due to the belated popularity of their formerly dismissed works.

And perhaps the most telling benefit of video was that torrent of movies old and new, domestic and foreign, which were made accessible to audiences starved for variety. It's no accident that Quentin Tarantino and Roger Avary's *The Video Archives Podcast*, celebrating their formative years as video store clerks, has hit a nerve with the burgeoning circle of VHS devotees.

Videotapes covered every genre, and if you couldn't find what you were looking for from the major suppliers, there were always boutique labels like Sinister Cinema, where dedicated film lovers still transfer obscurities from 35mm and 16mm prints. I dare anyone to check out their catalog and not find some unknown rarity that looks awfully tempting . . .

Personally, I prefer DVD and Blu-ray. As a filmmaker I'm always looking for the best possible presentation, and technically VHS has been surpassed for audio and visual clarity by the latest technology. But there's no denying that it was videotape that opened up a whole new world of movies to all of us.

For this, it deserves a special place in the pantheon of film history.

ABOVE: Having originally planned to be a cartoonist, Joe Dante brought that same sensibility to his 1984 comedy-horror movie *Gremlins* (Warner Bros. Home Video, 1985) when asked to direct by executive producer Steven Spielberg. It was a huge commercial success, and Dante followed it up with an even more maniacal sequel, *Gremlins 2: The New Batch* (1990).

THEY'RE COMING... FROM OUTER SPACE!

To bring you the ULTIMATE Science-Fiction Classic!

$54.95 each
plus $1.50 shipping. Visa and MasterCard accepted. California residents add 6% sales tax

If you like your video cassettes slighty cosmic, you'll love the latest addition to our catalog of super science-fiction, horror and fantasy films: the *original* 1956 version of INVASION OF THE BODY SNATCHERS!

Who can forget this classic chiller about a weird form of alien plant life that descends upon a small California town, murdering then replacing the townsfolk while they sleep with emotionless duplicates that emerge from giant seed pods!

It's enough to make the greenest bug-eyed monster pale with fright!

And speaking of bug-eyed monsters, don't forget that we have one of the largest selections of fantastic films available. Everything from the original KING KONG (and his son) to THE THING to CAT PEOPLE. And all are manufactured to our strict quality standards, assuring you of the finest quality available on these monster masterpieces!

To order your cassette of the original INVASION OF THE BODY SNATCHERS, contact your local Nostalgia Merchant retailer or call toll free (800) 421-4495.

We guarantee you won't fall asleep watching this one!

THE NOSTALGIA MERCHANT
6255 SUNSET BOULEVARD, SUITE 1019
HOLLYWOOD, CALIFORNIA 90028

CONTACT YOUR LOCAL NOSTALGIA MERCHANT RETAILER FOR THESE OUTSTANDING SCIENCE-FICTION FILMS.

KING KONG
105 minutes – B&W
starring Fay Wray, Bruce Cabot and Robert Armstrong

SON OF KONG
70 minutes – B&W – starring Robert Armstrong and Helen Mack.

THE LEOPARD MAN
66 minutes – B&W – starring Dennis O'Keefe and Margo

THE BODY SNATCHER
77 minutes – B&W – starring Boris Karloff and Bela Lugosi

AND NOW THE SCREAMING STARTS
87 minutes – Color
starring Peter Cushing, Herbert Lom and Patrick Magee

THE THING
80 minutes – B&W
starring Kenneth Tobey, Margaret Sheriden and James Arness.

CAT PEOPLE
75 minutes – B&W
starring Simone Simon, Kent Smith and Tom Conway.

CURSE OF THE CAT PEOPLE
70 minutes – B&W
starring Simone Simon, Kent Smith and Jane Randolph

ASYLUM
100 minutes – Color
starring Peter Cushing, Herbert Lom and Britt Ekland

ONE MILLION, BC
80 minutes – B&W
starring Victor Mature, Carole Landis and Lon Chaney, Jr.

MIGHTY JOE YOUNG
94 minutes – B&W
starring Terry Moore, Ben Johnson and Robert Armstrong.

THE VAULT OF HORROR
86 minutes – Color
starring Terry-Thomas, Curt Jurgens and Glynis Johns.

SINBAD THE SAILOR
117 minutes – Color
starring Douglas Fairbanks Jr., Maureen O'Hara and Anthony Quinn

I WALKED WITH A ZOMBIE
70 minutes – B&W
starring James Ellison, Frances Dee and Tom Conway.

BEDLAM
79 minutes – B&W
starring Boris Karloff, Anna Lee and Richard Fraser.

ISLE OF THE DEAD
72 minutes – B&W
starring Boris Karloff, Ellen Drew and Marc Cramer.

THE BEAST MUST DIE
93minutes – Color
starring Peter Cushing, Calvin Lockhart and Anton Diffring

ONLY $54.95 EACH. TO PLACE YOUR ORDER DIRECT CALL TOLL FREE (800) 421-4495

INTRODUCTION
BE KIND, REWIND
STEPHEN JONES

"VIDEOTAPES ARE ONE OF THE MOST DURABLE THINGS THAT WE'VE EVER CREATED TO STORE A MOVIE IN."
QUENTIN TARANTINO

IT IS HARD to imagine today, but at one time in the not-too-distant past, unless you were a specialist collector of 35mm and 16mm prints with deep pockets, it was almost impossible to actually own a copy of a movie that you could watch in the comfort of your own home.

As early as the 1900s, film distributors such as America's The Edison Manufacturing Company and France's Pathé had already recognized that there might be a lucrative market in the viewing of films in the home. Although they began selling projectors for this purpose, the exorbitant cost of producing release prints meant that the owners of these projectors invariably rented their films through the mail from the equipment manufacturer.

Unfortunately, neither enterprise was a success, and by the First World War this early experiment in home viewing was over.

As a result, for the next few decades, most feature films were basically inaccessible to the public after their initial run, unless they happened to be rereleased at a later date in revival theaters through distribution companies such as Realart Pictures and Favorite Films.

Although some motion pictures—usually low budget and independently produced ones—had been shown on television since the 1940s in many of the larger metropolitan areas, in those days very few people actually owned a television receiver to view them on. It was as a result of the boom in the market during the 1950s—when the falling cost of a TV set meant that they were finally within the grasp of ordinary working families—that people could eventually start watching feature films on a screen in their own homes.

Of course, these movies were broadcast live by the television network—there was no way of recording or keeping them—and so if you missed a film at the time of its initial broadcast, you would have to wait until it was shown again.

In 1923, Eastman Kodak had invented 16mm film—which, as the name implies, was half the gauge of the more bulky 35mm that was used in movie theaters—and by the 1950s and '60s this made the collection and preservation of films by private collectors much more likely, although they still needed a projector and a screen to show them on.

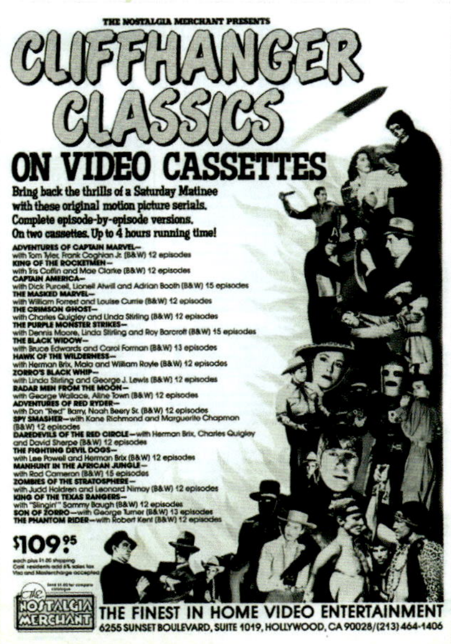

OPPOSITE PAGE: 1981 advertisement from California's The Nostalgia Merchant, a division of Home Media Entertainment, to buy its science fiction and horror videos through the mail for $54.95 each. Founded in 1977 by record producer Snuff Garrett, the label specialized in selling videos of vintage movies, including the original *King Kong* (1933) and various Val Lewton titles.

ABOVE: Advertisement for The Nostalgia Merchant's "Cliffhanger Classics" series on videocassette. They released many classic serials from Republic Pictures in full-length versions spread over two cassettes and packaged in a cardboard slipcase at a mail-order price of $109.95 per title.

Amex pioneered the first commercial videotape recording system in 1956. A reel-to-reel magnetic tape used for storing and retrieving analog or digital sound and vision, earlier attempts had resulted in a grainy or blurred image, while the equipment to record and playback the fourteen-inch reels of two-inch tape was, by necessity, physically bulky.

Though there were plans by the electronics division of singer and actor Bing Crosby's production company, Bing Crosby Enterprises, to have a commercial version on the market by 1954, it didn't happen.

Experimentation continued, and by the latter half of the 1950s, television networks such as NBC and CBS began using prerecorded videotape to play out programs to different time zones. Although many "live" television broadcasts had been recorded using the kinescope system (which used a motion picture camera to record directly from a video monitor), most of the early videotape recordings were not preserved because it was cheaper for broadcasters to simply erase what was on the tape and reuse it.

It was again Eastman Kodak who began developing the less expensive 8mm format (half the size again of 16mm) during the Great Depression, and they started marketing it in 1932 for home movie viewing.

It was the development of the videocassette, however, that finally led to a revolution in the home entertainment industry.

Sony had been the first on the market to introduce video players/recorders based around its U-matic technology. These VCR machines were soon followed by a bewildering choice of cassette formats—Sony's own Betamax, Phillips's Video 2000, and JVC's Video Home System (VHS)—which led to what became known as the "videotape format war."

As the prices of both equipment and videocassettes began to fall, Phillips's top-loading format soon fell by the wayside, and for much of the late 1970s and into the '80s, VHS and Betamax competed for supremacy in the home video market.

Although Sony's Beta format actually offered a higher picture resolution, it could only record two hours of material. On the other hand, JVC's VHS tapes ran for twice that long and were cheaper. As a result, this eventually became the standard format among domestic consumers and rental stores.

In what may well be an anecdotal story, it has long been held that the porn industry in America helped hasten the demise of Betamax when it decided to adopt the VHS format for the home viewing of its adults-only product.

Whatever the reason—and it is more likely to be down to the cost disparity—by 1980 sales of Betamax players in the United States had dropped to just a twenty-five percent share of the market and, as sales continued to decline, the format officially lost the "format war" in 1988, when Sony agreed to start using VHS tapes in its machines. Despite that, the format continued to be used in the professional broadcast industry up until 2002, when the last Sony Betamax unit was produced.

Michigan's Magnetic Video Corporation became the first company to release prerecorded motion pictures on Betamax and VHS cassette via direct mail in 1977, after doing a nonexclusive licensing deal with 20th Century Fox to release fifty of the struggling Hollywood studio's movies on video.

TOP: 1951 Realart rerelease poster for Tod Browning's *Dracula*, starring Bela Lugosi, which Universal Pictures opened in the US on Valentine's Day, 1931. Reissued many times over the years (most notably on a double-bill with *Frankenstein* in 1938), it finally came to television in 1957 as part of the original syndicated *Shock Theater* package distributed by Screen Gems.

BOTTOM: When *Dracula* (1931) was released in 8mm format by Castle Films in 1963 for home movie projection, it marked the first time it was possible for most people to own a version of the classic film—albeit a severely truncated, silent version—that they could view whenever they wanted to. 8mm excerpts remained a popular way to watch movies until the advent of home video.

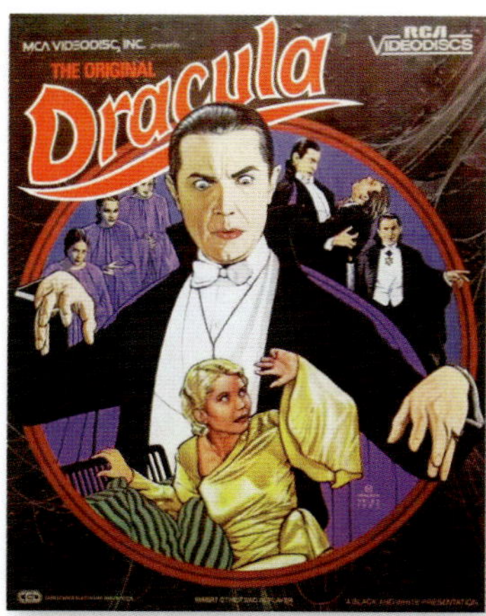

TOP: Walter Velez's cover for the 1983 *Dracula* Videodisc from RCA, which offered much better quality picture and sound than the rival videotape formats. The format never caught on with consumers because of the high cost of optical-disc players and their inability to record off television. By the early 2000s the videodisc system had been almost completely replaced by DVD.

BOTTOM: *Dracula* (MCA Home Video, 1991) was released as part of the Universal Monsters "Classic Collection" on video. The studio had finally caught on to the fact that there was a market for its classic monster movies from the 1930s to the 1950s, and it decided to reissue many of its most famous titles in a redesigned home video line with a new logo and a uniform package design.

In December that same year, George Atkinson, an enterprising businessman from Los Angeles, spent around $3,000 buying one copy in each format of all fifty Fox films offered by Magnetic Video. He then converted his storefront on Wilshire Boulevard into the first professionally managed video rental store, The Video Station, charging $50 for an annual membership that allowed customers to then rent out a videotape for $10 a day.

Despite the threat of lawsuits, Atkinson went on to establish the first major chain of retail video outlets which, at its peak, had more than 600 independently operated "affiliates" throughout the US and Canada. When he died in 2005 at the age of sixty-nine, Atkinson was hailed as "The father of movie video rental."

Bo Andersen, president of the Video Software Dealers Association, paid tribute at the time. "From George Atkinson's innovation, a tremendous industry has developed," he said. "In many respects he was a role model for the determined entrepreneurs who established the video rental business."

In 1980, fewer than three percent of US homes with television sets also owned a VCR. That figure had jumped closer to twenty percent just four years later.

As more and more studios began offering their movies—both old and recent releases—on videocassette, so the number of stores selling and/or renting prerecorded tapes began to expand exponentially. "Mom-and-pop" franchises started to proliferate across North America and beyond, as people decided to open their own video stores and get in on the "gold rush" that was coming.

Perhaps one of the most famous employees to work in a video rental store was future filmmaker Quentin Tarantino (*Reservoir Dogs*, *From Dusk Till Dawn*). In the mid-1980s he was working as a clerk at Video Archives, a video rental store in Manhattan Beach, California, where he met many future collaborators, including screenwriter Roger Avary.

The twenty-two-year-old soon gained a reputation in the neighborhood for being the most reliable person in the store to go to for movie suggestions. "We went to the movies all the time," Tarantino remembered, "we watched movies all the time in the store, we talked about them *ad nauseam*—people came in the store just to talk to us. It was just a lot of fun."

Video Archives closed its doors in 1995, but Tarantino purchased its video inventory and used it to rebuild the store in his home. In 2022, he and Avary launched *The Video Archives Podcast*, looking back at their days working at the store and talking passionately about watching movies on VHS.

David Cook opened the first Blockbuster Video in Dallas, Texas, in 1985. That first store carried 8,000 VHS and 2,000 Beta cassettes and was such a success that Cook built a $6 million warehouse to support future growth in the business.

"I determined there might be a bigger industry there," recalled Cook in a 2003 interview. "The first night we were so mobbed we had to lock the doors to prevent more people from coming in."

Within just a couple of years, it was estimated that Blockbuster was opening a new store every twenty-four hours as they aggressively bought up rival video chains. In early 1987 they had just thirty-five stores, but by the end of the year that figure had risen to 137.

The company's slogan was "Be Kind, Rewind," and when you returned a rental tape one the store clerks would check to see if you had been considerate enough to have done just that for the next customer. The phrase became so well known that it was used as the title of a 2008 comedy movie starring Jack Black.

Having pioneered a revenue-sharing agreement with the studios, Blockbuster would pay very little for a new release up front, and then share the rental fee in a 60/40 split with the distributor. Older releases would be sold off at a discount as "Previously Viewed" or recategorized as a "Blockbuster Favorite" and moved to the back of the store.

Videocassettes of big movies were still relatively expensive to buy at a flat fee of around $65–$100 per title. This resulted in a two-tier pricing system, where rental stores could purchase lower-priced tapes and then rent them out multiple times to make their money back and hopefully turn a profit, while consumers could buy the higher-priced ones to keep.

After a period of time following the initial release, the price would then be reduced for those who had decided to wait before they owned their own copy.

It was not long before independent distributors started popping up in competition to the big studios, invariably offering a more interesting and desirable selection of titles to the discerning *cineaste*. These included such now-forgotten labels as Burbank Video, Concord Video, GoodTimes Entertainment, Media Home Entertainment, The Nostalgia Merchant, Prism Entertainment, Simitar Entertainment, Trans-Atlantic Video, and VidAmerica, to name only a few, most of which did not survive much past the mid-1990s.

Many of these fly-by-night video distributors dealt in cheap-to-produce public domain titles such as *White Zombie* (1932), *The Terror* (1963), or *Night of the Living Dead* (1968). These releases were often graced with execrable box art and misleading liner notes, although many of the companies did not last long due to the stiff competition in the marketplace.

One production company whose business model was partly based around the direct-to-video format was Empire Pictures, which was founded by producer-director Charles Band and launched at the Cannes Film Festival in 1983.

"We *were* the video days," Band later recalled. "I was literally like the second guy on the block in 1976 with the home-video company. This was when no one knew what I was talking about. So, that was truly the pioneer days."

Over the next couple of years the company continued to expand, and at its height was on average releasing two movies a month—one theatrically and the other to home video. Unfortunately, the company overreached itself, and Empire Pictures closed down due to financial problems in 1988, with a number of films that were in production at the time having their releases delayed for several years.

Charles Band remained undeterred, and that same year he founded Full Moon Entertainment, based on much the same business model of

ABOVE: Blockbuster Video kept its costs down by buying in volume and obtaining early access or even exclusive distribution of new titles, stocking multiple copies of the more popular releases. This had the dual effect of cutting down customers' choice while, at the same time, putting many of the independently owned mom-and-pop video stores—which usually offered a much more eclectic selection of titles—out of business due to Blockbuster's dominance of the market.

producing low-budget horror, fantasy, and science fiction movies with a "big-budget" look.

"We were lucky that the label Full Moon had a good reputation," Band remembered. "It was easier for new filmmakers to exist in the direct-to-video world because it was real money. And if you shipped enough units, you had an invoice, you got paid. For a while we were making one movie every four weeks, which was a lot back in the days before technology made it easier."

Despite VHS having successfully seen off its rival Betamax format, new technologies were still being developed for the home video market.

The first recorded historical use of an optical disc was in 1884, and there were further examples in the 1930s of experimental recording devices using light to both record and play back vision and sound signals. An early analog optical disc used for video recording was patented in America in 1961, and a system for recording a digital signal on an optical transparent foil was granted a patent in 1970.

The LaserDisc was an optical disc storage and playback medium. It was initially sold and marketed as MCA DiscoVision and made its debut in December 1978, two years after the introduction of the Betamax and VHS systems. The first LaserDisc to be marketed in the USA was the DiscoVision release of *Jaws* (1975).

Pioneer Electronics purchased a majority stake in the format, while Philips produced the players and MCA created the discs. Although the system offered higher-quality video and audio than its videotape rivals, LaserDiscs never gained widespread popularity due to the high cost of the players and the system's inability to record off the television. By 1998, LaserDisc players were in only two percent of North American households, and just 16.8 million players were sold worldwide.

Far more popular in Asian markets and well received by videophiles, the system failed to catch on with the general public, and the last LaserDisc title to be released in America was Paramount Pictures' *Bringing Out the Dead* (1999) in October 2000.

Although the video boom quickly spread around the world—the first overseas Blockbuster Video store was opened in 1989 in South London after the company bought up the Ritz Video chain for $135 million, and further expansion continued into Canada, Australia, and Japan—all was not well with the video rental market.

Blockbuster had become a multibillion-dollar company. It had continued to expand throughout the 1990s, adding video game rental to its services, and by its peak in 2004 it had more than 9,000 stores around the world, all sporting the iconic blue-and-yellow ITC Machine font logo and shop fittings. However, changes in the market and the competition from video-on-demand and emerging streaming services such as Netflix saw a huge decline in revenue, and in 2010 the company was delisted from the New York Stock Exchange and forced to file for Chapter 11 bankruptcy protection with debts of $900 million.

As corporate support for the brand continued to be withdrawn, coupled with accusations of poor business decisions, so company-owned and franchise stores closed down around the globe until, by 2019, just a single franchise outlet still remained open in Bend, Oregon (the subject of the 2020 documentary *The Last Blockbuster*, from Netflix).

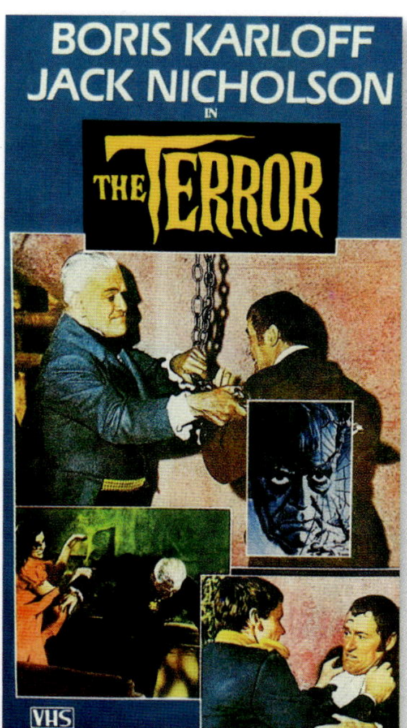

ABOVE: Because a copyright notice was inadvertently left off the credits for both Roger Corman's *The Terror* (GoodTimes Home Video, 1985) and George A. Romero's *Night of the Living Dead* (Video Treasures, 1985), both movies fell into the public domain. As a result, poor-quality copies were distributed by literally hundreds of fly-by-night home video labels over the years. Both films have subsequently been issued in "restored" versions to secure copyright protection.

Following the videotape format war, VHS had remained the dominant system in the home video market throughout the 1980s and '90s, but soon it was being replaced by newer technologies.

The killer blow to the format came in March 1997 with the introduction of the far more reliable and better quality Digital Versatile Disc (DVD). By the early 2000s, DVD had begun to completely replace VHS in the commercial prerecorded movie rental and sale markets. As bargain-basement stores remaindered their stocks for as little as a dollar apiece, so the final major Hollywood picture released on videotape in the US was David Cronenberg's *A History of Violence* (2005) at the very end of 2006.

Ironically, it was around the same time that the DVD format itself began to be replaced by its own high-definition successor, the Blu-ray Disc.

By now VHS and Betamax were almost forgotten video formats except among die-hard collectors, and piles of discarded used tapes could be found languishing on the shelves of thrift stores or being sold off at flea markets at knock-down prices due to the lack of public demand.

Then something unexpected happened. Like the revival of interest in vinyl records, long after those spiral-grooved discs had been replaced by CDs, so the prerecorded VHS tape began to enjoy something of a renaissance.

Many households still owned a video player—even if it was stored away, forgotten, in a dusty corner of an attic or basement—and newer movies such as *Paranormal Activity* (2007) and *The House of the Devil* (2009) had limited promotional distribution on VHS tapes as well as going to DVD and Blu-ray. Soon smaller, independent companies began tentatively putting out selected titles in limited edition releases.

Perhaps more importantly however, just as had happened with comic books a decade before, speculators began to recognize an investment opportunity in old—preferably factory-sealed—VHS tapes. A collectors' market in the rarer releases quickly sprang up, with professionally "slabbed" condition-graded tapes selling online or through auction houses, often for thousands of dollars.

Among some of the most valuable titles, according to an eBay survey conducted in mid-2023, are shrink-wrapped and sealed copies of *Raiders of the Lost Ark* ($12,679), *Back to the Future* ($7,900), *Indiana Jones and the Temple of Doom* ($7,600), *Star Wars* ($7,000), *Jaws* ($5,711) and *Ghostbusters* ($5,500).

Putting aside what some of these tapes could be worth—and, as with comic books, that speculative market could collapse at any time—there is an inherent beauty and historical significance to old videotape boxes that make them just as important to movie historians as the one-sheet posters and lobby cards of previous generations.

The technology may now be outdated, and streaming may largely have put an end to the "collecting" of movies in any format (at least until the next innovation comes along), but this book is a celebration of the art and design of those colorful cardboard slipcases and plastic clamshell boxes that once housed a spool of electronic tape containing a full-length feature film that could be played and replayed over and over again in your own home.

All you had to do was remember to rewind it afterwards.

ABOVE: As happened in the late 1950s, when Universal released its *Shock Theater* packages of old horror movies to American television—which directly inspired an explosion of monster magazines—so the video boom of the 1980s sparked a new generation of publications, both amateur and professional, devoted to covering this new generation of horror and exploitation films. The first issue of *Fangoria* was cover-dated August 1979, and the magazine quickly switched from a fantasy publication to one devoted to the horror genre. Under the initial editorship of Robert "Bob" Martin (1948–2020), and later Anthony Timpone, it grew to dominate the market and expanded into conventions and producing its own video films, until it ceased publication with issue #344 (October, 2015).

OPPOSITE PAGE: 1991 advertisement from British distributor Medusa Pictures to buy copies of its latest direct-to-video releases *Amityville 4: The Evil Escapes* (1989), *Retribution* (1987), and Guild Home Video's *Food of the Gods II* (1989).

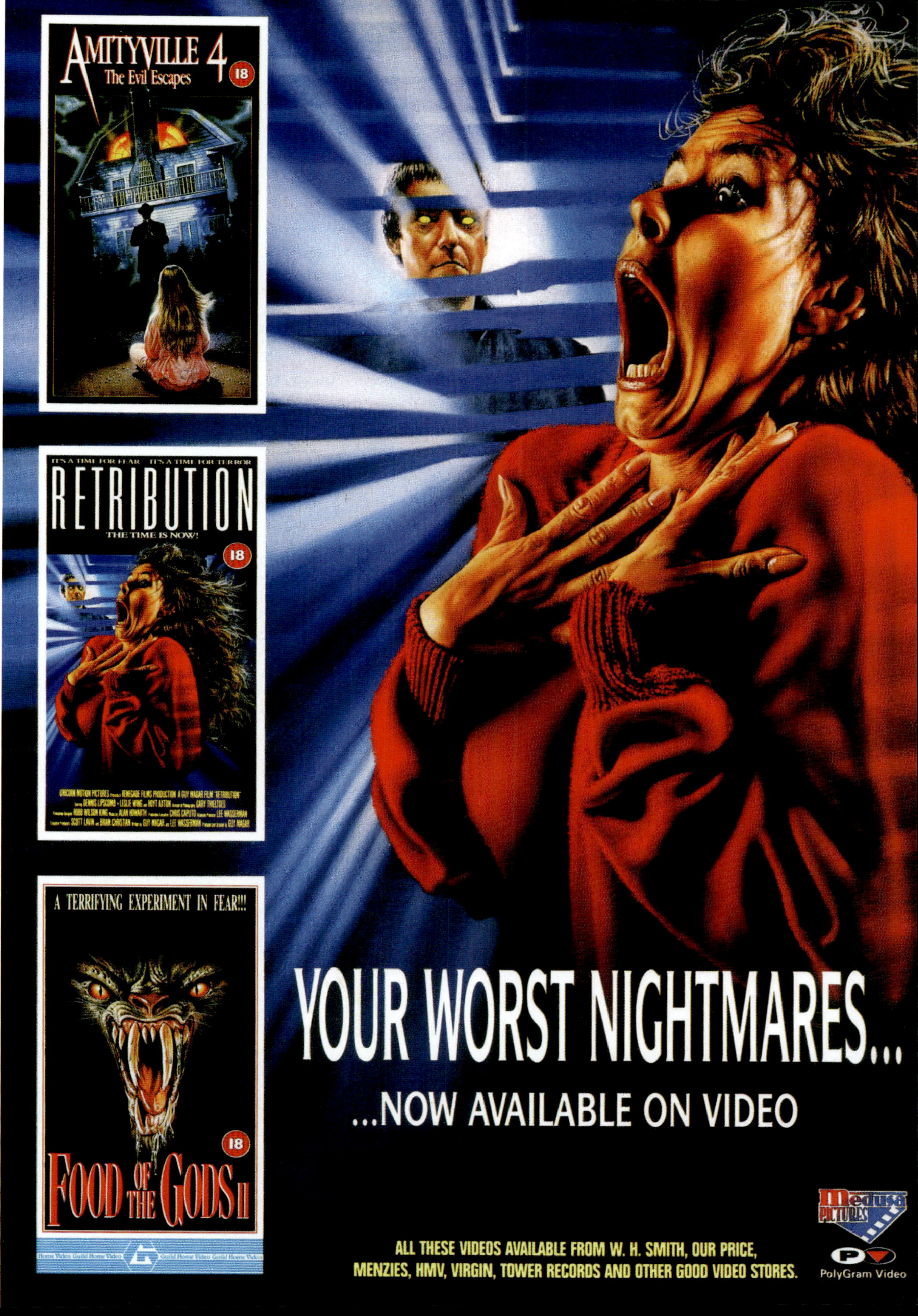

AMITYVILLE 4
The Evil Escapes
18

IT'S A TIME FOR FEAR IT'S A TIME FOR TERROR
RETRIBUTION
THE TIME IS NOW!
18

A TERRIFYING EXPERIMENT IN FEAR!!!
18
FOOD OF THE GODS II
Guild Home Video

Medusa
PICTURES
PolyGram Video

CLASSIC CREEPS

"Our position has never been more secure. Who in hell is going to look at those pygmy screens?"

Louis B. Mayer

"WHEN DISCUSSING THE CORRECT BALANCE OF REALITY AND FANTASY IN FILM, THE LAST TWO FILMS OF RONDO HATTON MUST CERTAINLY BE RECKONED WITH. RONDO HATTON WAS, IF YOU WILL, A REAL-LIFE 'ELEPHANT MAN.'"

THE BRUTE MAN VIDEO BOX BLURB (1982)

Before home video existed, the ways in which you could watch a classic movie were limited. Obviously, if you were lucky, you could see a film when it was first released in theaters, or perhaps later when it might be reissued, often on a double-bill with another older title.

Sixteen mm prints were a less expensive alternative and ideal for use in educational establishments (such as schools and museums) or by film clubs and private collectors. As a result, many movies that had been unavailable for decades had new prints struck in this cheaper format and were revived for audiences that had never seen them before.

As the popularity of television grew in the 1950s, so the studios began releasing syndicated "packages" of movies to the new medium. Probably the best known of these was Screen Gems' *Shock Theater* (a.k.a. *Shock!*), a package of classic pre-1948 horror films from Universal Studios that was released in October 1957 and included such titles as *Dracula* (1931), *Frankenstein* (1931), and *The Mummy* (1932), along with a few mysteries. The following year, a second package, *Son of Shock*, featured twenty films from both Universal and Columbia Pictures.

For many young horror fans, these screenings provided their first viewing of these movies, rekindling popular interest in the classic horror films and their stars, and also leading directly to the launching of Forrest J Ackerman's seminal *Famous Monsters of Filmland* magazine in early 1958.

By the early 1960s, companies such as Castle Films were offering "cut down" 8mm reels of feature films that could be projected in your own home. These 100-foot reels only ran for around ten minutes and were invariably silent and in black and white. It wasn't until 1965, and the introduction of the Super 8 format, that more titles were issued in color and with a magnetic soundtrack.

However, it was the development and marketing of videocassettes in the 1980s that led to a revolution in the home entertainment industry, as many of these classic films could finally be viewed again and reassessed in their full versions. When prices came down and the choice of titles dramatically increased, it became possible for anybody to not only acquire their own copy of a major motion picture for the first time, but also to gain access to many rediscovered rarities that had long been considered "lost" or kept out of circulation.

PREVIOUS SPREAD: *Frankenstein* (Dir: James Whale, 1931).

THIS PAGE: *The Brute Man* (Dir: Jean Yarbrough, 1946).

TOP LEFT: Believed "lost" until the late 1960s, this home video release of Paramount's 1931 version of *Dr. Jekyll and Mr. Hyde* (MGM/ UA Home Video-Turner Entertainment, 1989) restored seventeen minutes of previously censored material that was removed for a 1935 reissue. A critical and commercial success upon its initial release, Fredric March won an Oscar for his starring roles.

TOP RIGHT: Filmed at night on the same sets as Universal's better-known 1931 version and believed lost for many years, an incomplete print of the Spanish-language version of *Drácula* (MCA Universal, 1992) made its video debut as part of the "Universal Monsters: The Classic Collection." The box art depicted Carlos Villarías's hot-blooded Count bending over Lupita Tovar's heroine.

BOTTOM LEFT: Filmed in the early two-color Technicolor process, Michael Curtiz's *Mystery of the Wax Museum* (MGM/UA Home Video, 1987) was rediscovered in a long-lost print by the American Film Institute, and its videocassette debut marked the first time home viewers had an opportunity to see the movie in color since its original release through Warner Bros. in 1933.

BOTTOM RIGHT: Thought lost for many years until film historian William K. Everson located a battered, subtitled print in Czechoslovakia in the late 1960s, later home video releases of the 1933 British movie *The Ghoul* (Al Taylor Company/ Walterscheid Productions, 1990) were taken from a 35mm nitrate camera negative discovered in 1980 in a forgotten film vault at Shepperton Studios.

TOP LEFT: During the 1980s and '90s many movies with copyright that had lapsed (or never existed) were snapped up by numerous fly-by-night videotape distributors, in prints of varying quality, length, and speed. One such title to regularly receive this treatment was Robert Wiene's 1920 example of German Expressionism, *The Cabinet of Dr. Caligari* (Goodtimes Home Video, 1990).

TOP RIGHT: In 1988, actor Al Lewis, who portrayed Grandpa Munster in TV's *The Munsters* (1964–66) hosted a number of obscure "Grampa Presents" (note the variant spelling) releases in Amvest Video's "Vintage Video" public domain budget line. However, he didn't show up on this fuzzy American version of F.W. Murnau's *Nosferatu* (1922), which only ran sixty-seven minutes.

BOTTOM LEFT: Based on Victor Hugo's 1831 novel and starring Lon Chaney, Sr. as Quasimodo and Patsy Ruth Miller as Esmeralda, the 1923 version of *The Hunchback of Notre Dame* (Goodtimes Home Video, 1990) was Universal's most successful silent movie. Most public domain videotape releases used the shortened 16mm duplicate print distributed in the 1960s and '70s.

BOTTOM RIGHT: Christopher Lee introduced Video Treasures' 1993 videotape release of the 1925 version of *The Phantom of the Opera* starring Lon Chaney, Sr. Partially tinted and with the Technicolor sequences intact, this shortened version of the film also featured a new classical soundtrack composed and performed by British musician Rick Wakeman in 1989.

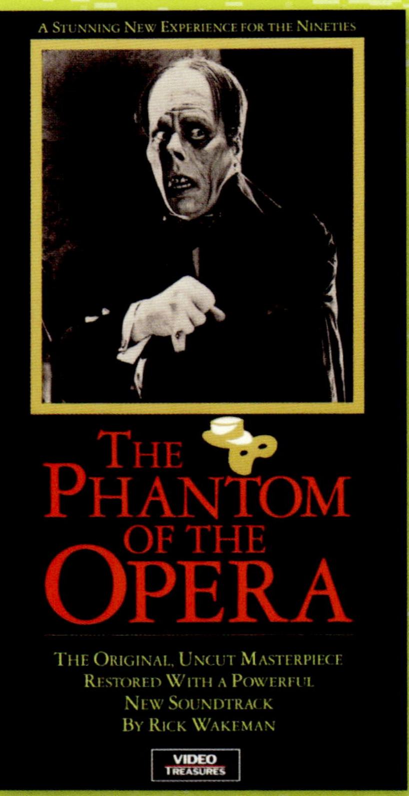

"THIS REVITALIZED *METROPOLIS* HAS ALL THE IMMEDIACY AND EXCITEMENT OF THE ORIGINAL WITH THE ADDED IMPACT OF GIORGIO MORODER'S VIBRANT SOUNDTRACK, SURGING NEW POWER INTO SOME OF THE MOST STRIKING AND MOVING IMAGES EVER PUT TO FILM."

METROPOLIS **VIDEO BOX BLURB (1985)**

ABOVE: In an attempt to recreate a silent movie that would appeal to a wider contemporary audience, the score to the heavily truncated eighty-seven-minute version of Fritz Lang's classic 1927 science fiction film *Metropolis* (Vestron Video International, 1986) was given a musical makeover by Giorgio Moroder in 1984, when the Oscar-winning Italian songwriter and composer recruited such rock performers as Pat Benatar, Freddie Mercury, Bonnie Tyler, Adam Ant, Loverboy, and others to record an electronic synth-pop soundtrack for a newly restored and tinted print of the movie. It was subsequently nominated for two Golden Raspberry Awards ("Razzies"), one for worst score and the other for worst song (Mercury's rendition of "Love Kills").

The leaning town of Holstenwall with its grotesque funfair; the shadow of the vampire climbing the stairs; the carved frontage of the cathedral of Notre Dame; Paris opera house complete with its all-important crystal chandelier; the furnace room of the modern city, fed by shuffling ranks of zombie workers: before the arrival of VHS videotape, I had to teach the greatest hits of film design in the silent era with untinted 16mm prints borrowed from the British Film Institute, purchased from Blackhawk Films or gleaned from bootleg reels of celluloid picked up at assorted film fairs—which always seemed to feature the same Muzak accompaniment on the same electric organ. Some of these prints had been chewed up by cack-handed projectionists—or by souvenir-hunters snipping their favorite frames—and most of them defied all attempts to screen them in focus or at the right speed.

Then came video. The tapes could be precisely cued up in advance; the prints still tended to be untinted (until Moroder's weird disco version of *Metropolis*), but the images looked better than even on the big screen; it was easier to slot the plastic cassettes into a playback machine than to thread up a projector; the boxes nestled comfortably next to film books on the shelves; and there was always the possibility of recording fresh versions off-air.

I located a long extract from the creation scene of Edison's *Frankenstein* (1910)—the one and only source in the 1980s—tucked inside a late-night TV series about Hollywood genres: there was a pleasing whodunit quality to those pre-Internet days.

Sure, the cues eventually turned into fuzzy white explosions on the tapes; over time the images began to resemble bad photocopies of family snapshots; and the soundtracks came to approximate Russ Conway recorded in a bathroom. But . . . one of my graduates helped to make a television commercial based on *Dr. Caligari*; several went on to direct rock videos which included esoteric references to silent films; two became fully-fledged production designers.

Video made these and other screen epiphanies possible.

Sir Christopher Frayling

TOP LEFT: Having first been released on LaserDisc in 1986, Universal Pictures' classic *Frankenstein* (1931) arrived on VHS from MCA Home Video the following year. Billed as "The Restored Version," it contained footage not seen since censors cut the film for its original release. It included some, but not all, of the missing material.

TOP RIGHT: A lengthy flashback sequence cut before the 1932 release of Universal's *The Mummy* (MCA Home Video, 1985) has never been restored and is now presumed lost. Unlike the studio's *Dracula* (1931) and *Frankenstein* (1931), which were based on novels, this was inspired by the opening of Tutankhamun's tomb in 1922.

BOTTOM LEFT: Released in a "Home Video Version" as a choice of flamboyant journalist and TV film critic Gene Shalit (who also wrote the back-of-the-box blurb), Universal's 1933 version of H.G. Wells's *The Invisible Man* (MCA Home Video, 1987) was originally set to star Boris Karloff before he was replaced by Claude Rains.

BOTTOM RIGHT: Universal Pictures' first horror sequel, *Bride of Frankenstein* (MCA Home Video, 1984), was originally released in 1935 and reunited *Frankenstein* star Boris Karloff and director James Whale. Elsa Lanchester played the dual roles of Mary Shelley and the titular character, while John Carradine had an uncredited part as a hunter.

OPPOSITE PAGE: Original artwork for *Dracula's Daughter* (MCA Home Video, 1992), which was severely cropped when it appeared on the video box. Universal's first sequel to *Dracula* was released in 1936 and featured Gloria Holden in the title role. Bela Lugosi was supposed to star, but only Edward Van Sloan returned from the original.

TOP LEFT: Paramount's *Island of Lost Souls* (MCA Universal, 1993) made its home video debut as part of "Universal Monsters: The Classic Collection." Charles Laughton starred as crazed vivisectionist Dr. Moreau, whose South Seas island was populated with "beast men" (and Kathleen Burke's seductive Panther Woman). Made in 1932, it was banned in Britain until 1958.

TOP RIGHT: Made only a year after *Dracula* (1931), the independent low-budget voodoo drama *White Zombie* (United American Video Corporation, 1985) was already an indication of the direction that Bela Lugosi's career was heading. Because the movie had fallen out of copyright protection, it became a favorite public domain title among early home video distributors.

BOTTOM LEFT: In an attempt to convince more people to watch old, black-and-white movies, RKO Radio Pictures' 1933 version of *King Kong* (Turner Entertainment, 1989) was one of a number of films that were reissued in digitally "colorized" versions on home video. Following a public campaign by filmmakers against colorization and the high cost of the process, it was eventually discontinued.

BOTTOM RIGHT: Despite the ownership of Metro-Goldwyn-Mayer's *Mad Love* (MGM/UA Home Video, 1992) falling into the hands of Turner Entertainment, Peter Lorre's first American movie was advertised as being "in glorious black & white" for its debut on home video. Following a disappointing initial release in 1935, MGM cut around fifteen minutes from the film.

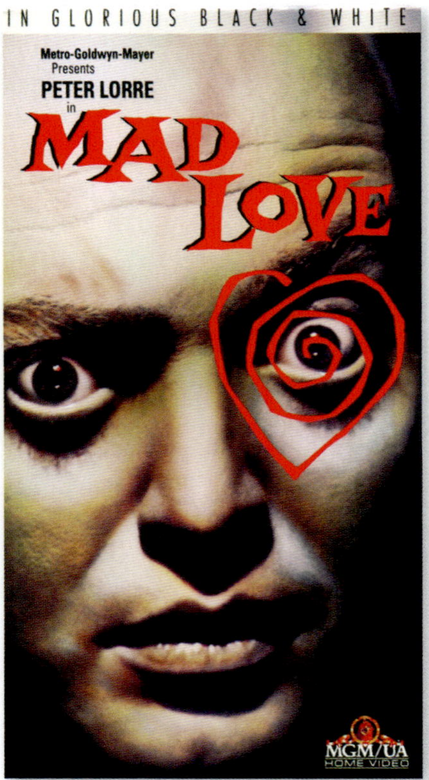

THIS PAGE: In 1943, Universal purchased the screen rights to "The Inner Sanctum Mysteries" from New York publisher Simon and Schuster, Inc. The book imprint, consisting mostly of mystery novels, had existed since 1930 and a popular series of radio programs ran under the title from 1941–52. Having already portrayed the Wolf Man, Frankenstein's Monster, the Mummy, and Count Dracula for the studio, Universal decided to star Lon Chaney, Jr. in the series of weird mystery movies, only one of which actually involved the supernatural. Without the monster makeup, Chaney proved to be an uneven leading man, and the series was cancelled after six titles. In 1997, Universal Home Video released all six films on VHS double-bills as part of its "Universal Horror Classics" line, with the same enhanced-photo covers used on all that series. Unfortunately, the *Inner Sanctum* films were not paired up in their original release order, which resulted in the tape combos *Weird Woman* (1944)/*The Frozen Ghost* (1945) [ABOVE LEFT], *Calling Dr. Death* (1943)/*Strange Confession* (1945) [TOP RIGHT], and *Dead Man's Eyes* (1944)/*Pillow of Death* (1945) [BOTTOM RIGHT].

OPPOSITE PAGE: Enhanced-photo cover artwork for Universal Pictures' 1941 "old dark house" horror-comedy *The Black Cat* (Universal Home Video, 1998), issued on video as part of the "Universal Horror Classics" series. Although actors Gale Sondergaard, Broderick Crawford, and Hugh Herbert are prominently featured, there is no sign of stars Basil Rathbone or Bela Lugosi.

TOP LEFT: Monogram's 1943 follow-up to *King of the Zombies* (1941), *Revenge of the Zombies* (Orbit Media, 1999), was supposed to star Bela Lugosi before John Carradine took over the role of a mad scientist attempting to create an army of zombies for the Nazis from his creepy home in the Bayou. Comedy relief Mantan Moreland played the same character he had in the earlier movie.

TOP RIGHT: Twelve years after he had starred in Universal's *Dracula* (1931), Bela Lugosi returned as another European bloodsucker in Columbia Pictures' *The Return of the Vampire* (GoodTimes Home Video, 1988). This time he was accidentally released from his tomb by a Nazi bomb, and with his werewolf servant he stalked the streets of a Blitz-ravaged London looking for victims.

BOTTOM LEFT: Despite his prominent billing, just one year later Bela Lugosi was reduced to playing a sinister-looking butler (a role originally intended for Boris Karloff) in Paramount Pictures' 1944 "old dark house" comedy *One Body Too Many* (Hal Roach Studios/Film Classics, 1985). This was another movie that fell out of copyright and was available on VHS in many poor quality versions.

BOTTOM RIGHT: Another title that found itself available on various public domain videotapes was the independently produced *Scared to Death* (Diamond Entertainment, 1991). Filmed in 1946 but not released until the following year by Screen Guild Productions, it was the only horror film to star Bela Lugosi that was made in color. George Zucco replaced a terminally ill Lionel Atwill.

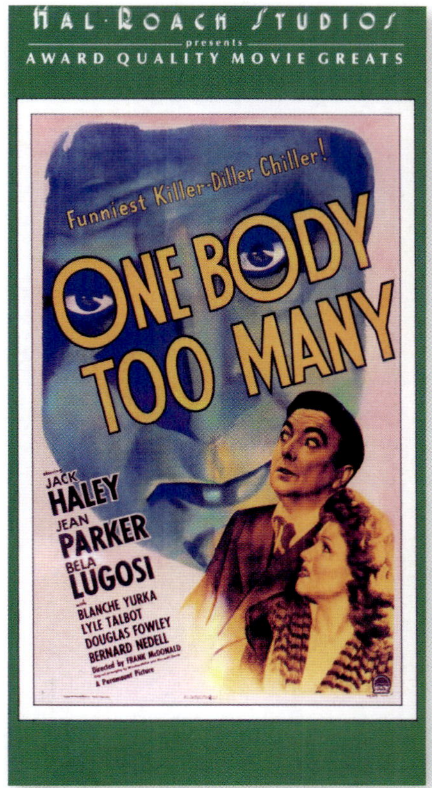

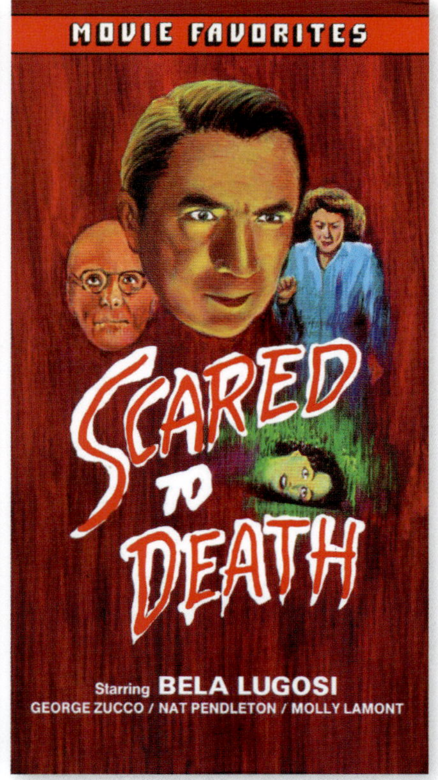

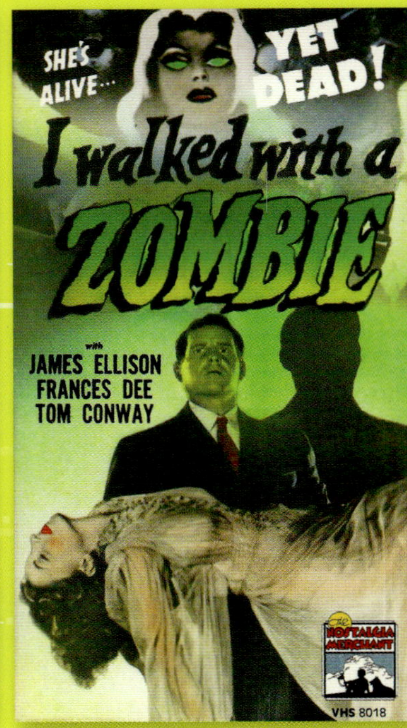

ABOVE LEFT: Having been put in charge of the failing RKO Radio Pictures' low-budget horror film division in 1942, visionary producer Val Lewton was saddled with the title *Cat People* (The Nostalgia Merchant, 1987) to work with. It was the first in a short series of intelligent and atmospheric movies that were the antitheses of Universal's monster mash-ups at the time.

ABOVE MIDDLE: When *Cat People* turned out to be a surprise hit for RKO, producer Val Lewton and director Jacques Tourneur reunited the following year for *I Walked with a Zombie* (The Nostalgia Merchant, 1980). Once again given a commercial title to work with, screenwriters Curt Siodmak and Ardel Wray partly based the script on Charlotte Brontë's 1847 novel *Jane Eyre*.

ABOVE RIGHT: Although marketed as a sequel in 1944 and featuring many of the same cast members, *The Curse of the Cat People* (The Nostalgia Merchant, 1985) was a very different film to *Cat People*. Gunther von Fritsch began directing the psychological fairy tale, but when he fell behind schedule he was replaced by editor Robert Wise, making his directorial debut.

When I got my first job in the film business, answering phones for the original *Star Wars* in 1977, it also allowed me to make my first purchase of note: a Toshiba Betamax videocassette recorder!

The magic of being able to record and watch a movie or show at any time was nothing less than supernatural. But the tapes were all priced for rental stores . . . until a company called The Nostalgia Merchant came along.

My very first purchase of a prerecorded videotape was of the Boris Karloff/Val Lewton/Mark Robson chiller, *Bedlam* (1946), for the then-unheard-of price of $19.95. It felt so good to be able to actually own a favorite classic film of mine, that I couldn't believe my luck!

Of course, the movie isn't a supernatural horror film or a monster movie, despite the presence of Karloff the Uncanny, but rather based on the actual story of how the mentally unfit were crammed into the hellhole that was St. Mary's of Bethlehem mental asylum, and the horrors that the criminally (and innocently) insane had to endure.

Karloff stars as the head of this snake pit, who runs the institution to suit his own desires . . . including having his way with a beautiful actress (Anna Lee) he's had committed to keep her from encouraging reforms to this wretched place.

As ever, producer Lewton was able to evoke a vivid period atmosphere that belies the low budget of this powerful film.

There was no specific box art back in the late 1970s, other than the generic Nostalgia Merchant montage they used on all their cardboard sleeves, but they were the first company to commit to sell-through movies, and I was happily among those early adopter customers, back when Beta was the only home video format, even before VHS existed.

Mick Garris

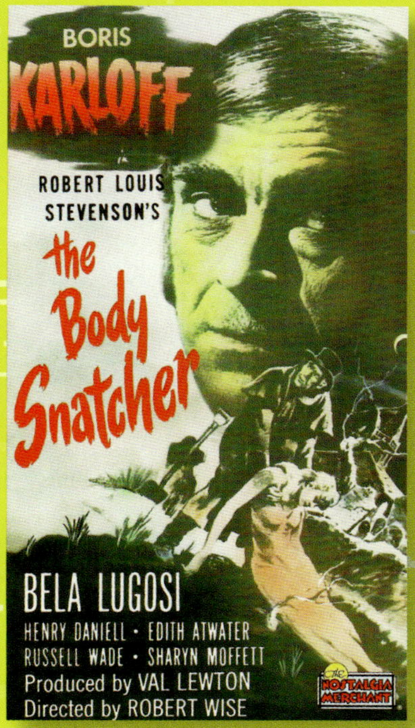

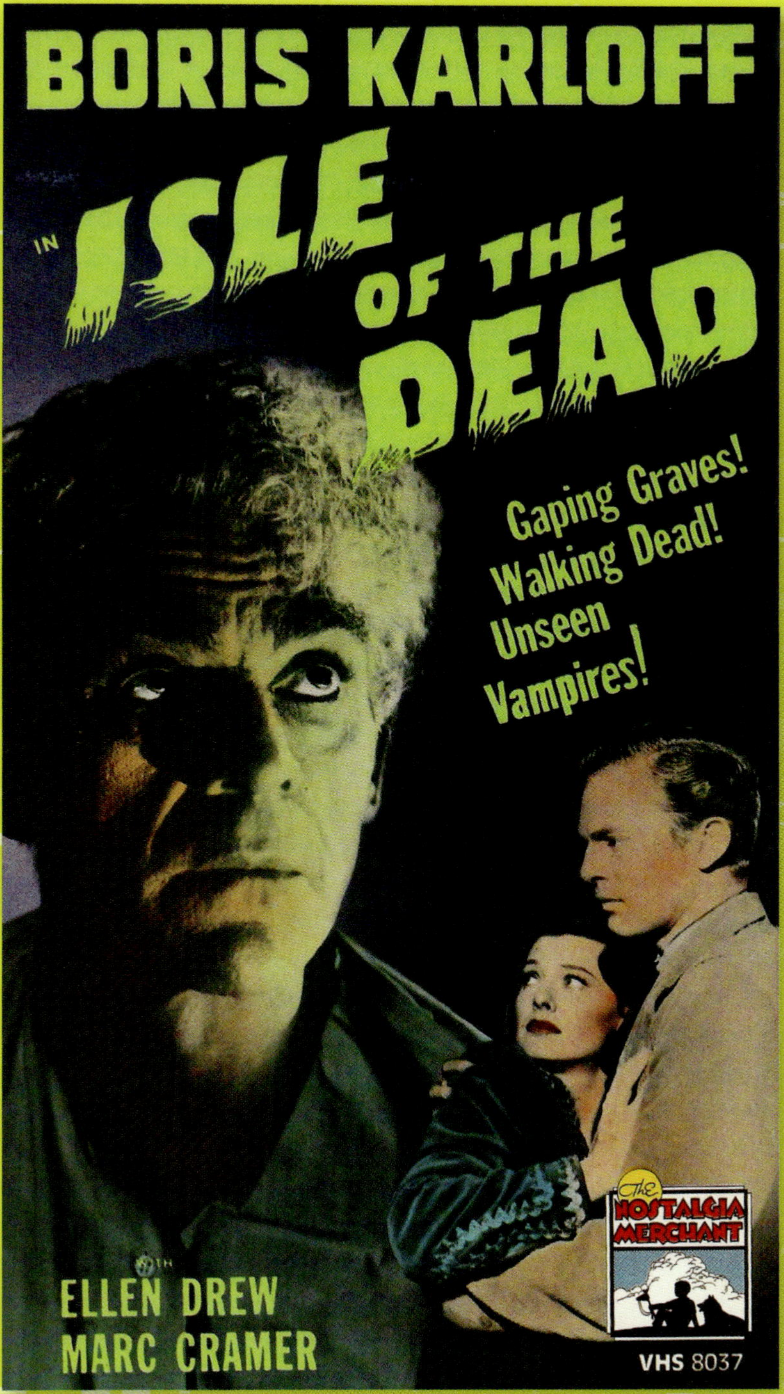

BORIS KARLOFF
IN
ISLE
OF THE
DEAD
Gaping Graves!
Walking Dead!
Unseen
Vampires!
WITH
ELLEN DREW
MARC CRAMER
VHS 8037

TOP LEFT: Producer Val Lewton and director Robert Wise reunited for the 1945 release *The Body Snatcher* (The Nostalgia Merchant, 1987), loosely based on an 1884 short story by Robert Louis Stevenson. The first of three films with Val Lewton that Boris Karloff made for RKO Radio Pictures, it also marked the final time that Karloff and Bela Lugosi appeared on screen together.

BOTTOM LEFT: Director Mark Robson and star Boris Karloff reunited for the 1946 release *Bedlam* (The Nostalgia Merchant, 1987), which was based on William Hogarth's 1732–34 painting series *A Rake's Progress*. After making a loss at the box office, it not only marked the final collaboration between Karloff and producer Val Lewton, but was also the last of RKO's B movie horrors.

ABOVE RIGHT: Directed by Mark Robson and inspired by a version of the painting of the same name by Arnold Böcklin, *Isle of the Dead* (The Nostalgia Merchant, 1980) was originally released by RKO in 1945 and was the second of Boris Karloff's three-picture deal. Although it had the highest budget of any Val Lewton horror movie to that time, it was not a big box office success.

TOP LEFT: *The Return of Chandu* (Rhino Home Video, 1989) was a follow-up to *Chandu the Magician* (1932), in which Bela Lugosi had played the villain. For this 1934 serial, the actor was recast as the mystical hero. The twelve chapters were released on home video in a two-tape set with a total running time of approximately 206 minutes. It was also edited down into two feature films.

TOP RIGHT: All fifteen episodes (267 minutes) of the 1940 serial *Mysterious Doctor Satan* (Republic Pictures Home Video, 1988) were released on home video. Originally planned as a Superman serial, the script was reworked so that a hooded hero named The Copperhead battled the criminal mastermind of the title and his army of robots. A cut-down version was released to TV in 1966.

BOTTOM LEFT: Roy Barcroft starred as the titular alien who possessed the body of a noted astronomer while he made preparations for an invasion from Mars in the 1945 serial *The Purple Monster Strikes* (Republic Pictures Corporation, 1986). All fifteen episodes (209 minutes) appeared on video, and a cut-down version was released to TV in 1966 under the title *D-Day on Mars*.

BOTTOM RIGHT: The hooded criminal mastermind of the title attempted to get his hands on an invention that could disable all electrical devices in the 1946 serial *The Crimson Ghost* (Republic Pictures Home Video, 1988). The complete twelve chapters (167 minutes) were released on videotape, while the edited-down 1966 TV version was retitled *Cyclotrode X*.

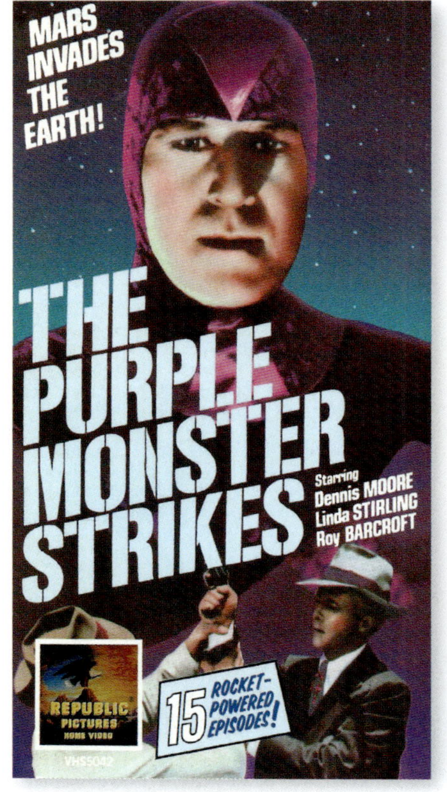

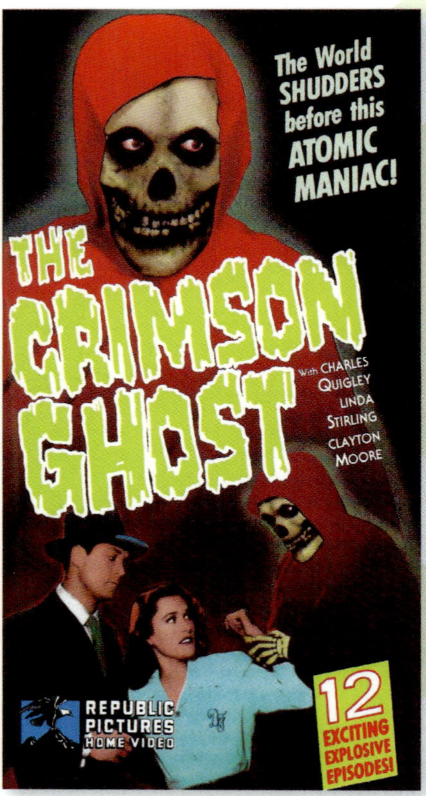

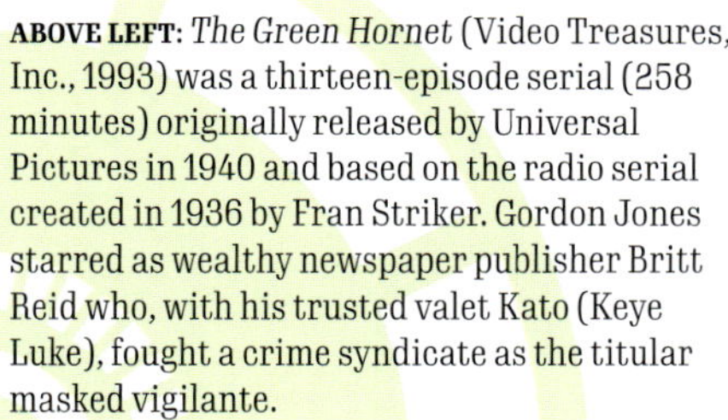

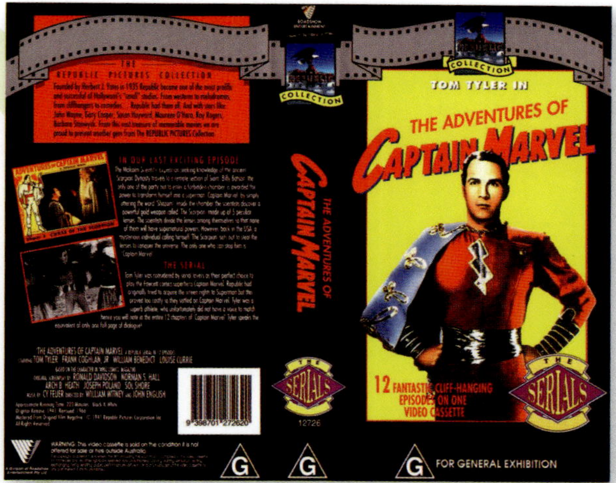

ABOVE LEFT: *The Green Hornet* (Video Treasures, Inc., 1993) was a thirteen-episode serial (258 minutes) originally released by Universal Pictures in 1940 and based on the radio serial created in 1936 by Fran Striker. Gordon Jones starred as wealthy newspaper publisher Britt Reid who, with his trusted valet Kato (Keye Luke), fought a crime syndicate as the titular masked vigilante.

ABOVE MIDDLE: Australian video sleeve for Republic Pictures' twelve-episode serial (223 minutes) from 1941, *Adventures of Captain Marvel* (Roadshow Entertainment, 1994). Based on the Fawcett Comics character, teenager Billy Batson transformed into the titular superhero (Tom Tyler) every time he said "Shazam!" to battle a hooded criminal mastermind called the Scorpion.

ABOVE RIGHT: The last Republic serial to be based on a comic-book character, *Captain America* (Video Treasures, Inc., 1993) was released in 1944 and ran for fifteen episodes (224 minutes). Timely Comics' patriotic hero (Dick Purcell) attempted to stop Lionel Atwill's arch-villain The Scarab from stealing the components to a secret weapon capable of destroying cities with sound vibrations.

CONTINUED NEXT WEEK . . .

Serials have been around almost since motion pictures began. In the decades before episodic TV, audiences would return to the movie theater every week to watch the next installment in a particular chapter play and see if the hero or heroine escaped from the certain doom that the "cliffhanger" ending of the previous episode had depicted.

After repeating the last few minutes of the preceding chapter, the protagonists usually evaded their terrible fate due, more often than not, to a judicious piece of film editing or even, in some cases, a direct cheat. The mostly young crowds that flocked to the Saturday morning matinees rarely minded though, as they sat through twelve to fifteen episodes of action-packed entertainment that usually lasted no longer than twenty minutes, except for the extended opening chapter that was around ten minutes longer.

Some of the earliest examples of successful serials were *The Perils of Pauline* (1914) starring Pearl White, along with Louis Feuillade's French-made *Fantômas* (1913–14), *Les vampires* (1915), and *Judex* (1916). There were also four Tarzan serials made during the silent era.

During the 1930s and '40s, many of the major Hollywood studios were churning out their own serials, often based on comic book and newspaper strip characters as in Universal's Flash Gordon trilogy (1936–40) and *Buck Rogers* (1939), Columbia's *Batman* (1943) and *Captain America* (1944), and the quartet of Dick Tracy serials (1937–41) and *Adventures of Captain Marvel* (1941) from Republic Pictures, the undisputed leader in serial production.

Genre icons such as Boris Karloff and Lon Chaney, Jr. appeared in serials at the beginning of their acting careers; Bela Lugosi starred in several at the height of his stardom, while Lionel Atwill was reduced to appearing in them towards the end of his career.

The popularity of the movie serials ended in the mid-1950s, when television began to replace motion pictures as the most popular form of household entertainment, although they received a new lease of life in the 1980s and '90s as numerous titles were reissued in their entirety in the new home video format.

The Original

CREATURE FROM THE BLACK LAGOON

TERRIFYING MONSTER RAVAGES MANKIND!

STARRING

RICHARD CARLSON · JULIA ADAMS

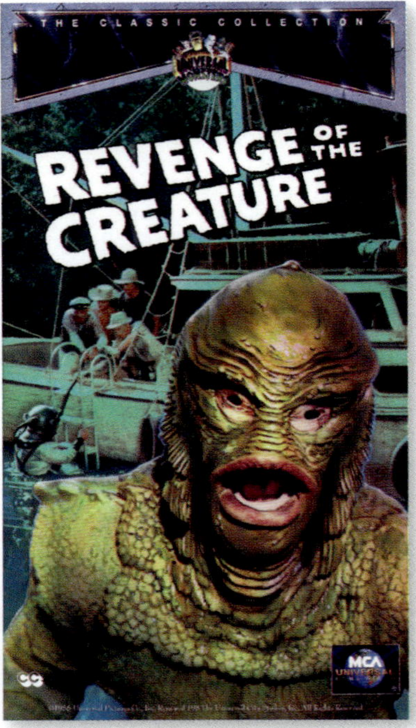

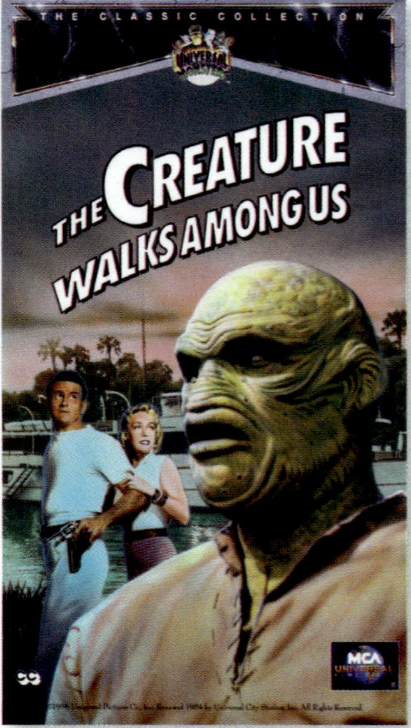

ABOVE LEFT: Universal's last truly iconic screen monster was probably the prehistoric "Gill Man" (played by Ben Chapman on land and Ricou Browning underwater) from *Creature from the Black Lagoon* (Goodtimes Home Video, 1987). It was originally released in 1954 in 3-D and appeared in that format on a VHS videocassette from MCA in 1980 with two sets of glasses.

TOP RIGHT: Released in 1955, *Revenge of the Creature* (MCA Universal Home Video, 1993) was the only 3-D sequel to a 3-D movie made during the process's height of popularity in the mid-1950s. This time stuntman Tom Hennesy played the Gill Man on land, while an uncredited Clint Eastwood made his screen debut as a lab technician with a mouse in his pocket.

BOTTOM RIGHT: The final installment in the Gill Man trilogy, *The Creature Walks Among Us* (MCA Universal Home Video, 1993) appeared in 1956 without any 3-D trickery. Don Megowan played the Creature on land, while Ricou Browning portrayed him underwater for the third time. In 1994, this film and *Revenge of the Creature* were released as a double-bill on LaserDisc.

TOP LEFT: Released in 1955 on a double-bill with *Revenge of the Creature*, Universal-International's *Cult of the Cobra* (MCA Universal Home Video, 1994) was about six American Air Force officers who, after witnessing a secret ritual in Asia, were hunted down by a seductive woman who could transform into a deadly snake. The video release included the film's original trailer.

BOTTOM LEFT: Originally released in black-and-white CinemaScope by Allied Artists in 1958, *Frankenstein 1970* (Warner Home Video, 1986) came to home video in an inferior pan-and-scan version. Almost twenty years after having last portrayed the Frankenstein Monster on screen, Boris Karloff played not only its creator but, in a surprise twist, the unbandaged creature itself.

ABOVE RIGHT: Released in 1958, the same year as Hammer's *Horror of Dracula*, United Artists' *The Return of Dracula* (MGM/UA Home Video, 1993) starred Francis Lederer as a contemporary Count preying on the residents of a small Californian town. Although mostly filmed in black and white, the videotape release restored a brief color shot when a female vampire was staked.

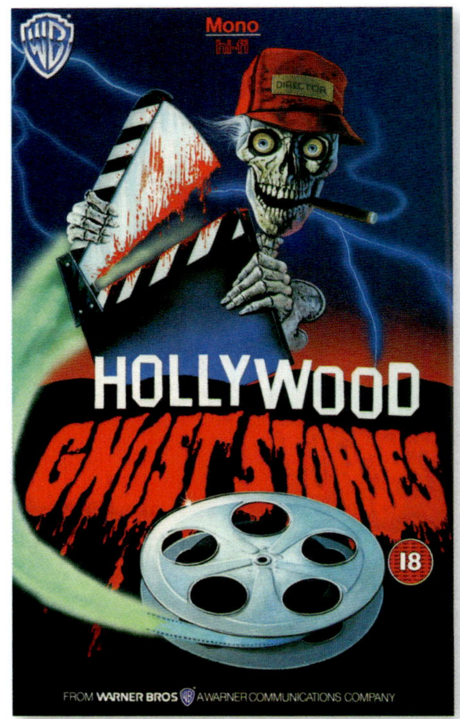

TOP: Japanese video sleeve for the hour-long 1982 documentary *Coming Soon!* (CIC Video, 1985), hosted by Jamie Lee Curtis from the Universal Studios back lot in California. Coscripted by producer Mick Garris and director John Landis, it featured scenes from fifty of the studio's greatest horror films, including Alfred Hitchcock's fun trailers for *Psycho* (1960) and *Frenzy* (1972).

BOTTOM LEFT: Ostensibly a documentary about haunted houses in Hollywood, James Forsher's *Hollywood Ghost Stories* (Warner Home Video, 1987) also included numerous clips from old movies. It was hosted by veteran actor John Carradine and featured interviews with Elke Sommer, William Peter Blatty, Susan Strasberg, Frank De Felitta, Robert Bloch, and others.

BOTTOM RIGHT: Produced for Halloween 1988 exclusively through Hallmark, Pamela Page's *Creepy Classics* was a half-hour video compilation of scenes and trailers from 1950s and '60s horror and science fiction films. Hosted from an empty movie theater by Vincent Price as the "Master of Scarimonies," the tape came with a Bonus Trivia Card featuring ten questions about the video.

TOP LEFT: Bryan Cohen's hour-long *Monsters We've Known and Loved* (Burbank Video, 1991) featured variable quality trailers from Universal, Hammer, American International Pictures, and others. The video documentary focused on mummies, vampires, and the Creature from the Black Lagoon, but also included some interesting behind-the-scenes clips from Hammer films.

TOP RIGHT: Bruce G. Hallenbeck's hour-long *Fangs! A History of Vampires in the Movies* (E.I. Independent Cinema, 1997) was hosted by Hammer starlet Veronica Carlson and featured numerous clips and trailers charting the evolution of vampire films over the decades, from *Nosferatu* (1922) and *Dracula* (1931), to a few obscurities and most of the Hammer titles.

BOTTOM: Ted Newsom's *Flesh and Blood: The Hammer Heritage of Horror* marked the final pairing of Christopher Lee and Peter Cushing, who narrated this visual history of the studio with on-screen interviews with many cast and crew. First broadcast on BBC-TV in 1994 in rough-cut form, it was subsequently reedited for release on video by Anchor Bay Entertainment in 1999.

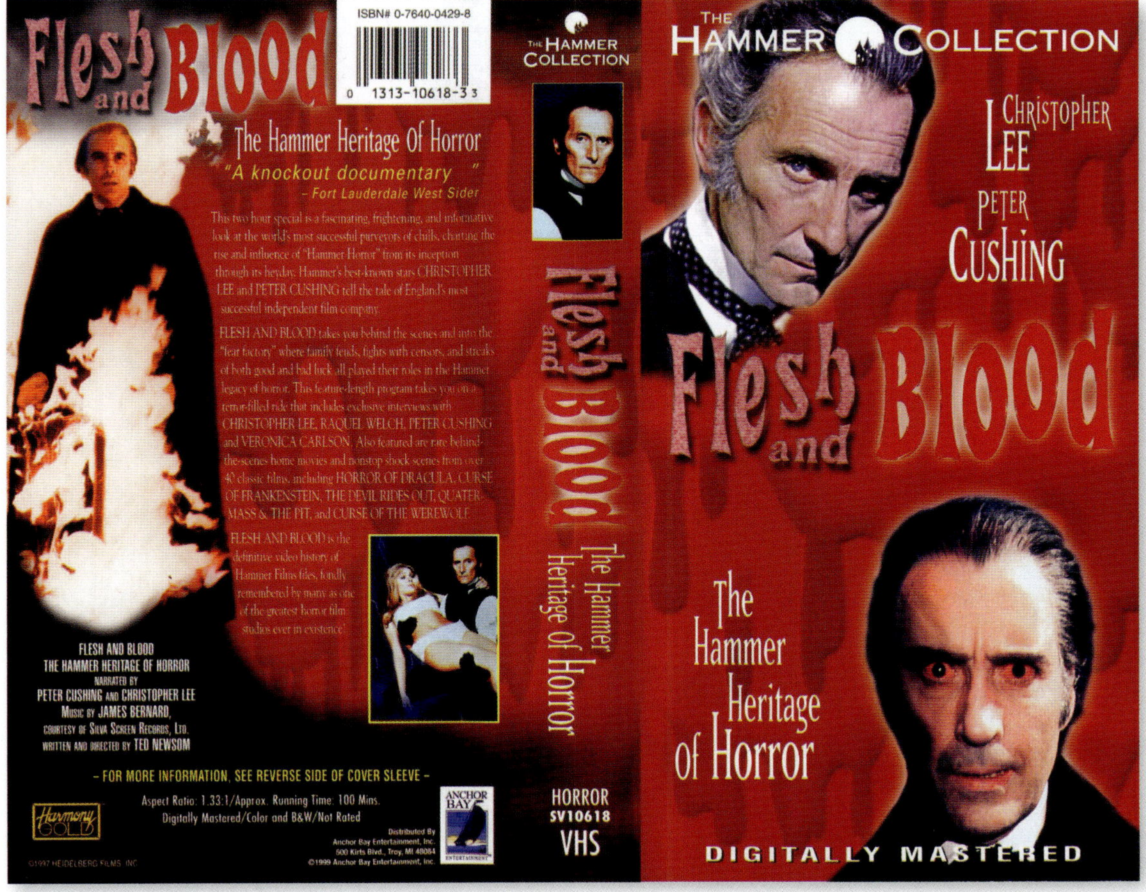

GRAY MORROW

CHAPTER 2

CHEAPO CHILLERS

"One of the worst things you can do is have a limited budget and try to do some big-looking film."

Roger Corman

> "*REVENGE OF DRACULA* IS A PRODUCT OF THAT STRANGE CINEMATIC PHENOMENON CALLED HORROR FILMS AND, AS SUCH, CAN BE REGARDED AS AN IMPORTANT WORK THAT ACCURATELY REFLECTS THE OBSESSIONS AND TENSIONS OF SOCIETY."
>
> *REVENGE OF DRACULA* VIDEO BOX BLURB (1987)

Low budget does not, necessarily, mean low quality, although that is often the case.

During the early days of the videotape revolution, it was perhaps inevitable that as the big Hollywood studios held their product back, waiting to see what effect the new technology would have on their bottom line, it was the smaller, independent distributors—who had basically nothing to lose—who dusted off their neglected, forgotten, and more obscure titles and launched them into the unknown waters of the nascent home video market.

This sudden influx of cheap and cheerful product often resulted in some surprising discoveries—whether they were such seldom-seen rarities as *Gallery of Horror* (1967/first released on video in 1985) and *Hillbillys in a Haunted House* (1967/circa 85), or titles that had been left unfinished or languished on the shelf, unreleased, like *The Mummy and the Curse of the Jackals* (1969/86), *House of the Black Death* (1965/99), or *Doctor Dracula* (1974/83).

It is no coincidence that all of the titles mentioned above featured old-time horror star John Carradine, and for many actors and filmmakers who may have thought that their careers were over, video directly resulted in their rediscovery and eventual reassessment.

Not just Carradine, but fellow horror actors Boris Karloff, Lon Chaney, Jr., Christopher Lee, and Basil Rathbone all appeared in forgotten films—and it might be argued that some should have remained forgotten—that probably would not have seen the light of day again, or at least never have reached a wider public, if they had not been resurrected on videotape to fuel a growing appetite for inexpensive product to rent or sell.

Meanwhile, Edward D. Wood, Jr., Al Adamson, Herschell Gordon Lewis, Andy Milligan, Ted V. Mikels, and Larry Buchanan were just a few of the forgotten filmmakers who suddenly found that their low-budget productions were in demand again, even if it was by a niche audience, as their work, often dismissed at the time, was actively sought out by a new generation of video viewers.

PREVIOUS SPREAD: *Brain of Blood* (Dir: Al Adamson, 1971)/*Vampire People* (Dir: Gerardo de Leon, 1964).

THIS PAGE: *Revenge of Dracula* (Dir: Al Adamson, 1971).

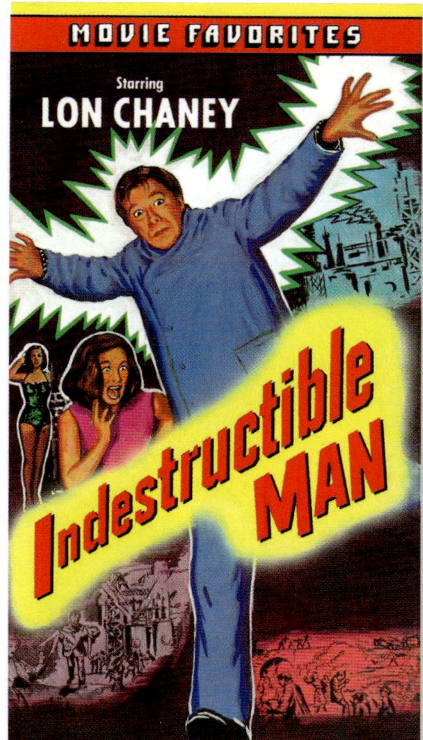

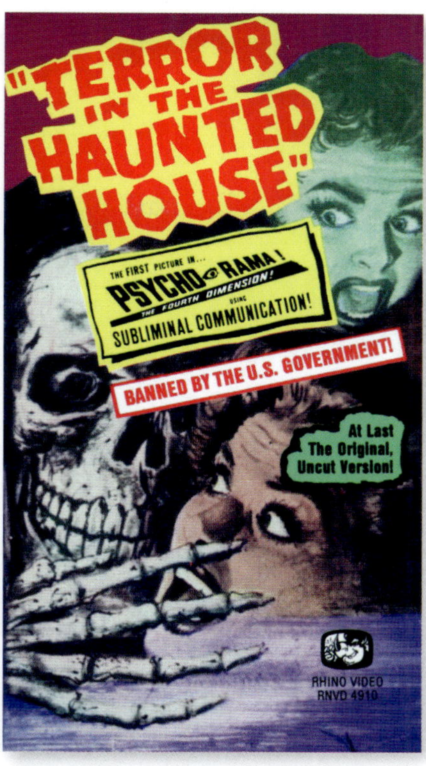

TOP LEFT: By 1956, Lon Chaney. Jr.'s career was on the wane, due in part to the actor's heavy drinking. Although he was top-billed as the resurrected murderer in Jack Pollexfen's woefully cheap *Indestructible Man* (Trans-Atlantic Video, 1987), Chaney was given almost no dialogue. Shoddy-looking prints of this public domain movie turned up on various bargain video labels.

TOP RIGHT: Originally released in 1958 as *My World Dies Screaming*, the video release of Harold Daniels's *Terror in the Haunted House* (Rhino Video, 1987) claimed to restore the movie's much-hyped "Psycho-rama" process, which supposedly projected subliminal images into the viewer's subconscious. In fact, the video featured much more obvious "supraliminal symbols."

BOTTOM LEFT: The shrink-wrap on the video release of Herbert L. Strock's *The Crawling Hand* (Acme Video, 1995) featured a "Fright Factor" sticker that claimed the 1963 movie was "Blood Curdling." It actually wasn't, as the severed arm of a dead astronaut came to life and started strangling people before it possessed the mind of the medical student who had taken it home as a souvenir.

BOTTOM RIGHT: Former Hollywood star Veronica Lake came out of retirement to coproduce and play a mad scientist experimenting with flesh-eating maggots to rejuvenate Adolf Hitler in Brad F. Grinter's *Flesh Feast* (Intercity Video, 1981). Filmed in 1967 in Florida, but not released until 1970, it marked the alcoholic actress's final movie prior to her death in 1973.

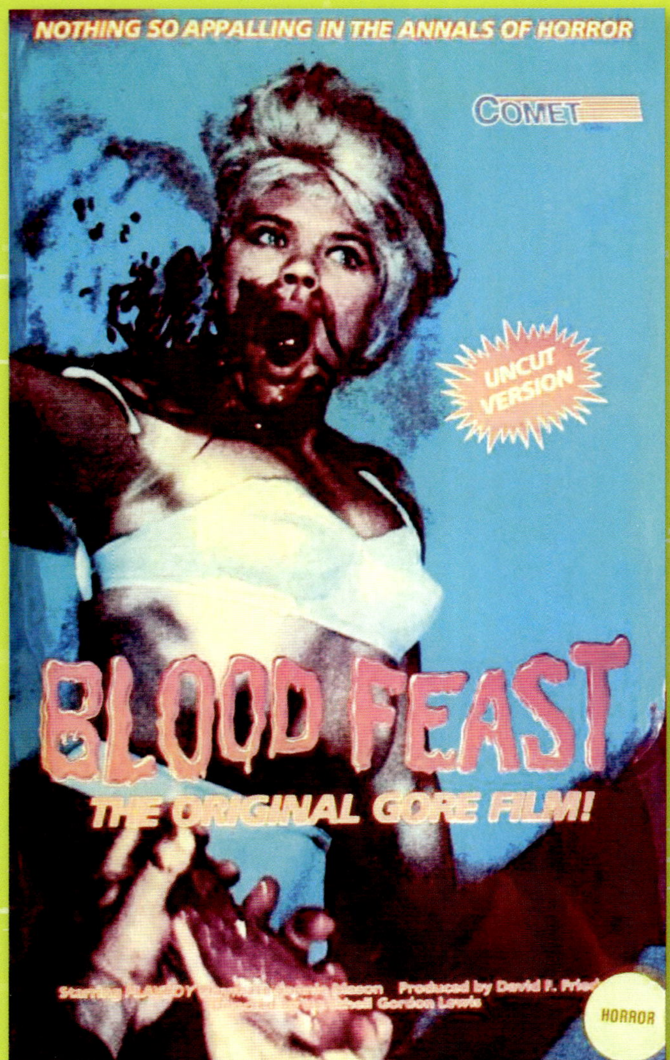

"THE BLOOD-CHURNING GORE EFFECTS IN *BLOOD FEAST* ARE SOME OF THE MOST CATASTROPHIC ACTS OF HORROR ON FILM . . . SO OUTRAGEOUS AND MERCENARY THAT MOST CONSIDER THIS FILM . . . IN A STRANGE, SATIRICAL WAY . . . TO BE QUITE FUNNY!"

***BLOOD FEAST* VIDEO BOX BLURB (1984)**

ABOVE LEFT: Former college teacher Herschell Gordon Lewis's splatter debut *Blood Feast* (Comet Video, 1984) was filmed over four days in Miami, Florida, in 1963 on a budget of $24,500. It earned more than $4 million upon release, thanks to some imaginative publicity stunts created by producer David F. Friedman, including the handing out of "vomit bags" to theatergoers.

ABOVE RIGHT: Australian video box for *Two Thousand Maniacs!* (Roadshow Home Video, 1983), the second in Herschell Gordon Lewis's unofficial "Blood Trilogy." *Playboy* Playmate Connie Wilson was among a group of tourists lured to a backwoods Southern town where the locals turned out to be the cannibal spirits of those massacred a century before.

I meant to see Herschell Gordon Lewis's *Blood Feast* (1963) at the Lisbon Drive-In, Lewiston, Maine, but my mother said no, and I couldn't go on my own because I didn't have a driver's license.

Years later I either rented it or bought it on video. I was amazed by the badness. My wife doesn't care for horror movies, but I got her attention by saying, "This is the absolute worst—and funniest—horror movie I've ever seen."

So she watched it.

We had a very good time.

The mad bad cannibal, Fuad Ramses (played by Mal Arnold), had these ridiculous eyebrows, and for years after, Tabby would waggle her own—far less ridiculous—eyebrows at me and say: "Steve! What about a real Egyptian *FEAST*?"

It got me every time.

Stephen King

BOTTOM LEFT: The third and final entry in Herschell Gordon Lewis's loose "Blood Trilogy," *Color Me Blood Red* (Comet Video, 1984) was originally released in 1965. Gordon Oas-Heim starred (under the name "Don Joseph") as a crazed artist who murdered his models so he could paint with their blood. Lewis cited Roger Corman's *A Bucket of Blood* (1959) as his main inspiration.

TOP: Herschell Gordon Lewis reportedly considered his 1967 film *A Taste of Blood* (Something Weird Video, 1996) as his "masterpiece." After drinking from two mysterious bottles of brandy, a Miami businessman turned into a vampire, a descendant of Count Dracula. Roger Corman was impressed with it enough to offer Lewis a job, which the director turned down.

BOTTOM RIGHT: A private investigator looked into a series of gruesome murders of strippers in the 1972 splatter comedy *The Gore Gore Girls* (Midnight Video/Select-a-Tape, 1985), which marked Herschell Gordon Lewis's swan song as the "Godfather of Gore" for three decades. He returned to filmmaking in 2002 with a sequel to *Blood Feast* and died fourteen years later at the age of ninety.

"HELLO, DARLING! IT'S ME. ELVIRA, MISTRESS OF THE DARK, WITH THE GREATEST HORROR AND SCI-FI CLASSICS FROM THE GOLDEN AGE IN MY EXCLUSIVE 'MIDNIGHT MADNESS' SERIES."

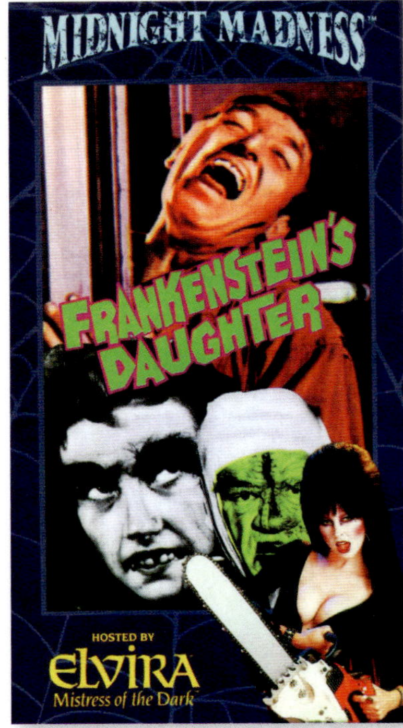

THIS PAGE: Vampiric TV horror hostess "Elvira"—a combination of camp humor and juvenile sex appeal—is the creation of actress Cassandra Peterson. After hosting a series of videos in the mid-1980s for International Home Video, she returned in 1990 to introduce a number of B movie video releases under the series title "Midnight Madness" for Rhino Home Video.

TOP LEFT: Originally released in 1958 to cash in on the "teenage monster" craze, Donald Murphy's "Oliver Frank" set about creating a female monster in the low-budget *Frankenstein's Daughter*, which was reportedly filmed in just six days.

TOP RIGHT: Also released in 1958, and from the same director (Richard E. Cunha), *She Demons* involved experiments by a Nazi scientist on a desert island to restore his disfigured wife's beauty. It was just as bad as *Frankenstein's Daughter*.

BOTTOM: *The Mask* was a 1961 Canadian movie about a mask that caused the wearer to experience weird nightmares. In an attempt to replicate the original 3-D sequences, the "Midnight Madness" video was issued with two pairs of 3-D glasses.

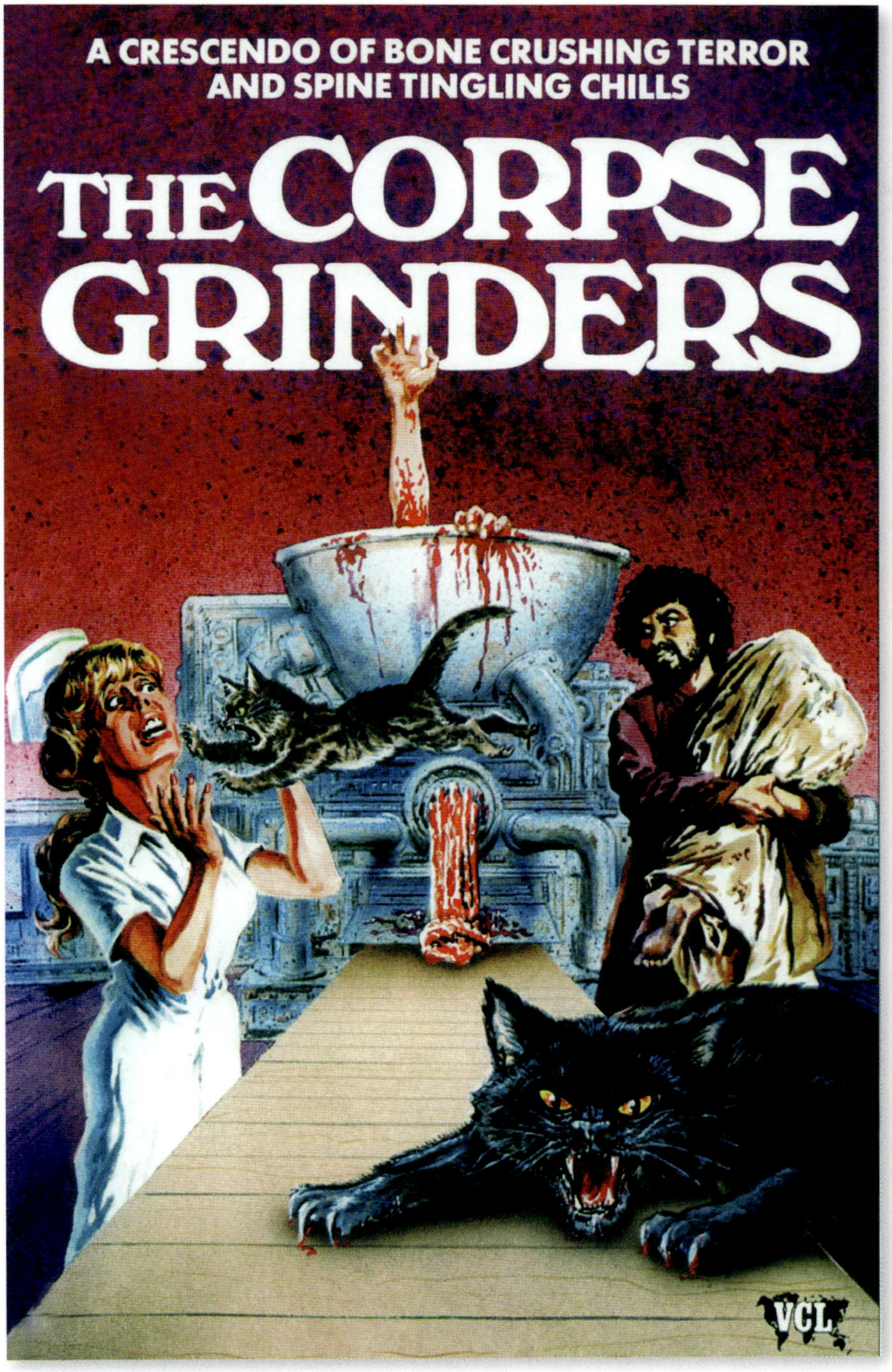

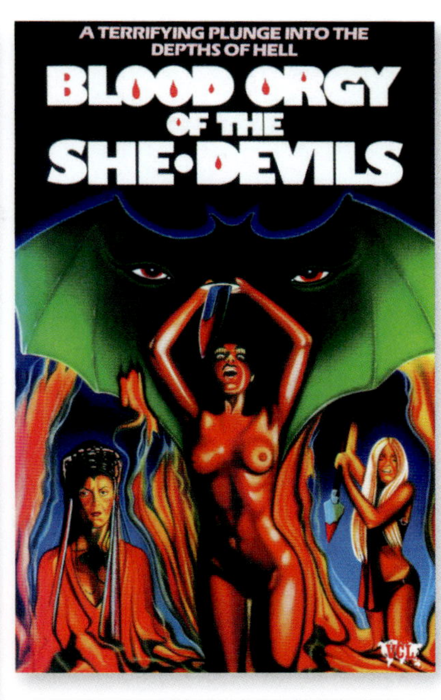

ABOVE LEFT: After the owners of a cat food company began using dead bodies in their product to cut costs, some feisty felines developed a taste for human flesh in Ted V. Mikels's 1971 comedy-horror movie *The Corpse Grinders* (VCL, 1982). Thanks to the title, it was a rare box-office hit for the independent director, coscripted by Joe Cranston, the father of actor Bryan Cranston.

TOP RIGHT: Ted V. Mikels's follow-up movie, *Blood Orgy of the She-Devils* (VCL, 1982) was released in 1973. Unfortunately, despite another terrifically commercial title, this modern-day tale of witchcraft did not do so well as his previous production. Filmed at the director's "castle" home in Glendale, California, it was reissued on video in 1988 under the title *Female Plasma Suckers*.

BOTTOM RIGHT: Producer William Mishkin took Andy Milligan's 16mm movie *Curse of the Full Moon*, filmed in England in 1969, and asked the independent filmmaker to pad it out with new scenes of flesh-eating rats before releasing it in 1972 under the far more commercial title *The Rats Are Coming! The Werewolves Are Here!* (Midnight Video/Select-a-Tape, 1982).

THIS SPREAD: Veteran Hollywood character actor John Carradine (Richmond Reed Carradine) had something of a late-career resurgence thanks, in part, to the home video boom of the 1980s. In movies since 1930, the prolific stage and screen actor appeared in more than 350 films and TV shows during his long career, and he was still working up to his death in Milan, Italy, in 1988 at the age of eighty-two.

TOP LEFT: : John Carradine appeared alongside Lon Chaney, Jr. and Basil Rathbone in the 1967 musical comedy *Hillbillys in a Haunted House* (GoodTimes Home Video, 1989), which marked director Jean Yarbrough's final theatrical credit.

BOTTOM LEFT: John Carradine starred as another mad scientist in Ted V. Mikels's *The Astro-Zombies* (1968), which turned up on home video as *Space Zombies* (Wizard Video, 1985).

ABOVE RIGHT: Produced, written, composed, edited, and directed by Jerry Warren, *Frankenstein Island* (Ambassador Video, 1982) was the final movie from the veteran filmmaker. Only John Carradine's floating head and shoulders appeared as the spirit of Dr. Frankenstein, while the cast also included old-timers Cameron Mitchell, Andrew Duggan, Steve Brodie, Robert Clarke, and Katherine Victor as the doctor's descendant.

ABOVE LEFT: Robin Groves's author of Gothic mysteries moved into a remote Victorian mansion and was haunted by the ghosts of the former brothel's inhabitants in Armand Weston's *The Nesting* (Warner Home Video, 1986). Originally seized as a "video nasty" in the UK, it featured cameos by Hollywood veterans John Carradine and Gloria Grahame in her last movie.

TOP RIGHT: Striking Danish video cover for Al Adamson's 1969 release *Blood of Dracula's Castle* (Video International, 1984), which surprisingly starred former Dracula John Carradine as the family butler to fellow old-timers Alexander D'Arcy's Count and Paula Raymond's vampire Countess. Despite the film's copyright date, it was apparently filmed in August 1966.

BOTTOM RIGHT: John Carradine costarred with British horror icon Peter Cushing in the 1977 movie *Shock Waves* (StarMaker Entertainment, 1989), filmed in Florida. The survivors of a shipwreck encountered a former SS commander and his group of zombie super-soldiers on a desert island. Carradine reportedly kept the cast and crew entertained with stories about his Hollywood days.

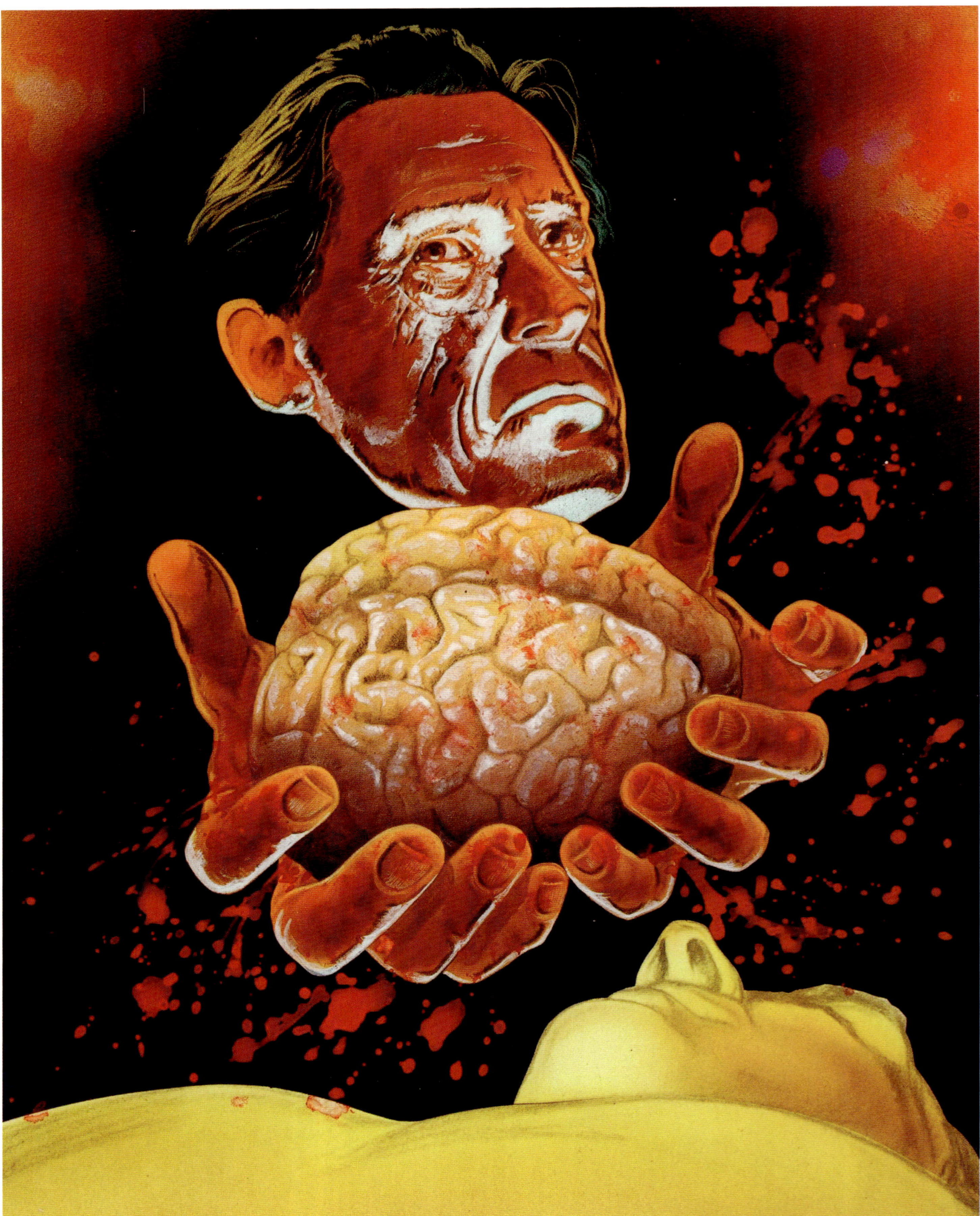

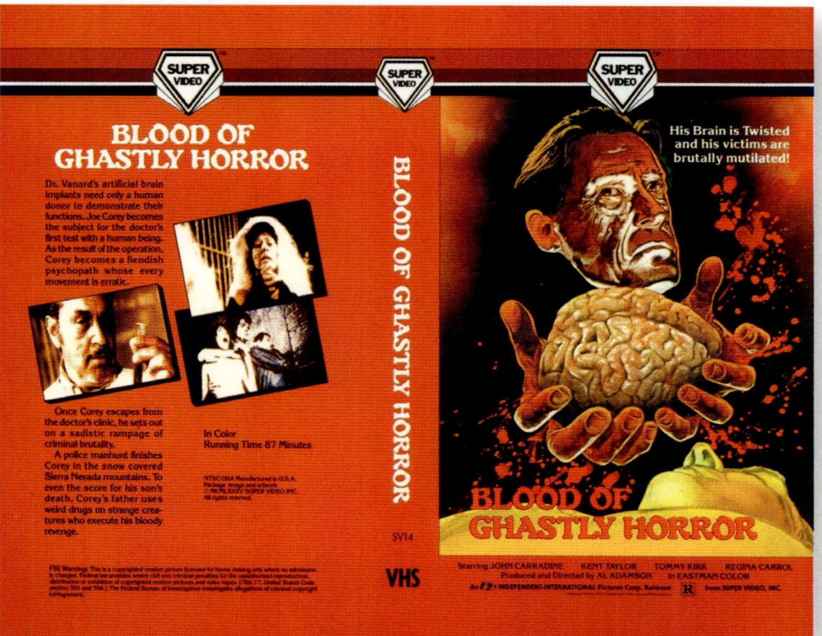

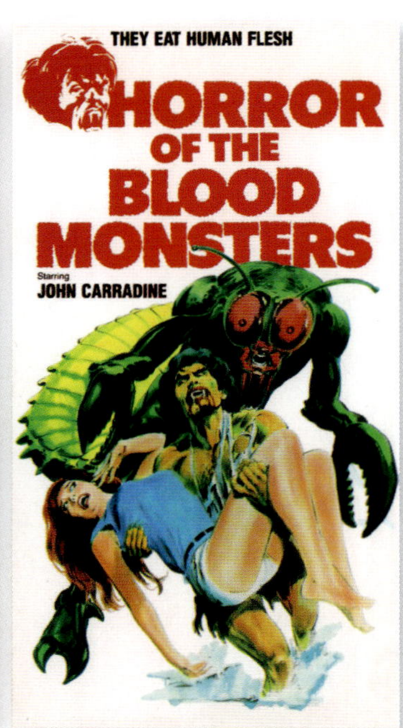

OPPOSITE PAGE & ABOVE LEFT: Al Adamson's *Blood of Ghastly Horror* (Super Video, 1984) started out as a reedited version of his 1965 crime thriller *Psycho A-Go-Go* (a.k.a. *Echo of Terror*). In 1969 he added additional footage of veteran horror actor John Carradine playing a mad scientist and it was reissued under the new title *The Fiend with the Electronic Brain*. However, Adamson was still not satisfied, and so two years later he added even more footage featuring actors Kent Taylor, Tommy Kirk, and Regina Carrol. This was then reedited into an entirely new film entitled *Blood of Ghastly Horror* (a.k.a. *The Man with the Synthetic Brain*).

ABOVE RIGHT: When a friend sold Sam Sherman the rights to a Filipino caveman movie, Al Adamson and future Oscar winner Vilmos Zsigmond shot additional footage featuring actors Robert Dix, Vicki Volante, and John Carradine that was inserted into the film to pad out its running time. Now retitled *Horror of the Blood Monsters* (a.k.a. *Vampire Men of the Lost Planet*, along with many other titles), noted comic-book artist Neal Adams designed the 1970 poster art, a detail of which was used on this 1988 home video release in the "World's Worst Videos" series from VidAmerica.

AL ADAMSON'S GHASTLY HORRORS

The son of silent film stars, Al Adamson (Albert Victor Adamson, Jr., 1929–95) was a prolific director of low-budget horror, softcore sex, and exploitation movies.

After assisting his father on a Western, he began his solo directing career in the mid-1960s with the crime movie *Psycho A-Go-Go* (1965), which he later reworked into *The Fiend with the Electronic Brain* and, later, as *Blood of Ghastly Horror*. With producer and film distributor Sam Sherman, he cofounded Independent-International Pictures, which distributed many of Adamson's productions, such as *Blood of Dracula's Castle* (1967), *The Female Bunch* (1969, filmed on the infamous Manson Family ranch in Southern California), *Satan's Sadists* (1969), *Dracula vs. Frankenstein* (1971), and *Brain of Blood* (1971).

These productions served as late-career vehicles for such veteran Hollywood actors as John Carradine, Lon Chaney, Jr., Kent Taylor, Russ Tamblyn, Scott Brady, Robert Dix, and Paula Raymond, among others.

Despite many of his films being the mainstay of the early home video boom, Adamson mostly retired from the movie industry at the beginning of the 1980s and with his wife, former waitress turned actress Regina Carrol, decided to pursue a career in real estate.

In 1985, five weeks after Adamson was reported missing by his housekeeper, law enforcement officials discovered his remains beneath the concrete and tile-covered floor in his home, where his hot tub once stood. His live-in contractor Fred Fulford was subsequently convicted of murder and sentenced to twenty-five years to life in prison.

In a bizarre echo of his death, it was reported that Adamson had earlier written an unproduced script about a man who was murdered and buried beneath his own house over a financial dispute.

ABOVE LEFT: Originally intended to be a biker film called *Satan's Bloody Freaks* starring Russ Tamblyn, Al Adamson's *Dracula vs. Frankenstein* (Rainbow Video/Vertex Video, 1982) marked the final film credit for ailing Hollywood veterans J. Carrol Naish and Lon Chaney, Jr. It had a lively life both theatrically and on early home video under various titles, including *Blood of Frankenstein* and *They're Coming to Get You*.

TOP RIGHT: *Revenge of Dracula* (Cine Video, 1987) was yet another variant title in the UK. Filming began in spring 1969, although the movie was not released until 1971 due to reshoots and changes during postproduction. J. Carrol Naish starred as the last descendant of Dr. Frankenstein, who attempted to revive the original Monster (played by both John Bloom and Shelly Weiss in footage shot at different times).

BOTTOM RIGHT: In scenes added a year after production began on *Dracula vs. Frankenstein* (Super Video, 1984), "Zandor Vorkov" (Raphael Peter Engel) portrayed Count Dracula.

OPPOSITE PAGE: Advertisement for the direct-to-video horror-comedy *Bloodsucking Pharaohs in Pittsburgh* (Nightmare Home Video/ Paramount Home Video, 1991), which was filmed in 1988.

BLOODSUCKING PHARAOHS IN PITTSBURGH

Bloodsucking Pharaohs In Pittsburgh

They had a deadly appetite for life.

Cannibalistic crazies looking for eternal life try to turn Pittsburgh into blood soup.

- Hilarious, "campy" feature-length horror film in the tradition of *The Rocky Horror Picture Show* and *Pink Flamingos.*
- Genre: Horror/Comedy

#12905   1991   Color   89 Min.
R   Stereo

Order Cut-Off: April 9
Street Date: May 2

VHS Priced for Rental.
Beta $29.95 Suggested Retail Price.
Priced Slightly Higher in Canada.

Distributed and marketed exclusively by Paramount Home Video.

This art is featured on the cassette box.

VHS UPC 9736-12905-3 / ISBN 7921-1930-4
BETA UPC 9736-12905-5 / ISBN 7921-1931-2

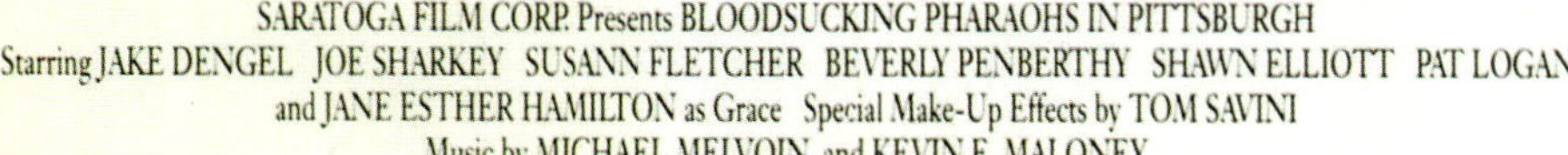
SARATOGA FILM CORP. Presents BLOODSUCKING PHARAOHS IN PITTSBURGH
Starring JAKE DENGEL JOE SHARKEY SUSANN FLETCHER BEVERLY PENBERTHY SHAWN ELLIOTT PAT LOGAN
and JANE ESTHER HAMILTON as Grace Special Make-Up Effects by TOM SAVINI
Music by MICHAEL MELVOIN and KEVIN E. MALONEY
Director of Photography PETER RENIERS Story by TOM TULLY
Screenplay by DEAN TSCHETTER
Produced by BEVERLY PENBERTHY and LAURENCE BARBERA
Directed by ALAN SMITHEY

NIGHT MARE HOME VIDEO

ABOVE LEFT: Inspired by his love of obscure exploitation movies, when former movie theater projectionist Mike Vraney founded Something Weird Video in Seattle, Washington, in 1990, he not only appropriated the title of Herschell Gordon Lewis's 1967 film—which featured LSD, ESP, a serial killer, and an ugly witch who could transform into a beautiful woman—but also the distinctive logo that appeared on the poster art.

ABOVE RIGHT: Cult movie director Frank Henenlotter (*Basket Case*) selected *Mondo Keyhole* (Something Weird Video, 1994) to be #29 of his "Sexy Shockers from the Vault." Written and codirected by Jack Hill (with John Lamb), this 1966 "nudie" is another mind-boggling example of low-budget filmmaking, as Nick Moriarty's serial rapist finally received his just rewards at the hands of one of his former victims.

Back in the 1990s, if you were seeking the best, sleaziest, strangest exploitation movies to experience at home, there was only one place to go: Something Weird Video.

Founded in 1990 by former theater projectionist Mike Vraney, Something Weird came up with the gems that you just wouldn't find anywhere else; when you plugged in one of those cassettes and that swirling logo with the electronic sounds (it wasn't really music) came up, you knew you were in for a wild ride.

Something Weird also worked with many of the filmmakers behind the great exploitation films of the past: David F. Friedman, who directed "roughies" like *The Defilers* (1965) and produced Herschell Gordon Lewis's *Blood Feast* (1963), provided many of the works that got Something Weird up and running, and the company didn't just carry Frank Henenlotter's *Basket Case* (1982), they gave the director his own line ("Frank Henenlotter's Sexy Shockers").

One of the pleasures of Something Weird's videos was the way history was captured in these films: *Mantis in Lace* (1968), a genuinely entertaining romp about a stripper who takes LSD and goes on a murder spree, spiced up its psychedelic sections with footage of the late great Disneyland attraction Adventure Thru Inner Space; other flicks, like *Mondo Keyhole* (the 1966 debut of codirector Jack Hill), offer footage that's a look back at long-gone locations.

Although Mike Vraney sadly passed away in 2014, Something Weird continues on, offering Blu-ray discs, downloads, and vinyl soundtrack albums featuring the work of Doris Wishman (the most prolific female filmmaker since talkies took over), Lewis, Henenlotter, Friedman, and many more.

Lisa Morton

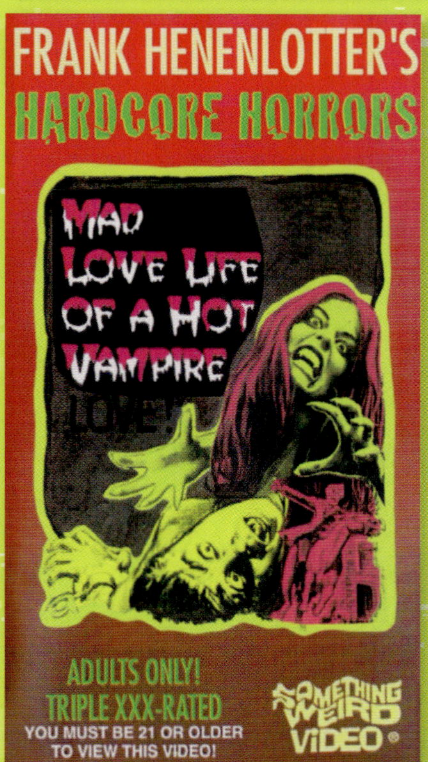

TOP LEFT: William Nigh's *House of Mystery* (Something Weird Video, n.d.) was an obscure 1934 poverty row release from Monogram Pictures, based on Adam Hull Shirk's stage play *The Ape*. It was filmed again in 1940 by the same studio and director. A group of people in a creepy old house was being killed off by a gorilla supposedly possessed by "the spirit of Kali."

TOP RIGHT: American rockabilly musician and wrestling manager "Johnny Legend" (Martin Margulies) also curated his own line of "Untamed Video" releases from Something Weird, including James Landis's cult 1963 movie *The Sadist*, which starred Arch Hall, Jr. and Marilyn Manning as a pair of psychopaths menacing a trio of stranded high school teachers on their way to Los Angeles.

BOTTOM LEFT: #10 in Frank Henenlotter's "Sexy Shockers from the Vault" was John A. Bushelman's rarely seen 1965 psycho-transvestite thriller *Day of the Nightmare* (Something Weird Video, 1993). Photographed by Ted V. Mikels, it featured Hollywood veterans John Ireland, John Hart, and Elena Verdugo, along with mobster's moll "Liz Renay" (Pearl Elizabeth Dobbins).

BOTTOM RIGHT: As the name suggests, Frank Henenlotter's other series, "Hardcore Horrors," featured more sexually explicit films. *The Mad Love Life of a Hot Vampire* (Something Weird Video, n.d.) was a 1971 porno movie made by Ray Dennis Steckler (as "Sven Christian"). Not even an hour long, it starred Las Vegas TV horror host Jim Parker as Count Dracula.

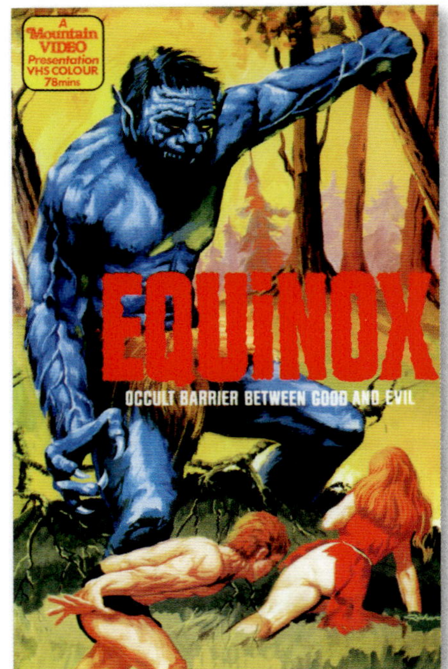

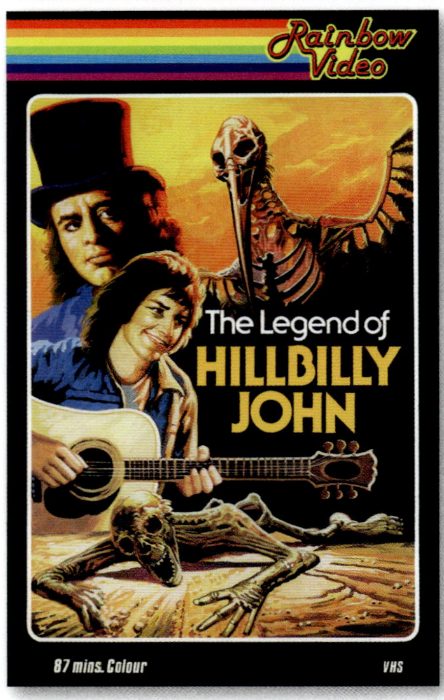

TOP LEFT: *Equinox* (Mountain Video, 1980) started out as a short 16mm student film shot in 1967 by director Dennis Muren with help from his friends, stop-motion animators Dave Allen and Jim Danforth. Producer Jack H. Harris hired Jack Woods to film additional material and blew it up to 35mm for a limited release in 1970. Author Fritz Leiber, Jr. appeared in a supporting role.

BOTTOM LEFT: Based on the stories by Manly Wade Wellman and filmed in North Carolina, John Newland's *The Legend of Hillbilly John* (Rainbow Video, 1982) was originally shown as *Who Fears the Devil* in 1972, before being reedited and receiving a limited release under its new title two years later. The impressive cast of character actors included Severn Darden and R.G. Armstrong.

ABOVE RIGHT: Michael Findlay's *Shriek of the Mutilated* (Iver Film Services, 1982) involved a cannibalistic cult that used supposed sightings of a Yeti creature to lure victims to a remote island. After the director reportedly suffered a nervous breakdown, his estranged wife Roberta Findlay was brought on as cinematographer. The film received a limited theatrical release in 1974.

TOP: A pair of con men and a gang of bikers attempted to rescue a group of women kidnapped by a family of backwoods Sasquatch creatures in the 1970 movie *Bigfoot* (World Video Pictures, n.d.), which starred the ubiquitous John Carradine. It marked the last screen appearance of both his costars: Joi Lansing and veteran Western star Ken Maynard.

BOTTOM LEFT: A lonely Bigfoot creature seeking a mate kidnapped a number of naked women from a remote Northern California hippie commune in the 1974 obscurity *The Beauties and the Beast* (Applause Productions, 1985), which starred Swedish porno actress Uschi Digard. The only directing credit of actor Ray Nadeau, it is also known as *The Beast and the Vixens*.

BOTTOM RIGHT: A small town was in danger of losing its lucrative tourist industry when a local businessman decided to finally trap the local Sasquatch in Bill Rebane's *The Capture of Bigfoot* (Active Home Video, 1986), which was filmed in Wisconsin and released in 1979. Lloyd Kaufman listed this film as one of the five worst movies his company Troma ever distributed.

TOP LEFT: Japanese VHS cover for Joel M. Reed's notorious 1976 movie *The Incredible Torture Show*, which was reissued by Troma Entertainment in the early 1980s in a reedited version entitled *Blood Sucking Freaks* (Tokuma Communications Co., n.d.). "I may have possibly secured my place in Hell by just watching it," said Troma cofounder Lloyd Kaufman.

TOP RIGHT: Codirected by Richard W. Haines and "Samuel Weil" (Lloyd Kaufman), *Class of Nuke 'Em High* (Troma Video Universe, n.d.) was a 1986 horror-comedy in which a nuclear accident at a New Jersey power plant turned some students of Tromaville High School into sex-crazed psychopaths while also creating a mutated monster. It has to date spawned four sequels.

BOTTOM LEFT: Filmed in Belgium as *Les mémés cannibales*, the 1988 horror-comedy *Rabid Grannies* (Virgin Vision, 1990) was released on VHS in a cut version by Troma Entertainment. Catherine Aymerie and Caroline Braeckman portrayed two elderly sisters who were transformed into cannibalistic demons during a birthday party given by their grasping relatives.

BOTTOM RIGHT: The unrated director's cut of *Redneck Zombies* (Troma Team Video, 1996) was released on VHS in a special "Troma Collectors' Edition." This 1989 horror-comedy, in which contaminated hillbilly hooch turned those who drank it into zombies, was one of the first independent films to be shot entirely on videotape and released into the home video market.

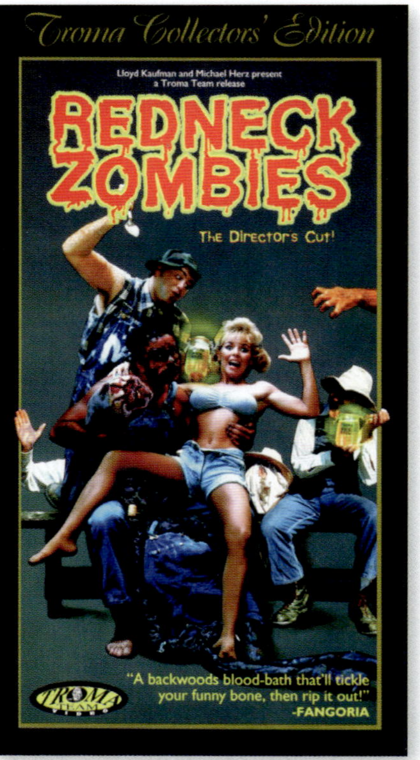

TOP LEFT: The 1984 horror-comedy *The Toxic Avenger* (Troma, 1996), directed by company cofounders Michael Herz and Lloyd Kaufman (under his "Samuel Weil" alias), is probably Troma Entertainment's most recognizable and successful franchise. A New Jersey janitor was transformed into a monstrously mutated crime-fighter after falling into a drum of toxic waste.

BOTTOM: Released five years after the original, New Jersey's first superhuman hero was tricked by an evil corporation into traveling to Tokyo to find his estranged father in *The Toxic Avenger Part II* (Shochiku Home Video, 1989). This Japanese video featured the uncut version, containing ten minutes of extra violence and gore that was missing from the initial American release.

TOP RIGHT: Also released in 1989, the second sequel, *The Toxic Avenger Part III: The Last Temptation of Toxie* (Vestron Video, 1991), pitted New Jersey's deformed superhero against a corrupt chemical corporation headed by the Devil himself. It was followed by a third sequel, a stage musical production, a video game, a children's TV cartoon series, a line of toys, and a 2023 theatrical reboot.

CHAPTER 3

DRIVE-IN DELIRIUM

"I could do without all of the *Children of the Corn* sequels."

Stephen King

"JESSE HASN'T BEEN HIMSELF LATELY. EVERY NIGHT, HE'S BEEN HAUNTED BY DARK, OVERPOWERING VISIONS OF AN EVIL PRESENCE TRYING TO POSSESS HIS BODY. AND IT ISN'T JUST A CASE OF BAD DREAMS. IT'S A NIGHTMARE COME TRUE."

A NIGHTMARE ON ELM STREET PART 2: FREDDY'S REVENGE VIDEO BOX BLURB (1986)

By the mid-1980s, VHS had established itself as the dominant videotape format and the Hollywood studios had accepted the new technology as an additional—and increasingly important—revenue stream.

The floodgates had finally opened.

As the prices of equipment and the tapes themselves plummeted, a video player/playback machine became *de rigueur* in most middle-class homes. Not only could consumers now watch their favorite movies whenever they wanted, or even record material off their television sets to keep and view at a later date, but it was now also possible to start *collecting* videos as well—building up a library of titles by actor, director, or genre, that could be pulled off the shelf at any time like a favorite book, and rewatched as many times as the owner wished.

Most people still wanted to rent their tapes from the big chains like Blockbuster or independent mom-and-pop corner stores—there was a bigger choice and it was still easier and cheaper—but the writing was already on the wall. The video rental business model was doomed, whether it knew it yet or not.

Meanwhile, as the time between a film's theatrical release and its video debut became shorter—in Britain, Sam Raimi's *The Evil Dead* (1981) was released simultaneously in cinemas and on video, causing an outcry—traditional television broadcasters and the new cable networks found themselves being left behind. As a result, they started creating more of their own exclusive content, much of which was subsequently released to home video, especially in overseas markets.

Another phenomenon around this time was the "direct-to-video sequel." If a movie had done well during its initial theatrical run, but perhaps not as well as the studio had been expecting, then they would often green-light a lower budget follow-up, possibly with different actors, and release the result directly to video in the hope that title recognition alone would generate sales.

There was no doubt that video was here to stay . . . at least for now.

PREVIOUS SPREAD: *Creepshow* (Dir: George A. Romero, 1982).

THIS PAGE: *A Nightmare on Elm Street Part 2: Freddy's Revenge* (Dir: Jack Sholder, 1985).

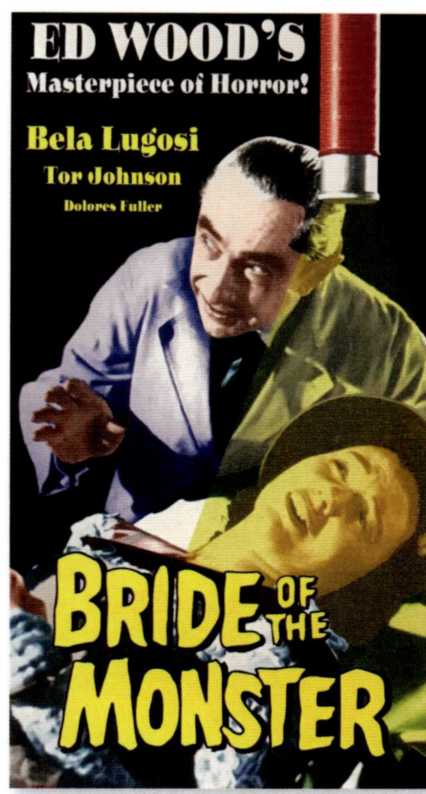

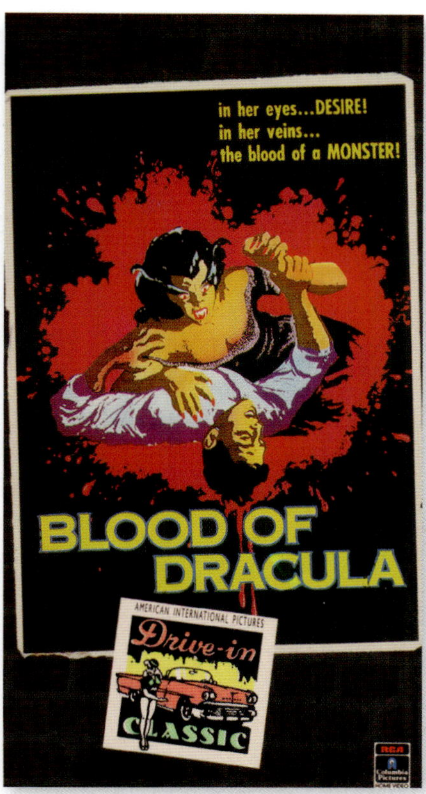

TOP LEFT: Writing in *Famous Monsters of Filmland* in 1962, Joe Dante included Edward D. Wood, Jr.'s *Bride of the Monster* (Rhino Home Video, 1995) on his list of the worst horror movies of all time. Filming began in 1954 (as *Bride of the Atom*), but because of financial problems it was not completed and released until 1955. It marked Bela Lugosi's final speaking role in a feature film.

TOP RIGHT: Originally released in 1957, Herbert L. Strock's *Blood of Dracula* (RCA/Columbia Pictures Home Video, 1991) was a companion piece to American International Pictures' teenage werewolf and Frankenstein movies that same year. About a schoolgirl who was hypnotized into becoming a vampire, in Britain it was released under the much classier title *Blood is My Heritage*.

BOTTOM LEFT: Also released in 1957, Fred F. Sears's *The Giant Claw* (GoodTimes Home Video, 1989) was about a giant monster bird from another galaxy attacking and destroying aircraft. Unfortunately, when the producers found they could not afford Ray Harryhausen's stop-motion animation effects, they hired a low-budget studio in Mexico City to come up with the puppet creature.

BOTTOM RIGHT: Irvin Berwick's independent 1959 movie *The Monster of Piedras Blancas* (Republic Pictures Home Video, 1990) took its inspiration from Universal-International's *Creature from the Black Lagoon* (1954). That's because first-time producer Jack Kevan had worked in the studio's makeup department and helped to create the Gill Man's iconic monster suit.

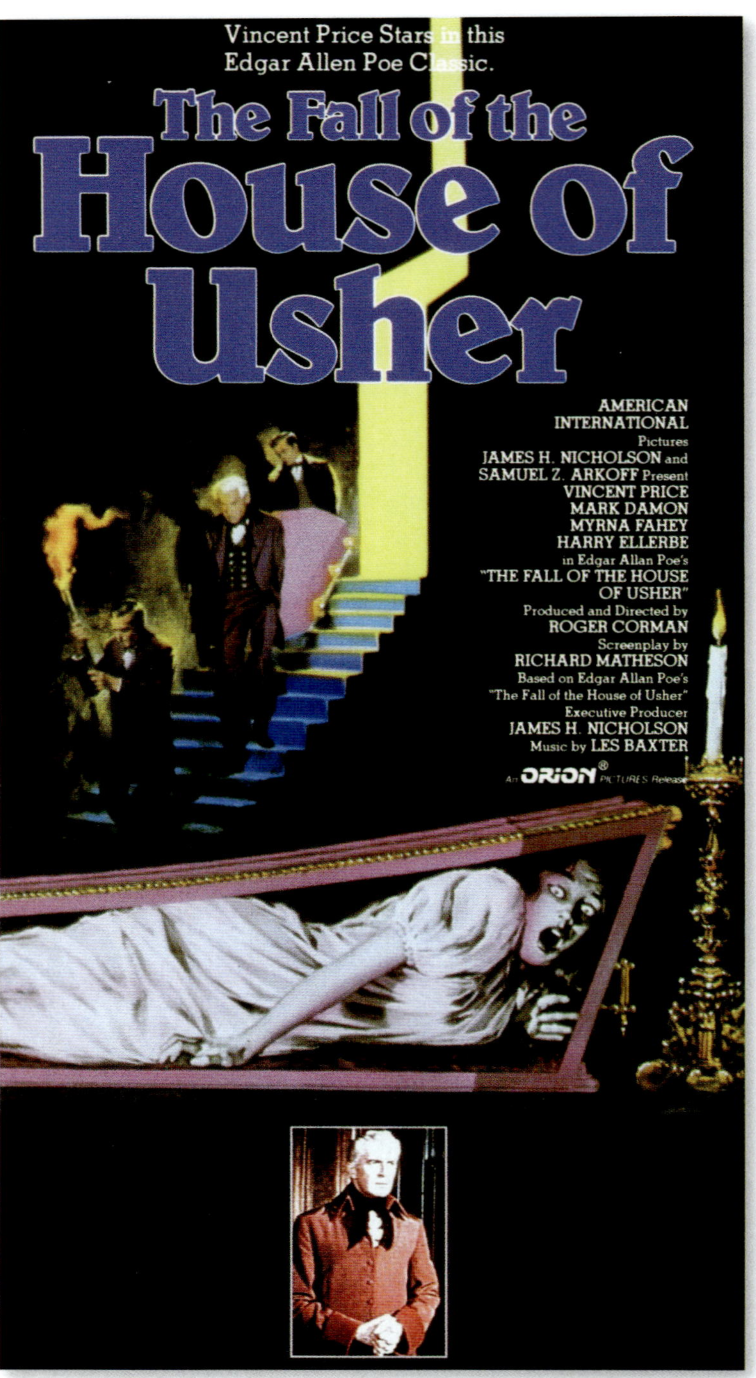

TOP LEFT: Shot over three weeks in 1962 on a budget of just $33,000 on location in and around the then-abandoned Saltair Pavilion in Salt Lake City, Utah, *Carnival of Souls* (Goodtimes Home Video, 1990) was the only feature film of industrial and educational filmmaker Herk Harvey. Because the movie fell into the public domain in the US, it was available on VHS from various video labels.

BOTTOM LEFT: Filmed in Pennsylvania in 1968 on a budget of approximately $100,000 by TV commercial and industrial filmmaker George A. Romero, *Night of the Living Dead* (Media Home Entertainment, 1992) grossed $12 million domestically and became a cult classic. Because the theatrical distributor failed to copyright the film, it slipped into the public domain.

ABOVE RIGHT: *The Fall of the House of Usher* (Warner Home Video, 1988) was filmed in color in just fifteen days on a budget of $300,000 and released by American International Pictures in 1960. Scripted by Richard Matheson, it was the first of a celebrated series of Edgar Allan Poe adaptations from AIP that were directed by Roger Corman and starred Vincent Price.

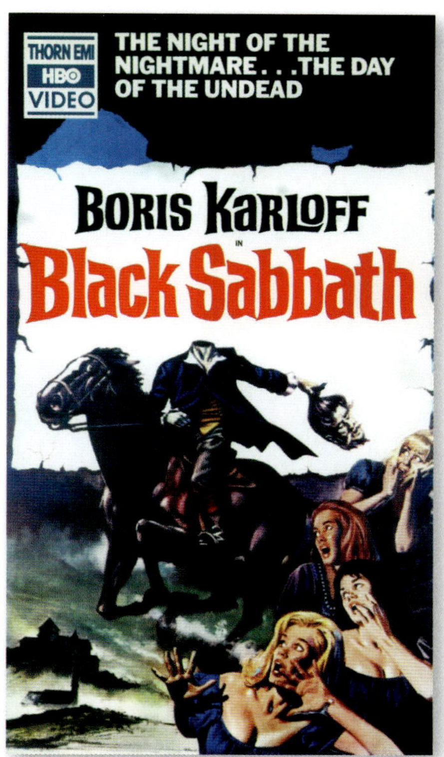

TOP LEFT: Mario Bava's 1963 Italian-made *Black Sabbath* (Thorn EMI/HBO Video, n.d.) was a coproduction with American International Pictures, who secured Boris Karloff to star in the vampire episode and also host the anthology movie. AIP subsequently reedited the film, changing the order of the stories and adding a new soundtrack for US audiences. The VHS release was in pan and scan.

TOP RIGHT: Jerry Jameson's low-budget *The Bat People* (Intervision Video, n.d.), also known as *It Lives By Night*, was distributed by American International Pictures in 1974. Stuart Moss starred as a newly married doctor who was bitten by a bat on his honeymoon and soon began to transform into a man-sized vampire bat. Future Oscar winner Stan Winston created the special makeup effects.

BOTTOM: Robert Quarry was back as the titular vampire in American International Pictures' 1971 release *The Return of Count Yorga* (Orion Home Video, 1993), director Bob Kelljan's sequel to his *Count Yorga, Vampire* the year before. Veteran actor George Macready, who appeared in his last role as an eccentric vampire expert, was the father of the film's producer, Michael Macready.

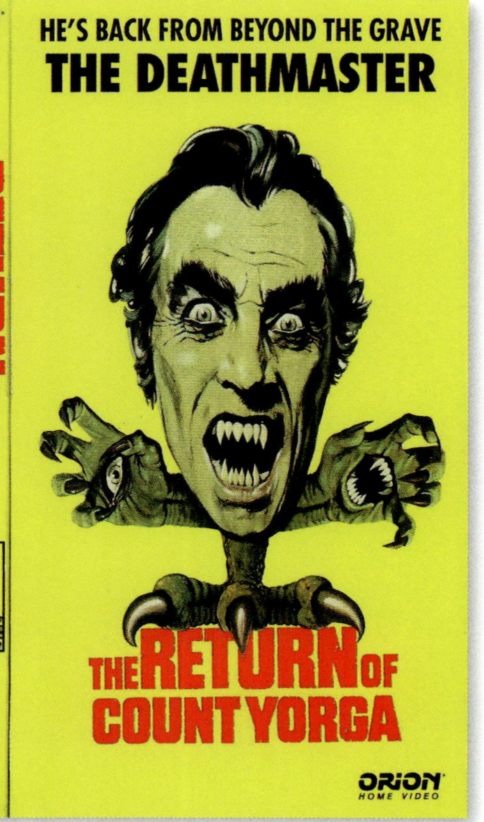

"*THE EVIL DEAD* WILL PULL SCREAM AFTER SCREAM FROM THE BASE OF YOUR SPINE AND FROM THE DEPTHS OF YOUR SOUL."
***THE EVIL DEAD* VIDEO BOX BLURB (1998)**

ABOVE: The UK video poster for Sam Raimi's 1981 directorial debut *The Evil Dead* repurposed Graham Humphreys's original artwork from the quad poster, which was credited with turning the film into a cult classic in Britain. After horror author Stephen King saw a preview at the Cannes Film Festival he gave the movie a rave review, later describing it as "The most ferociously original film of the year," a quote that was used prominently on the publicity material. Raimi credited King for making the sequels possible, after the writer convinced producer Dino De Laurentiis over dinner to finance *Evil Dead II* through his company DEG (De Laurentiis Entertainment Group).

When I was commissioned to design and paint the original poster for *The Evil Dead* (1981), my design was constructed specifically for the UK quad format (forty inches width, thirty inches depth).

When the client announced that a VHS sleeve would immediately follow, it was obvious that the quad format would not work. At that time, home video entertainment was still a relatively new and growing industry and appropriate considerations for poster art were often neglected.

The commission predated affordable desktop computing, so there was no way of scanning the image and rearranging the elements in Photoshop—as one might do today. I was left with no choice but to repaint the entire image for the VHS format. The urgent deadline resulted in a sub-standard painting that still makes me embarrassed.

There are various tricks you can employ that will accommodate reformatting, but I find them rarely satisfying. Designing for a specific format presents its own challenges, but trying to apply the same solutions to another betrays any considered composition. The vertical and horizontal formats are two different worlds.

When I worked on *Evil Dead II* (1987), I again had to resolve the separate formats with two paintings. The same with *A Nightmare on Elm Street* (1984) and subsequently *A Nightmare on Elm Street Part 2: Freddy's Revenge* (1985). In each case, I specifically designed for one format, having to make difficult compromises for the second. As first considerations, the quads were the inevitably the more successful compositions . . . with the exception of *Freddy's Revenge* which began as a portrait format, specifically for the subsequent video release.
Graham Humphreys

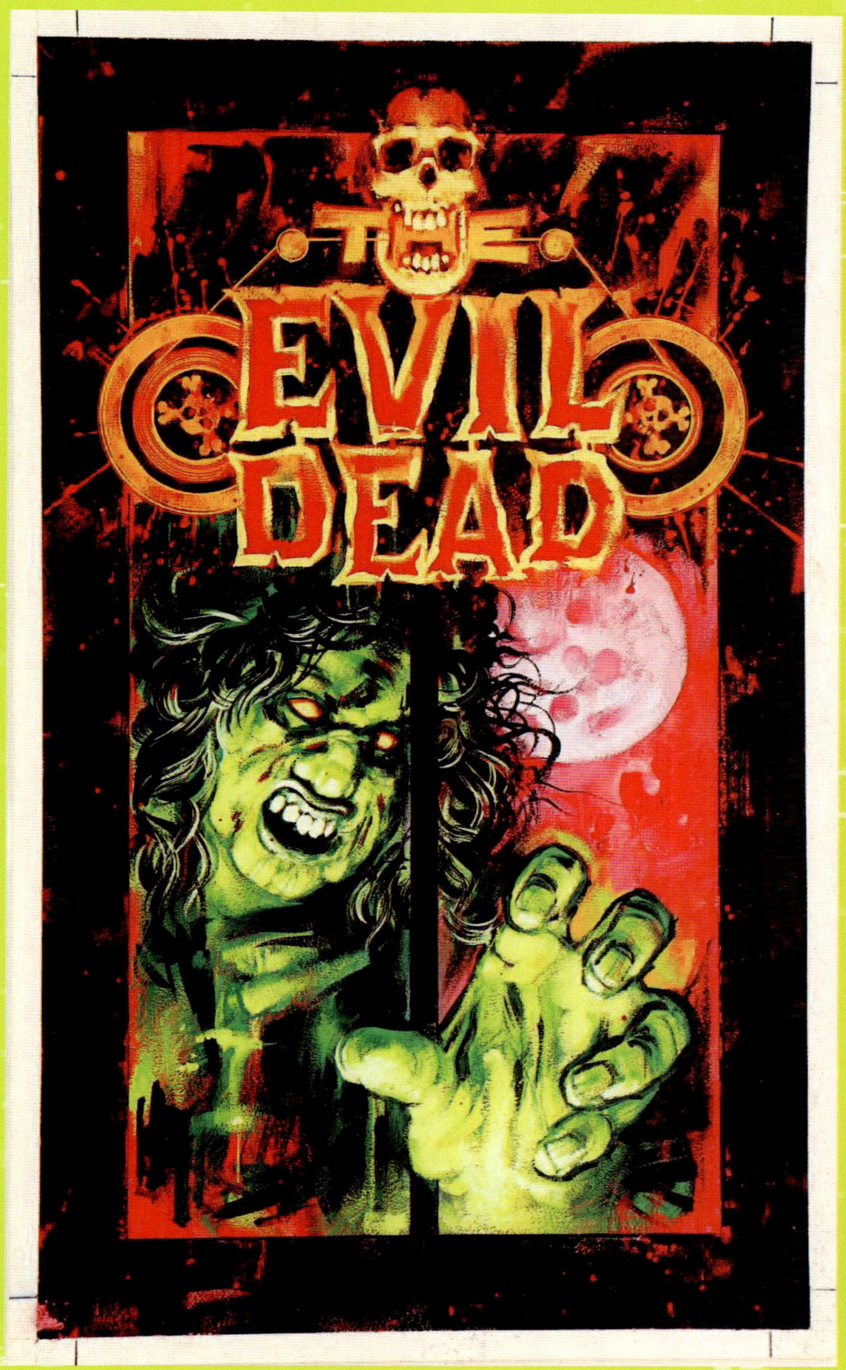

ABOVE LEFT: Although Graham Humphreys was unhappy with his original reworking of his theatrical poster for *The Evil Dead* video sleeve in 1983, he was given another opportunity in 1990 when Palace Pictures reissued the film in the UK. It had been unavailable since 1985, after spending a long time on the "video nasty" list before all threats of prosecution were dismissed.

TOP RIGHT: As had happened with the first film, Graham Humphreys was asked to recreate his quad poster art for the UK video sleeve of *Evil Dead II* (Palace Premiere, 1987). For the theatrical poster he had included a creepy clock and splattered the whole image with green and red gore. The final video design went for a more traditional look by concentrating on the characters of Ash and Annie.

BOTTOM RIGHT: Australian video sleeve cover for *Army of Darkness* (FoxVideo, 1993), the third installment in Sam Raimi's *Evil Dead* trilogy. This adapted Michael Hussar's original one-sheet poster design of a chainsaw-wielding Ash (Bruce Campbell) trapped in the Middle Ages and surrounded by "Deadites." The movie's original postapocalyptic ending was subsequently reshot.

TOP LEFT: As with his work on *The Evil Dead*, artist Graham Humphreys had to repaint his artwork for the 1984 UK quad poster when Wes Craven's *A Nightmare on Elm Street* (CBS/Fox Video, 1988) was released on video. For this first movie in the franchise, Freddy Krueger was only silhouetted in the background, although his signature metal-clawed glove was prominently featured.

BOTTOM LEFT: Renato Casaro's art was used on the Dutch video sleeve for the fifth entry in the series, Stephen Hopkins's *A Nightmare on Elm Street: The Dream Child* (CNR Video, 1991). "Splatterpunk" writers John Skipp, Craig Spector, and David J. Schow all worked on drafts of the script, in which Freddy Krueger attempted to return through the dreams of an unborn baby.

ABOVE RIGHT: Graham Humphreys's UK video cover for *A Nightmare on Elm Street Part 2: Freddy's Revenge* (Warner Home Video, 1987). Video releases of Jack Sholder's 1985 sequel in overseas markets were often heavily censored, while many versions omitted Bing Crosby's song "Did You Ever See a Dream Walking?" over the end credits, presumably due to copyright concerns.

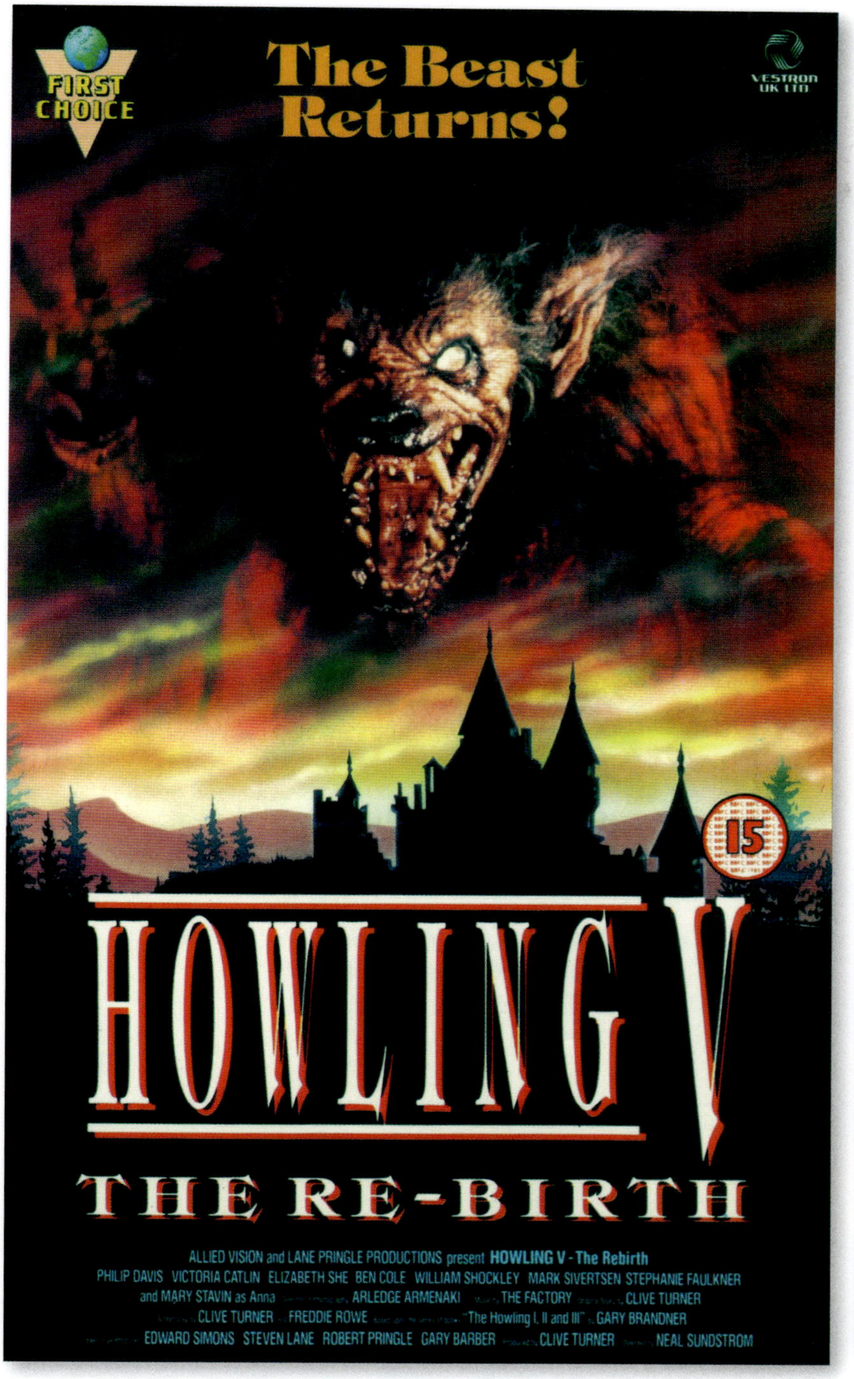

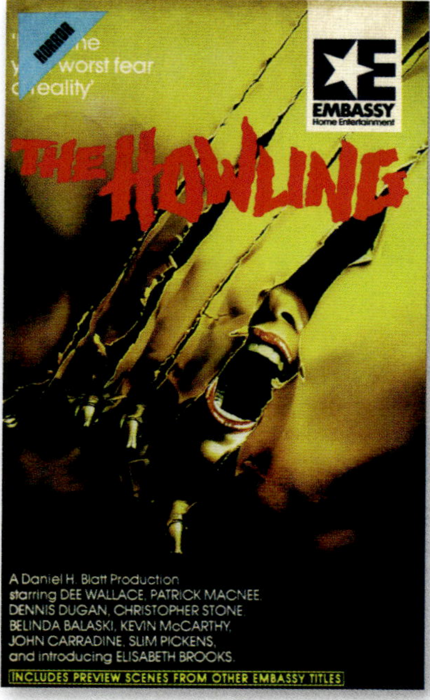

ABOVE LEFT: Filmed in Hungary, the direct-to-video *The Howling V: The Rebirth* (Vestron Video, 1990) was the fifth entry in the sometimes-connected series. Considered to be one of the better stand-alone sequels, it was more of an "old dark castle" mystery, as a group of strangers was killed off by an unknown werewolf. It has been followed by three more sequels to date.

TOP RIGHT: Based loosely on the 1977 novel by Gary Brandner, Joe Dante's revisionist 1981 werewolf movie *The Howling* (Embassy Home Entertainment, 1982) led to a series of direct-to-video sequels. Rob Bottin's transformation effects were state of the art at the time, and there are fun cameos by Kevin McCarthy, John Carradine, Kenneth Tobey, Roger Corman, and others.

BOTTOM RIGHT: Spanish video sleeve cover for John Hough's troubled *Howling IV: The Original Nightmare* (CBS/Fox Video, 1990), which was a more faithful adaptation of Gary Brandner's original novel, produced by Harry Alan Towers in South Africa. Coproducer and scriptwriter Clive Turner reshot, reedited and revoiced the film in postproduction after Hough's departure.

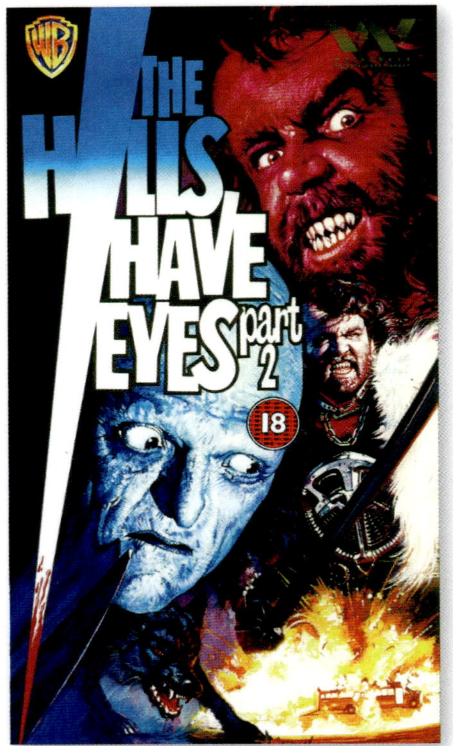

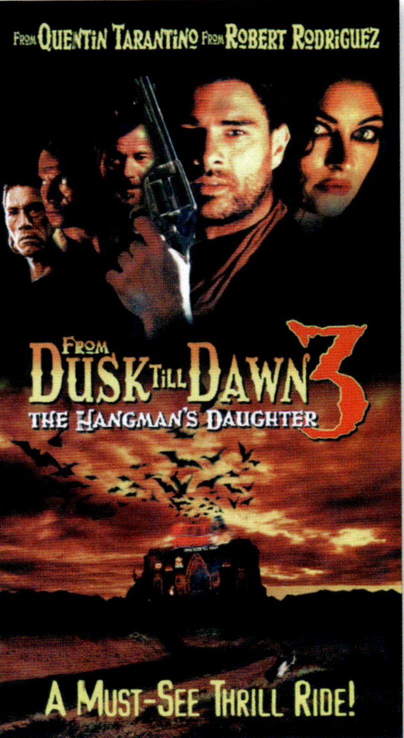

TOP: Australian video sleeve for American International Pictures' *Scream Blacula Scream* (CBS/Fox Video, 1990), director Bob Kelljan's 1973 blaxploitation sequel to his own *Blacula*, released the previous year. William Marshall returned for the second and final time as vampire Prince Mamuwalde/Blacula, revived by voodoo magic in contemporary Los Angeles.

BOTTOM LEFT: Wes Craven disowned *The Hills Have Eyes Part II* (Warner Home Video, 1989), a cheaply made 1984 sequel to his own 1977 movie. After shooting was halted when the production ran out of money, he had to edit the film together from the existing footage and flashback clips from the original. Following a brief limited theatrical run in the US, it went straight to video and pay-TV.

BOTTOM RIGHT: Robert Rodriguez only cowrote the original story for *From Dusk Till Dawn 3: The Hangman's Daughter* (Dimension Home Video, 2000), a direct-to-video prequel to his *From Dusk Till Dawn* (1996). Set in 1913 Mexico and filmed in South Africa, Michael Parks starred as "lost" author Ambrose Bierce, who found himself trapped in an isolated inn full of vampires.

TOP: Graham Humphreys's UK video sleeve design for Dan O'Bannon's *The Return of the Living Dead* (Vestron Video International, 1986), a 1985 comedy-horror "reimagining" that was loosely based on a novel by *Night of the Living Dead* (1968) cocreator John Russo. This movie is credited with introducing the concept that zombies specifically ate the brains of their victims.

BOTTOM LEFT: The sixth film in the "Children of the Corn" series based on the short story by Stephen King, the direct-to-video *Children of the Corn 666: Isaac's Return* (Dimension Home Video, 1999) was notable for featuring actor and cowriter John Franklin, who reprised his role as religious cult leader Isaac Chroner from the first film, *Children of the Corn* (1984).

BOTTOM RIGHT: Originally developed as a stand-alone script called *The Curse*, Katt Shea's *The Rage: Carrie 2* (MGM Home Entertainment, 1999) was subsequently rewritten to be a direct sequel to *Carrie* (1976), which was based on the novel by Stephen King. Amy Irving reprised her role as a survivor from the first film, while original star Sissy Spacek turned up in flashback clips.

TOP LEFT: Stephen King's second published novel was filmed by Tobe Hooper in 1979 as a two-part miniseries for CBS-TV. It was edited down for a theatrical release in overseas markets as *Salem's Lot: The Movie* (Warner Home Video, 1987), which also used slightly more gruesome takes of some scenes. The look of Reggie Nalder's vampire was inspired by *Nosferatu* (1922).

TOP RIGHT: Australian video sleeve cover for *Silver Bullet* (RCA/Columbia Pictures/Hoyts Video, 1986), which was based on Stephen King's 1983 novella *Cycle of the Werewolf*, illustrated by Bernie Wrightson. Following disagreements with executive producer Dino De Laurentiis over the werewolf suit, original director Don Coscarelli resigned and was replaced by Dan Attias.

BOTTOM LEFT: Michael Gornick's 1987 sequel *Creepshow 2* (Anchor Bay Entertainment, 1999) was written by George A. Romero from an outline by Stephen King. Although it consists of three stories, there were originally supposed to be five, as in the first movie. Romero's script for one of these, "The Cat from Hell," was later used in *Tales from the Darkside: The Movie* (1990).

BOTTOM RIGHT: Mick Garris's *Sleepwalkers* (Columbia TriStar Home Video, 1992) was based on Stephen King's first screenplay written specifically for the screen. It was about a mother and son who were the last of a species of vampiric shape-shifters that fed off the lifeforce of virgins. King, John Landis, Joe Dante, Clive Barker, and Tobe Hooper all appeared in cameo roles.

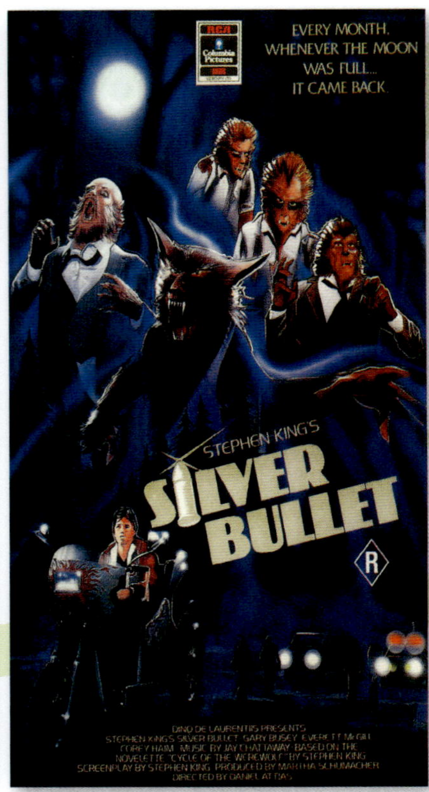

ABOVE: Joann Daley's original 1982 poster design was used on the VHS cover for George A. Romero's *Creepshow* (Warner Home Video, 1987), which marked Stephen King's screenwriting debut. Conceived as a homage to the EC horror comics of the 1950s, King himself starred in the title role of the second segment, "The Lonesome Death of Jordy Verrill" (based on his short story "Weeds"), about a backwoods yokel whose body was slowly covered by a growth of alien vegetation that originated from a crashed meteorite. Bernie Wrightson adapted and illustrated a tie-in comic book published by Penguin Books/Plume.

"SALEM'S LOT, MAINE. A SLEEPY NEW ENGLAND VILLAGE, THE KIND YOU SEE ON PICTURE POSTCARDS. BUT IF YOU VISITED HERE, YOU'D USE THOSE POSTCARDS TO SEND OUT DESPERATE PLEAS FOR SOMEONE—ANYONE—TO HELP YOU GET OUT OF TOWN . . . ALIVE."

***SALEM'S LOT: THE MOVIE* VIDEO BOX BLURB (1987)**

KING OF THE CASTLE ROCK

Stephen King's first novel, *Carrie,* was published in 1974 in a hardcover printing of 30,000 copies. A paperback edition appeared a year later, but it was Brian De Palma's 1976 movie adaptation that really launched the author and his work into the mainstream when it became both a critical and commercial success.

By then, King had already published *'Salem's Lot* (turned into a TV miniseries by Tobe Hooper in 1979) and he quickly followed it with *The Shining,* which was controversially filmed in 1980 by Stanley Kubrick. King was not happy with the adaptation, and he scripted his own three-part miniseries for ABC-TV in 1997, directed by Mick Garris.

David Cronenberg's *The Dead Zone* and Lewis Teague's *Cujo* were both set in the author's fictional town of Castle Rock, Maine. Both were released in 1983, the same year as John Carpenter's version of *Christine.*

Subsequent novels such as *Firestarter, The Running Man* (as by "Richard Bachman"), *It, Misery, The Dark Half, The Tommyknockers, Needful Things, Dolores Claiborne, Thinner,* and *The Green Mile* were all filmed.

Children of the Corn (1984), *Cat's Eye* (1985), *Silver Bullet* (1985), *Stand By Me* (1986), *Pet Sematary* (1989), *Graveyard Shift* (1990), *Sometimes They Come Back* (1991), *The Lawnmower Man* (1992), *The Shawshank Redemption* (1994), *The Mangler* (1995), *The Langoliers* (1995), *The Night Flier* (1996), and *Apt Pupil* (1998) were based on the author's short fiction.

King teamed up with George A. Romero for the anthology movies *Creepshow* (1982) and *Creepshow 2* (1987), based around his short stories. Mick Garris's *Sleepwalkers* (1992) was an original screenplay, while King and Garris partnered with ABC again in 1994 for an eight-hour miniseries of the postapocalyptic epic *The Stand.*

By now the studios were churning out their own often direct-to-video sequels without King's involvement. These included *A Return to Salem's Lot* (1987), *Children of the Corn II: The Final Sacrifice* (1992), *Children of the Corn III: Urban Harvest* (1995), *Children of the Corn: The Gathering* (1996), *Sometimes They Come Back . . . Again* (1996), *Children of the Corn V: Fields of Terror* (1998), *Sometimes They Come Back . . . for More* (1998), *Children of the Corn 666: Isaac's Return* (1999), and the inevitable *The Rage: Carrie 2* (1999).

Maximum Overdrive (1986) was Stephen King's only directorial credit. Loosely based on his short story "Trucks," it was part of a three-picture deal with executive producer Dino De Laurentiis.

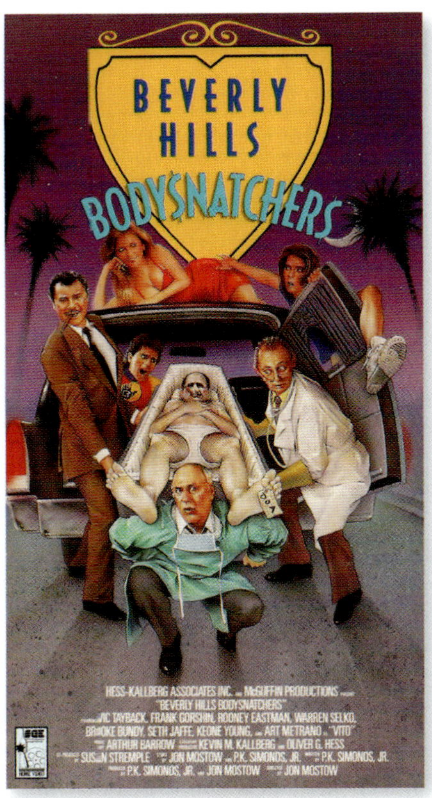

TOP LEFT: Boris Karloff and Phyllis Diller headed the voice cast of Rankin-Bass's stop-motion "Animagic" musical comedy *Mad Monster Party?* (Embassy Home Entertainment, 1985), which was originally released in 1967. Artist Jack Davis, who worked with coscriptwriter Harvey Kurtzman at *Mad Magazine* and EC Comics, designed many of the recognizable monster characters.

TOP RIGHT: When Vic Tayback's greedy mortician and Frank Gorshin's mad scientist created a formula for bringing *wealthy* dead people back to life, they accidentally revived a recently murdered Mafia boss in the horror-comedy *Beverly Hills Bodysnatchers* (Shapiro Glickenhaus Entertainment Home Video, 1989), which had a limited theatrical release before going to video.

BOTTOM LEFT: Susan Blakely's suburban housewife was bitten by John Saxon's urbane lycanthrope in the horror-comedy *My Mom's a Werewolf* (Prism Entertainment, 1989). When she began to transform into a supernatural creature, her teenage daughter and her daughter's horror-loving best friend set out to kill the wolf-man before the moon set and so put an end to the curse.

BOTTOM RIGHT: Taking its title from the 1962 hit novelty song by Bobby "Boris" Pickett and based on a 1967 stage musical, *Monster Mash: The Movie* (Turner Home Entertainment, 1996) was about a teenage couple who took refuge in the home of Dr. Frankenstein (played by Pickett), where they encountered all the classic Universal monsters, including Count Dracula and his wife.

OPPOSITE PAGE: Trade advertisement for the 1989 direct-to-video zombie comedy *Night Life*, released in the UK as *Grave Misdemeanours* (Medusa Pictures, 1991). Scott Grimes's teenage mortuary assistant was harassed by some fellow high school students who had been turned into the living dead by a toxic spill and lightning strike. With veterans John Astin and Severn Darden.

IT'S A HELL OF A WAY
TO KILL
AN EVENING
Grave
Misdemeanours
18
AVAILABLE AT ALL GOOD VIDEO STORES FROM FEBRUARY 8
RCA
Columbia Pictures
Medusa
PICTURES

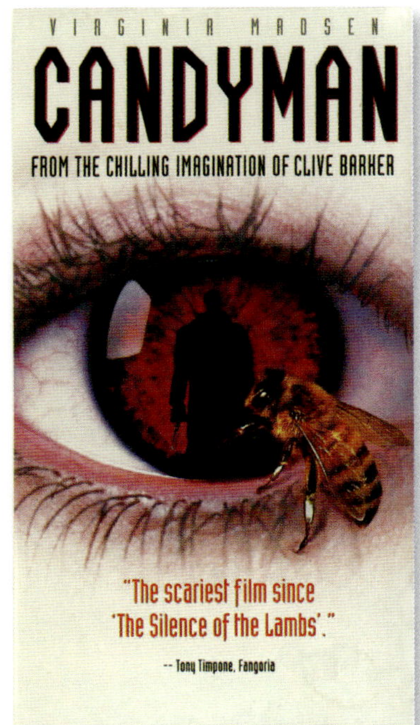

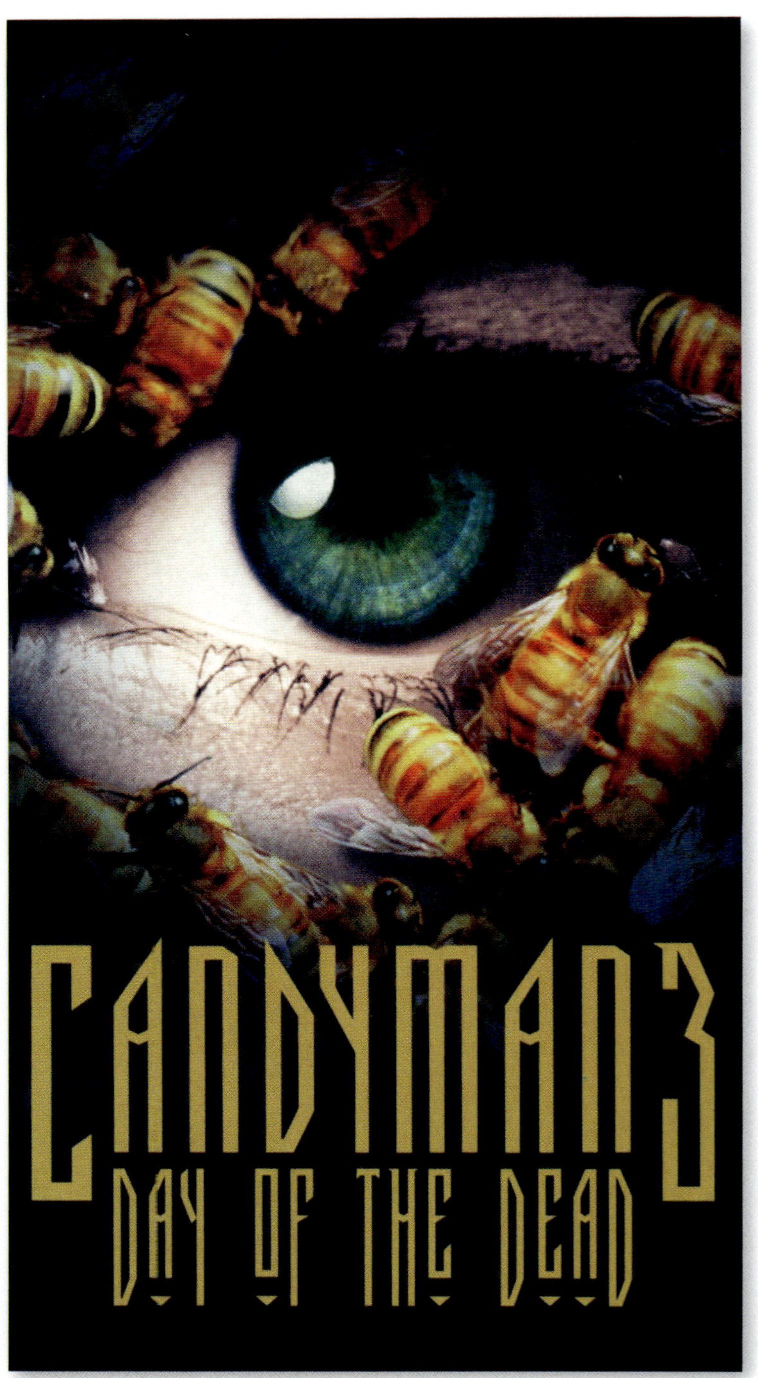

TOP LEFT: Based on executive producer Clive Barker's 1985 short story "The Forbidden," Bernard Rose's movie adaptation changed the location from Liverpool to Chicago and was retitled *Candyman* (Columbia TriStar Home Video, 1992), after the vengeful spirit of Tony Todd's hook-handed urban legend, who was summoned by repeating his name five times in front of a mirror.

BOTTOM LEFT: Clive Barker also executive produced and came up with the original story for Bill Condon's sequel *Candyman II: Farewell to the Flesh* (PolyGram Video, 1995). This time Tony Todd's ghost of a nineteenth-century murder victim pursued Kelly Rowan's New Orleans art teacher. Original director Bernard Rose's concept for a prequel was rejected by the studio.

ABOVE RIGHT: Clive Barker was not involved with Turi Meyer's direct-to-video sequel, *Candyman: Day of the Dead* (Artisan Home Entertainment, 1999). This time, coproducer Tony Todd's bee-covered bogeyman menaced the grown-up daughter of the heroine from the previous movie. It was followed by *Candyman* (2021), a reboot/sequel to the original 1992 film.

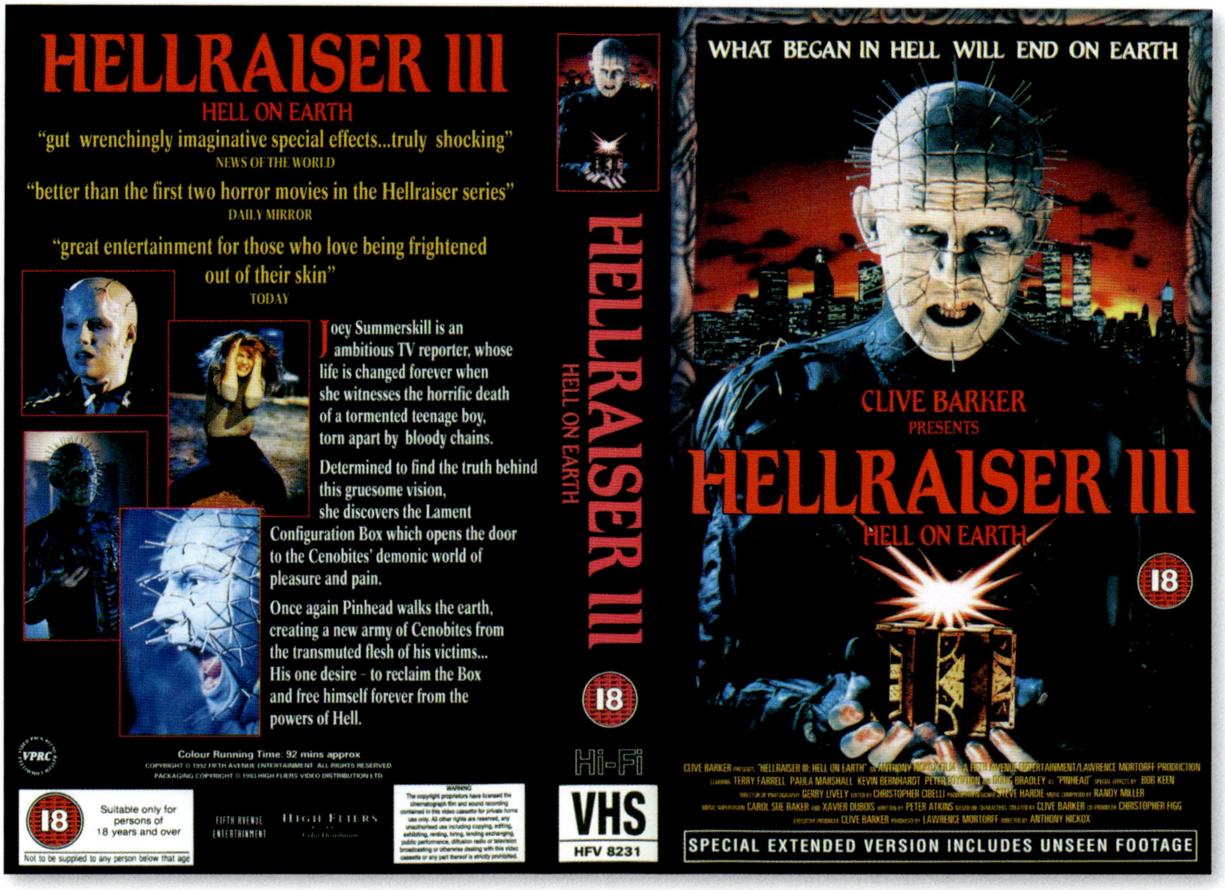

HELLRAISER III

HELL ON EARTH

"gut wrenchingly imaginative special effects...truly shocking"
NEWS OF THE WORLD

"better than the first two horror movies in the Hellraiser series"
DAILY MIRROR

"great entertainment for those who love being frightened out of their skin"
TODAY

Joey Summerskill is an ambitious TV reporter, whose life is changed forever when she witnesses the horrific death of a tormented teenage boy, torn apart by bloody chains.

Determined to find the truth behind this gruesome vision, she discovers the Lament Configuration Box which opens the door to the Cenobites' demonic world of pleasure and pain.

Once again Pinhead walks the earth, creating a new army of Cenobites from the transmuted flesh of his victims... His one desire - to reclaim the Box and free himself forever from the powers of Hell.

Colour Running Time: 92 mins approx

18 Suitable only for persons of 18 years and over

Not to be supplied to any person below that age

HELLRAISER III HELL ON EARTH

18

Hi-Fi

VHS HFV 8231

WHAT BEGAN IN HELL WILL END ON EARTH

CLIVE BARKER PRESENTS

HELLRAISER III

HELL ON EARTH

18

SPECIAL EXTENDED VERSION INCLUDES UNSEEN FOOTAGE

TOP: Clive Barker executive produced Anthony Hickox's *Hellraiser III: Hell on Earth* (High Fliers Video Distribution, 1993), which was the first movie in the franchise to be filmed in the US. As with the previous entry, Peter Atkins (who also played a Cenobite) scripted this second sequel to Barker's 1987 original, which revealed the origins of Doug Bradley's iconic Pinhead character.

BOTTOM LEFT: Dutch video sleeve cover for *Hellraiser: Bloodline* (RCV, 1997), the last film in the series to be theatrically released before going to video. Clive Barker again executive produced, while Peter Atkins contributed his third and final screenplay to the franchise. When Miramax asked for reshoots, director Kevin Yagher took his name off the film and it is credited to "Alan Smithee."

BOTTOM RIGHT: Clive Barker's third and (to date) final film as writer/director, *Lord of Illusions* (MGM/UA Home Entertainment, 1996) was based on his 1985 short story "The Last Illusion," which introduced occult detective Harry D'Amour. Although MGM/UA cut the movie for theatrical release, it was subsequently issued on video in a longer "director's cut" version.

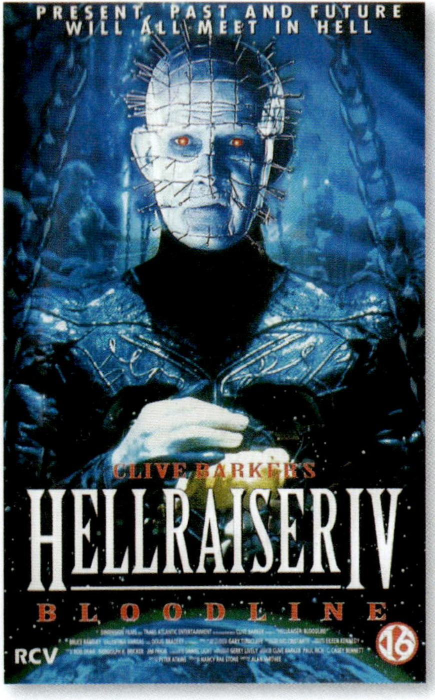

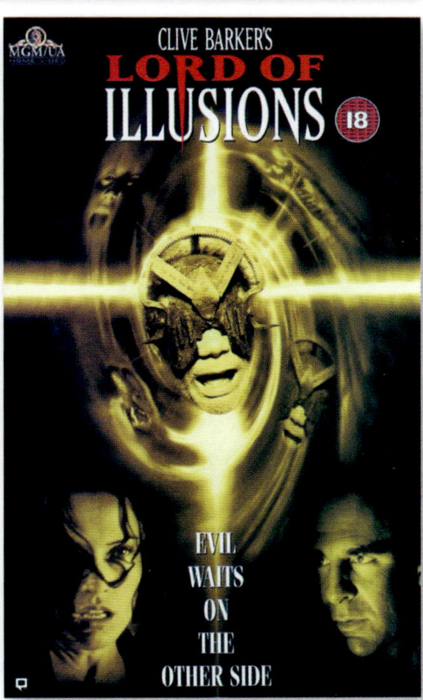

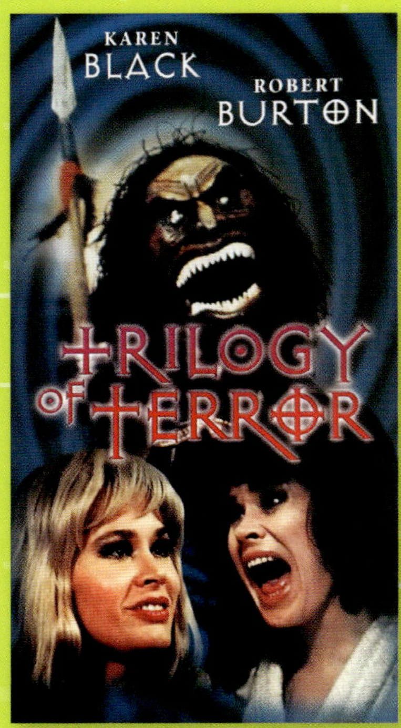

ABOVE LEFT: Produced and directed by Dan Curtis as an "ABC Movie of the Week" in 1975, *Trilogy of Terror* (Anchor Bay Entertainment, 2000) was a three-part made-for-TV film scripted by William F. Nolan and Richard Matheson, based on three stories by the latter. The third story, "Amelia," famously featured a homicidal Zuni fetish doll.

ABOVE MIDDLE: British video sleeve cover for Dan Curtis's *Dead of Night* (PMA Video, n.d.), which premiered on NBC-TV in 1977. It consisted of three stories scripted by Richard Matheson and was the pilot for a TV series that was never picked up. The third segment, "Bobby," was later remade for *Trilogy of Terror II* with different actors.

ABOVE RIGHT: *Trilogy of Terror II* (Paramount Home Entertainment, 1998) was first broadcast on the USA Network in 1996. Scripted by William F. Nolan and director Dan Curtis, it again featured three unconnected stories, with the third one, "He Who Kills," being a sequel to the Zuni doll episode in the original made-for-TV movie.

For film junkies and scheduling despisers, the jailbreak of cable and TV movies to VHS was akin to man crawling from sea and walking upright; liberation and deliverance gone retail. With push-button fates, plots and stars lived, dreamed, and died at our convenience. Our sofas were the pews, VHS players gulping cassettes like communion wafers, FAST FORWARD, REWIND, RECORD, PLAY, STOP, and PAUSE taking the pulpit, like narrative gods.

The HBO movie *Full Eclipse* (1993) was an edgy tale of werewolves on the police force I cowrote with the late Michael Reaves, and also executive produced. It snarled with rabid editing, and when released on VHS, I watched it on my big-screen TV, freeze-framing lycanthropic mojo, blazing FAST FORWARD through the so-so, hooked on full-moon, rewound rush. I reveled in digital-counts, even had the feral VHS box art blown-up to full poster size, framed in my office.

I loved that the movie was easy to rent or buy; paroled from servitude and schedule. That's what films should be. Watched when you want. With the "King of TV Movies" added to his golden quiver, my father was devout on the subject, collecting his films on VHS, including *Trilogy of Terror* (1975) and *Dead of Night* (1977)—adrenaline fixes he'd pop in when the mood hit. Take *that*, programming despots.

These days, you can get *Full Eclipse* on DVD or Blu-ray. Or just order it up if you're jonesing for some badge and fur. But once, not so long ago, when cable and TV schedules bullied space and time, and owning film copies was forbidden, VHS descended from the heavens and, as if prayer-answered, we could dim the lights, press PLAY and sin to our heart's content.

R.C. Matheson

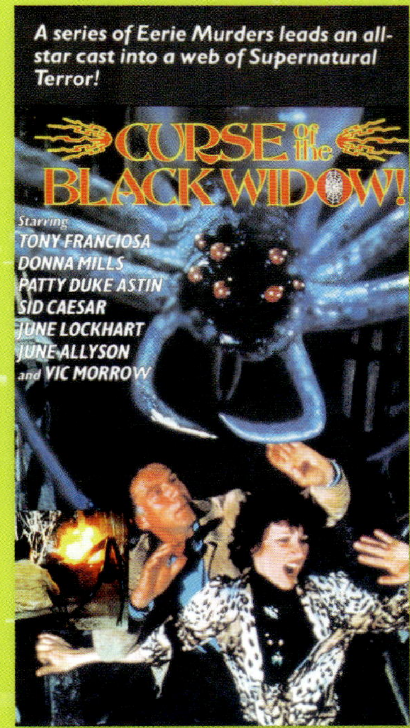

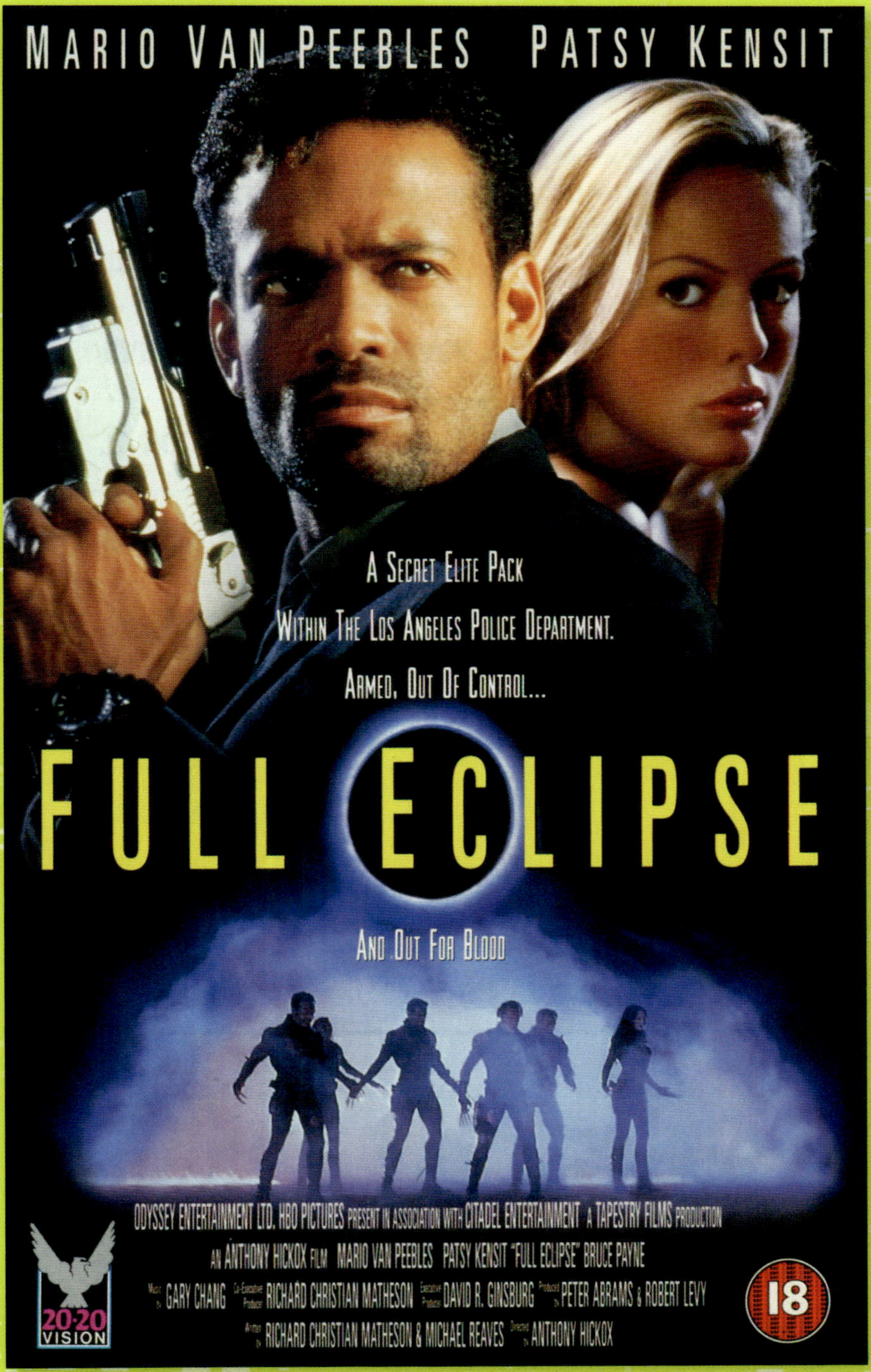

TOP LEFT: Canadian video box cover of *Curse of the Black Widow* (VEC, n.d.), which was made by Dan Curtis as a contractual obligation to ABC-TV. This originally started out as a Harlan Ellison project entitled *Dark Destroyer*, but no trace of Ellison's original remained in this story of a woman who changed into a giant spider under the full moon. It was later reissued as *Love Trap*.

BOTTOM LEFT: Canadian video box cover for Gordon Hessler's made-for-TV movie *KISS Meets the Phantom of the Park* (HGV Video Productions, 1992), which was first broadcast on NBC in 1978. The four members of the real-life rock band used their superpowers to save a California amusement park. An overseas theatrical version featured additional footage and an alternative soundtrack.

ABOVE RIGHT: British video sleeve cover for Anthony Hickox's made-for-cable *Full Eclipse* (Odyssey Entertainment, 1994), which was originally shown on HBO in 1993. Coscripted by Richard Christian Matheson and Michael Reaves, a renegade Los Angeles policeman used a serum to turn himself and others into vigilante werewolves so they could clean up the streets of criminals.

DRACULA
Ray

CHAPTER 4

HAMMER'S HORRORS

"There was no foul language, no gratuitous violence and, in the end, good always triumphed over evil."

Peter Cushing

"BARON FRANKENSTEIN IS DEAD, RIGHT? THAT'S PRECISELY WHAT HE WANTS FOLKS TO THINK. HE'S HAD IT UP TO HERE WITH A PUBLIC THAT DOESN'T APPRECIATE THE TROUBLE A MAD SCIENTIST GOES THROUGH TO SNATCH GOOD BODY PARTS."

***FRANKENSTEIN AND THE MONSTER FROM HELL* VIDEO BOX BLURB (1992)**

The revival in the British horror film industry began in the 1950s with a small company based in Bray, a village in the county of Berkshire set on the banks of the River Thames. Hammer Film Productions actually grew out of a company founded in 1934 by comedian and businessman William Hinds (a.k.a. "Will Hammer") and the distribution company Exclusive Films, which he cofounded with former cinema manager Enrique Carreras the following year.

Although Hammer initially turned out cheaply made "quota-quickies," invariably designed to fill the lower half of a double-bill, in 1955 they adapted a BBC-TV serial as *The Quatermass Xperiment,* which not only led to a sequel but also to color reimaginings of such classic horror characters as Baron Frankenstein, Count Dracula, The Mummy, and other proven franchises.

The use of a "repertory company" of actors (notably Peter Cushing, Christopher Lee, and Michael Ripper) and talent behind the camera (including director Terence Fisher, scriptwriter Jimmy Sangster, and composer James Bernard) helped cement Hammer's reputation among the cinema-going public.

It wasn't long before other producers noticed Hammer's success at the box office and decided to emulate them. Companies such as Eros Films, Amalgamated Productions, Baker and Berman, Amicus Productions, Planet Film Productions, Tigon British Film Productions, and even American International Pictures started making movies in Britain in the "Hammer style," which led to a renaissance in UK horror films that lasted until around the mid-1970s, when they were superceded by more "realistic" films coming out of the US, such as *Rosemary's Baby* (1968) and *The Exorcist* (1973).

Ironically, because the rights in most of Hammer's titles were tied up with different distributors, many of their rivals got in on the video boom first.

PREVIOUS SPREAD: *Dracula Has Risen from the Grave* (Dir: Freddie Francis, 1968).

THIS PAGE: *Frankenstein and the Monster from Hell* (Dir: Terence Fisher, 1974).

TOP LEFT: Terence Fisher's *The Curse of Frankenstein* (Warner Home Video, 1989) was the movie that kicked off the Hammer horror boom in 1957. Peter Cushing was cast as Baron Victor Frankenstein (the first of six occasions he would portray the character for the studio) and Christopher Lee played the "Creature" he created. This was one of the more difficult to obtain of the Hammer films on videotape during the heyday of the VHS format.

TOP RIGHT: Following the box office success of its Frankenstein revival, the following year Hammer reteamed Peter Cushing and Christopher Lee with director Terence Fisher for a color version of *Dracula*. Retitled *Horror of Dracula* (Warner Home Video, 1989) in America to avoid confusion with Universal's 1931 movie, Lee's portrayal of the vampire Count was the first of seven appearances as the character for the studio.

BOTTOM LEFT: A photo of Oliver Reed's reluctant lycanthrope graced the video box cover of Terence Fisher's *The Curse of the Werewolf* (MCA Home Video, 1987). Released in 1961 and loosely based on Guy Endore's novel *The Werewolf of Paris*, the action was moved to eighteenth-century Spain to take advantage of a number of standing sets that had been built for a movie about the Spanish Inquisition that was never made.

BOTTOM RIGHT: Filmed in 1964 by Terence Fisher as an attempt to create a new screen monster, *The Gorgon* (GoodTimes Home Video, 1988) reunited Hammer's dream team of Christopher Lee and Peter Cushing in a decidedly mittel-European version of the ancient Greek myth. Barbara Shelley was the unsuspecting shape-changer who transformed into a snake-headed monster whose gaze turned her victims to stone.

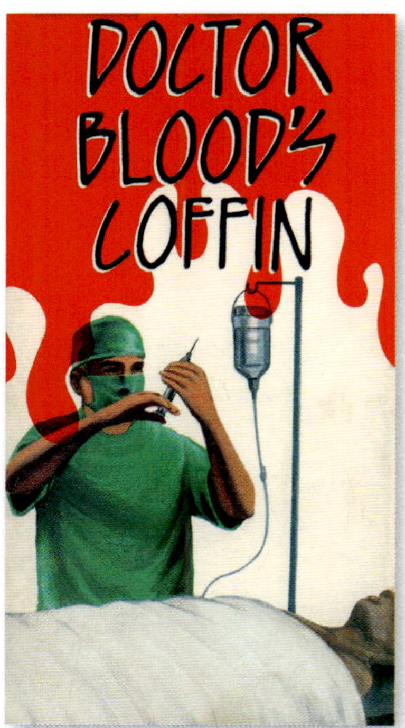

ABOVE LEFT: Based on the classic story "Casting the Runes" by M.R. James and filmed by Jacques Tourneur in England as *Night of the Demon* in 1957, the American video of *Curse of the Demon* (RCA/Columbia Pictures Home Video, 1986) was the edited theatrical version, running almost thirteen minutes shorter. The demon shown on the box cover was added in postproduction.

TOP RIGHT: Sidney Hayers's *Circus of Horrors* (Thorn EMI/HBO Video, n.d.) starred Anton Diffring as a crazed plastic surgeon who used a traveling circus as a cover for his experiments. It marked the only time that Hammer starlets Yvonne Monlaur and Yvonne Romain appeared in the same film. The song "Look for a Star" became a minor hit on both sides of the Atlantic.

BOTTOM RIGHT: In a rural Cornish village, Kieron Moore's obsessive biochemist was experimenting with reviving the dead using still-living hearts in *Doctor Blood's Coffin* (Alpha Video Distributors, 1991), filmed in the UK by Canadian director Sidney J. Furie. Although shot in color, the film was only shown in black and white during its limited American theatrical run in 1961.

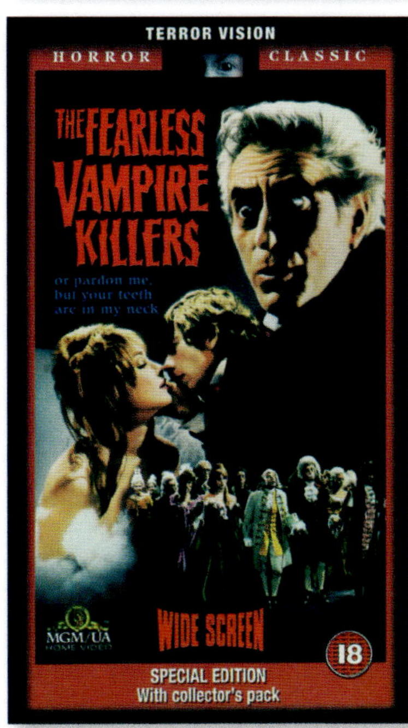

TOP LEFT: German Betamax sleeve for Lance Comfort's final film, *Devils of Darkness* (Hunter Home Video, n.d.), in which members of a secret French vampire cult led by Hubert Noël's Count Sinistre pursued William Sylvester's skeptical tourist to England to recover a golden talisman. Made by Planet Film Productions, this was the UK's first contemporary vampire movie.

ABOVE RIGHT: *Island of Terror* (MCA Home Video, 1994) was also made by Planet Film Productions. Directed by Hammer veteran Terence Fisher, it was set in a remote island community off the coast of Ireland where scientifically created "silicates" liquefied the bones of their victims. Peter Cushing's eminent London pathologist was forced to hack his own hand off with an axe.

BOTTOM LEFT: The 1967 Hammer spoof *The Fearless Vampire Killers* (MGM/UA Home Entertainment, 1995) was filmed in England and Italy as *Dance of the Vampires*. The original US theatrical release was cut by around twenty minutes and some actors' voices redubbed to make them sound more American without director Roman Polanski's approval.

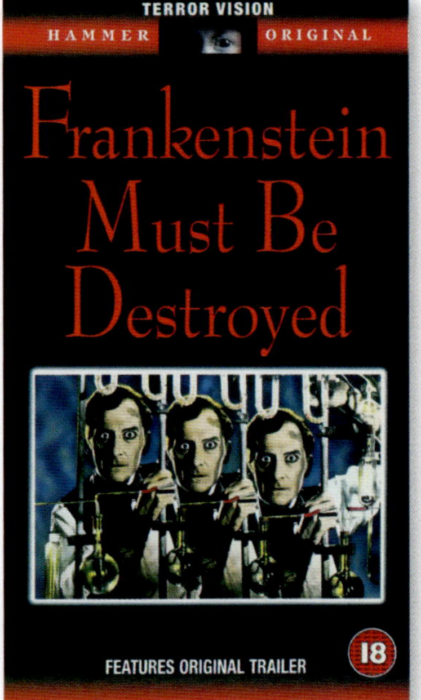

OPPOSITE PAGE: Original video box art for Hammer's *The Brides of Dracula* (MCA/Universal Home Video, 1992), a not-really-*Dracula*-sequel in which Peter Cushing's indefatigable Dr. Van Helsing attempted to save a naïve young schoolteacher (Yvonne Monlaur) from the clutches of the Count's disciple, Baron Meinster (David Peel).

ABOVE LEFT: Originally intended as Hammer's third Dracula film, *Kiss of the Vampire* (MCA Universal, 1990) was a stand-alone vampire movie made in 1962. Edward de Souza and Jennifer Daniel played the newlyweds who stumbled upon a Bavarian cult of bloodsuckers, and Clifford Evans's obsessed vampire-hunter was their only hope.

TOP RIGHT: *Dracula Has Risen from the Grave* (Warner Home Video, 1988) marked the third time that Christopher Lee portrayed the Count for Hammer Films. During filming, Hammer became the first movie studio to be presented with the Queen's Award for Industry, and this became the most successful movie in the company's history.

BOTTOM RIGHT: *Frankenstein Must Be Destroyed* (Warner Home Video, 1996) was Peter Cushing's fifth outing as the Baron for Hammer Films. The actor deplored the film's controversial rape scene between his character and Veronica Carlson's innocent landlady, which was added at the last minute to appease the US distributor.

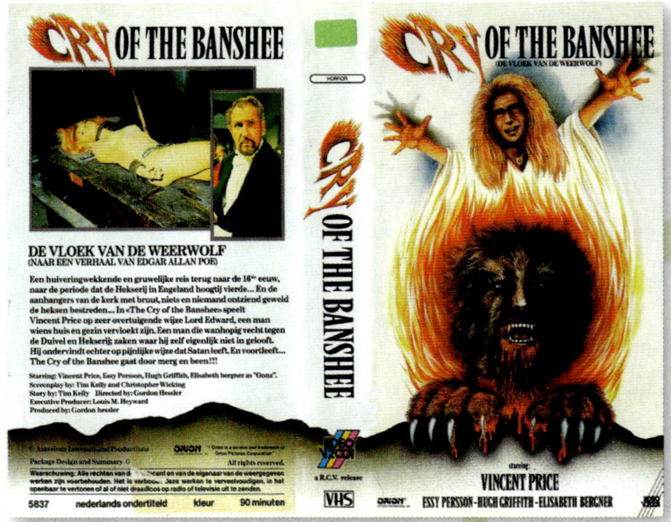

THE PRICE IS RIGHT

After studying at the University of London's Courtauld Institute of Art, American horror icon Vincent Price began his acting career in the mid-1930s, initially on the London and New York stage and then as a character actor in Hollywood movies.

Price eventually returned to England to star in Roger Corman's *The Masque of the Red Death* (1963), and over the next several years appeared in a string of further Edgar Allan Poe-inspired productions filmed in the UK by American International Pictures. These included *The Tomb of Ligeia* (1964), *War-Gods of the Deep* (a.k.a. *City Under the Sea*, 1965), *The Conqueror Worm* (a.k.a. *Witchfinder General*, 1968), *The Oblong Box* (1969), and *Cry of the Banshee* (1970).

Splitting his time between both sides of the Atlantic, in the early 1970s Price was back in Britain to star in *Scream and Scream Again* (1970), *The Abominable Dr. Phibes* (1971), *Dr. Phibes Rises Again* (1972), *Theatre of Blood* (1973), and *Madhouse* (1974), as well as various projects for British television and radio.

Some of these films were coproductions between AIP and such UK studios as Tigon British and Amicus Productions.

The Monster Club (1981) saw Price teamed with John Carradine in an anthology movie based on short stories by "Britain's Prince of Chill," R. Chetwynd-Hayes, while Pete Walker's *House of the Long Shadows* (1983) added Hammer stalwarts Christopher Lee and Peter Cushing to the quartet of horror heavies in yet another version of the hoary old mystery novel *Seven Keys to Baldpate*.

The actor's last UK movie role was in the comedy *Bloodbath at the House of Death* (1984), in which he played second fiddle to British TV and radio personality Kenny Everett. He continued working for another decade, until his death in 1993 at the age of eighty-two.

His final acting credit was Richard Williams's animated Arabian Nights fantasy *The Thief and the Cobbler* (1993), although Price had actually recorded most of his dialogue in London back in 1973.

"THIS ACTOR DOESN'T JUST BREAK A LEG. HE KNOCKS 'EM DEAD . . . ONE BY ONE."

***THEATER OF BLOOD* VIDEO BOX BLURB (1992)**

ABOVE LEFT: The Dutch video sleeve for Gordon Hessler's *Cry of the Banshee* (Video 2001/R.C.V., n.d.) reflects the movie's "folk horror" theme as Vincent Price's sixteenth-century magistrate was cursed by a witch for his brutality against local villagers. Despite his name appearing prominently on the American poster, except for a few lines of poetry this has nothing to do with Edgar Allan Poe.

ABOVE RIGHT: *Theatre of Blood* (Warner Home Video, 1987) was reportedly Vincent Price's favorite film. It's not hard to see why, as he relished playing hammy actor Edward Lionheart, who exacted a gruesome revenge on the critics who snubbed him (a star-studded cast of British character actors) through a series of slayings based on those found in Shakespeare's plays.

TOP LEFT: Australian video sleeve cover for Robert Fuest's *The Abominable Dr. Phibes* (Roadshow Home Video, n.d.), in which Vincent Price portrayed the demented and disfigured Dr. Anton Phibes who took a grisly revenge–inspired by The Ten Plagues of Egypt from the Old Testament–on the doctors he believed responsible for the death of his wife.

TOP RIGHT: Vincent Price was back as Dr. Anton Phibes in Robert Fuest's even more outlandish sequel, *Dr. Phibes Rises Again* (Vestron Video, 1985). This time he was in a race against time with Robert Quarry's centuries-old Biederback to find the River of Life buried below an Egyptian tomb so that he could resurrect his late wife. Once again, those in his way met a series of inventive deaths.

BOTTOM LEFT: Pete Walker's *House of the Long Shadows* (Guild Home Video, 1983) was a lightweight old dark house mystery that wasted the combined talents of Vincent Price, Christopher Lee, Peter Cushing, John Carradine, and Sheila Keith. Desi Arnaz, Jr. played the American author who traveled to a remote mansion in Wales to fulfill a bet with his publisher (Richard Todd).

BOTTOM RIGHT: Ray Cameron's *Bloodbath at the House of Death* (Video Treasures/Video Cassette Sales, 1988) was an old dark house comedy that starred TV and radio personality Kenny Everett. Vincent Price's "Sinister Man" headed a Satanic cult out to kill a group of paranormal investigators staying at a creepy manor. It was the actor's final British film.

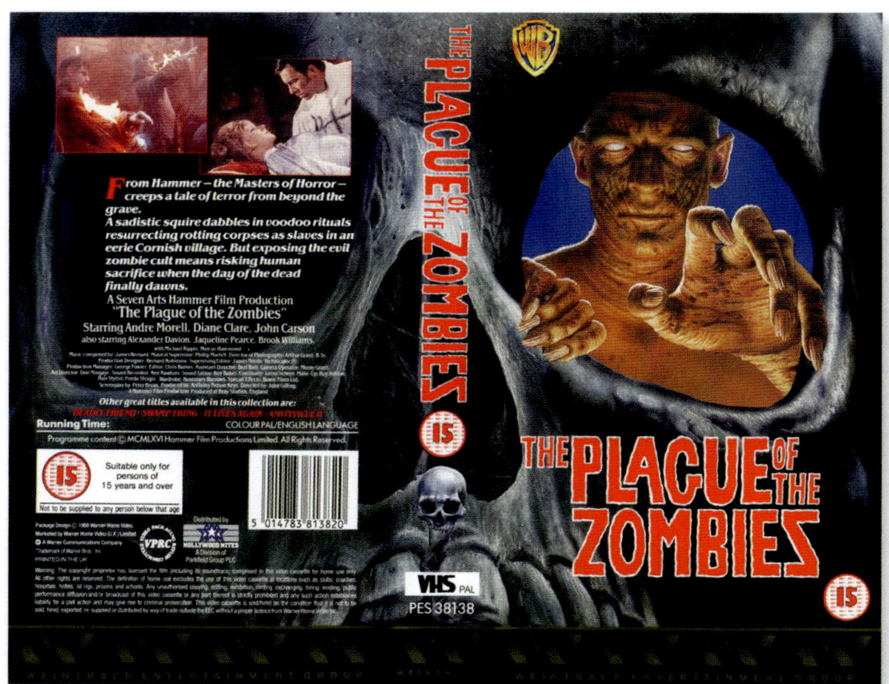

TOP: John Gilling's *The Plague of the Zombies* (Warner Home Video, 1988) was a very Hammer version of the West Indies mythology, with the location shifted to a rural village in Cornwall. It was filmed back-to-back with Gilling's *The Reptile* (1966) and used many of the same sets on the back lot at Bray Studios. To promote the film's release in 1966, girls were offered zombie-eyes glasses to defend themselves.

BOTTOM: Terence Fisher's *Frankenstein Created Woman* (Castle Pictures, 1991) was released in 1967 and was the fourth in Hammer's series starring Peter Cushing's Baron Frankenstein, who had become bored with swapping body parts and was now experimenting with transferring a soul from one body to another. As expected, it didn't turn out well for anyone when his female recipient went on a murderous rampage of revenge.

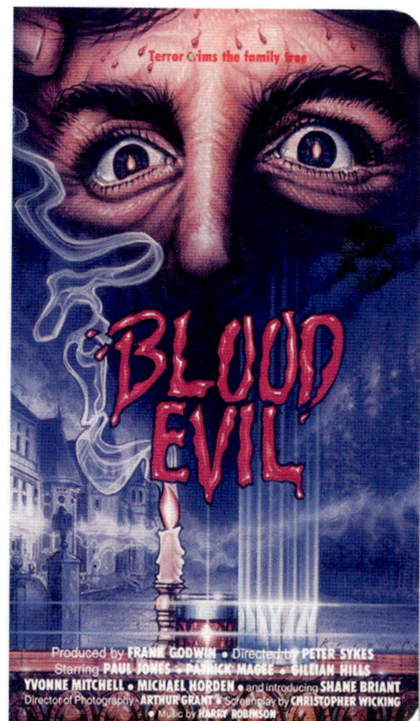

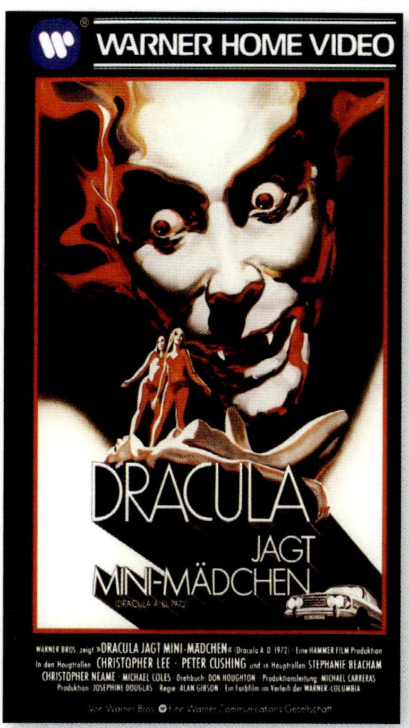

TOP LEFT: *Blood Evil* (Academy Home Entertainment, 1986) was actually a video retitling of Hammer's troubled Gothic mystery *Demons of the Mind*. Filmed in 1971 under the title *Blood Will Have Blood*, the film's UK release was delayed for a year after management upheavals at the studio, while it barely received a theatrical release in the US two years later.

BOTTOM LEFT: German video sleeve cover for Hammer's *Dracula A.D. 1972* (Warner Home Video, 1985), the first of two films directed by Alan Gibson that put Christopher Lee's Dracula and Peter Cushing's Van Helsing into "swinging seventies" London. Filmed as *Dracula Today*, the final title had to be changed in some European markets where it was released a year later.

ABOVE RIGHT: Box cover artwork by Spanish comics artist Rafael Cortiella Juancomarti, reportedly done for a 1980s video release of *Frankenstein and the Monster from Hell*. Released in 1974, it was not only the sixth and final entry in Hammer's series starring Peter Cushing as Baron Frankenstein, but it also marked Terence Fisher's final film as a director.

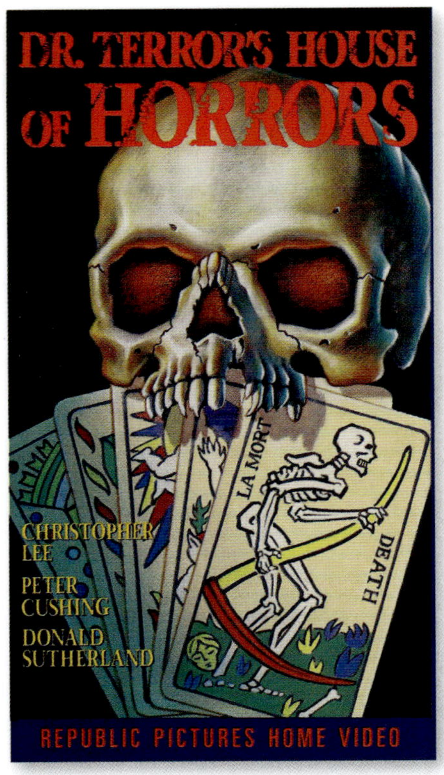

TOP LEFT: Under producers Milton Subotsky and Max J. Rosenberg, Amicus Productions was Hammer's closest rival in Britain during the 1960s and early '70s. Their first big hit was the 1965 portmanteau *Dr. Terror's House of Horrors* (Republic Pictures, 1989), which starred the rival studio's Peter Cushing and Christopher Lee and became a template for future Amicus films.

TOP RIGHT: The second Amicus anthology movie, *Torture Garden* (RCA/Columbia Pictures Home Video, 1985) was based on four short stories by screenwriter Robert Bloch. Because the US distributor insisted on two American stars, Christopher Lee and Peter Cushing's roles were given to Jack Palance and Burgess Meredith (who played "Dr. Diabolo" in the framework story).

BOTTOM: Impulse Productions "borrowed" the tagline from *Hellraiser* for its 1989 video release of *Black Werewolf*, a more exploitative retitling of Amicus's 1974 werewolf mystery *The Beast Must Die*. Calvin Lockhart's big game hunter invited six guests to his country estate to discover which of them was a lycanthrope. A "Werewolf Break" allowed the audience to make up its own mind.

TOP: Tony Tenser's Tigon British Film Productions was another major rival to Hammer in the 1960s and '70s. Written and directed by James Kelley in 1970, *The Beast in the Cellar* (Paragon Video Productions, 1985) starred veteran actresses Beryl Reid and Flora Robson as two spinster sisters who kept something nasty in the basement that was killing soldiers stationed in a country army base.

BOTTOM LEFT: Originally filmed under the title *Curse of the Crimson Altar* in 1968, *The Crimson Cult* (HBO Video, 1984) was a coproduction between Tigon British and American International Pictures and costarred Boris Karloff, Christopher Lee, Barbara Steele, and Michael Gough. It was loosely based on H.P. Lovecraft's uncredited short story "The Dreams in the Witch House."

BOTTOM RIGHT: Tigon's follow-up to the critically acclaimed *Witchfinder General* (1968), *The Blood on Satan's Claw* (Paragon Video Productions, 1985) is now justly regarded as an early film example of the "folk horror" genre. Patrick Wymark's seventeenth-century judge set out to discover why the children of a rural village had turned into a coven of Devil-worshippers.

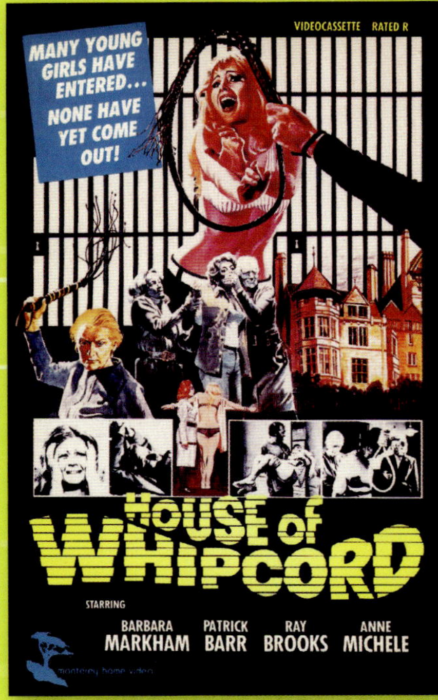

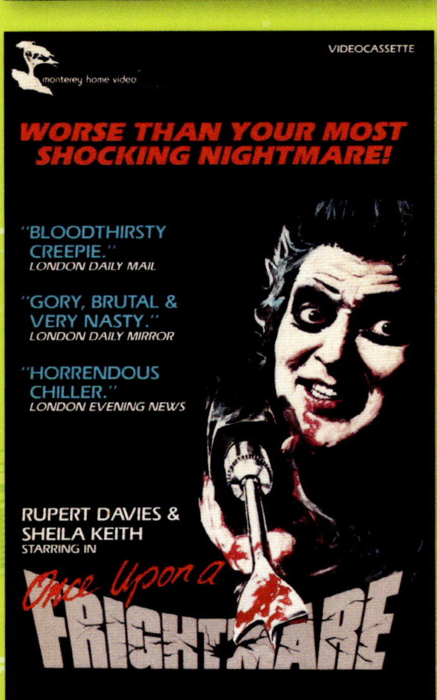

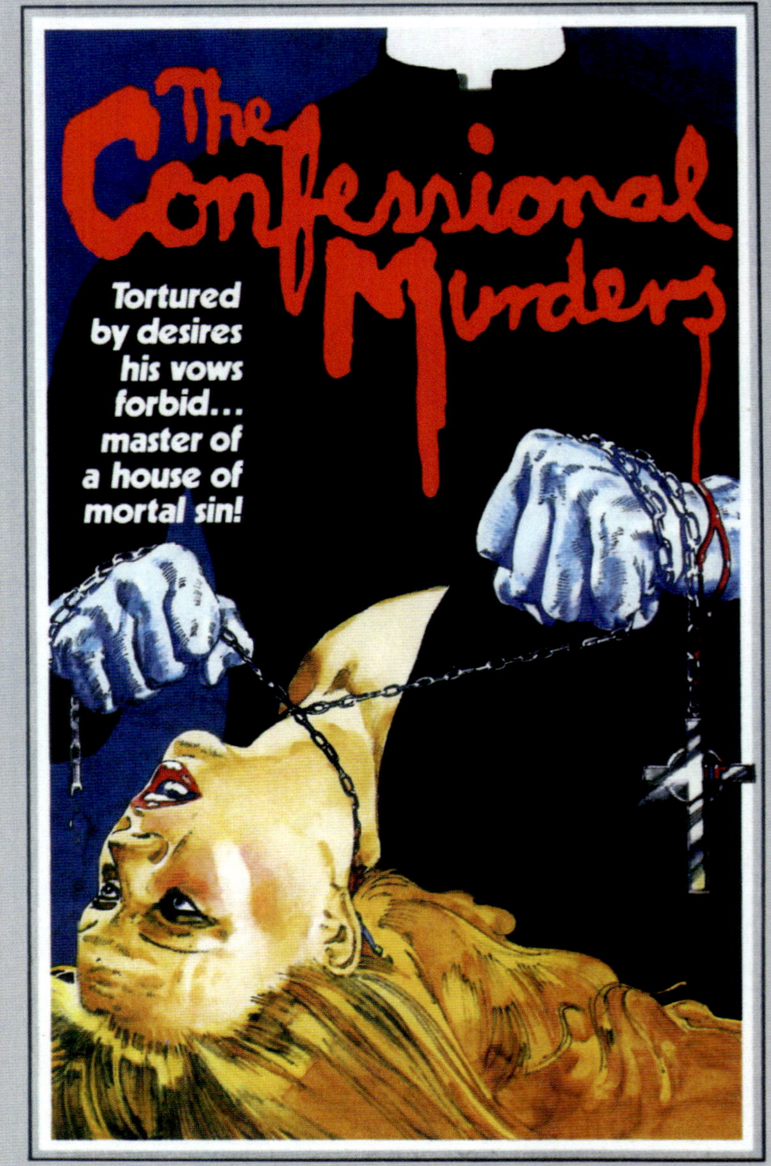

TOP LEFT: British film director Pete Walker and screenwriter David McGillivray were responsible for a quartet of transgressive horror films made in Britain in the 1970s. The first of these was *House of Whipcord* (Monterey Home Video, 1986), in which Barbara Markham's moral campaigner and her sadistic warder Sheila Keith ran a correctional institution for wayward young women.

BOTTOM LEFT: Sheila Keith was back as a homicidal cannibal in Pete Walker and David McGillivray's next collaboration, *Frightmare* (Monterey Home Video, 1985). Despite the often gruesome and exploitative nature of their films, they always managed to attract respectable British actors to appear in them, in this case Rupert Davies, Leo Genn, and Gerald Flood.

ABOVE RIGHT: Pete Walker again teamed up with scriptwriter David McGillivray for *House of Mortal Sin*, which was released in 1976. It finally turned up uncut on video in the UK as *The Confessional Murders* (RCA/Columbia Pictures International Video, 1983). Anthony Sharp played the priest obsessed with a vulnerable girl in a role that was originally offered to Peter Cushing.

"ONLY THE DEPRAVED MINDS OF A MORALLY CORRUPT FEW COULD DREAM UP SUCH A PLAN."
***HOUSE OF WHIPCORD* VIDEO BOX BLURB (1986)**

I have lived through only one period of complete upheaval in the film industry. I first saw a video recorder in the 1970s. A friend showed me a box the size of a fridge freezer that took tape reels like something a weightlifter might use. I looked with disdain at the fuzzy, black-and-white image the box reproduced and thought nothing more about home video for the next few years.

By 1980 I had a VCR because we were in the middle of the video revolution. I answered readers' questions for several film magazines and was well aware of how *cinéastes* had become obsessed with watching films not on the big screen but on their TVs. I was convinced that this new technology meant the end of cinema as we knew it.

My fears were unfounded. Cinema had survived radio and television and it survived video too. Although certainly a lot more picture palaces now existed only as Art Deco façades for pubs and dance clubs.

But the upheaval that video created spilled over into my own life, changing it forever. In the 1980s I became part of an exciting underground community that traded illegal tapes. In 1983 the Director of Public Prosecutions published a list of films that, because they contained something unpleasant—a decapitation or a castration or that sort of thing—were therefore not allowed to be shown. These films, as we know only too well, were dubbed by the press "video nasties." I wanted to see them all, and eventually I did.

The hysterical attitude of the media towards popular entertainment angered me so much that, for the first time in my life, I became politically aware. I published *Scapegoat* magazine and have remained an anti-censorship campaigner.

Today, when I think about the video revolution, the first thing that comes to mind is horror. But it's the horror of the favorite tape irretrievably enmeshed in the workings of the box. Bring me the scissors!

David McGillivray

ABOVE LEFT: The final teaming of Pete Walker and David McGillivray, *Schizo* (United Home Video, 1986) starred Lynne Frederick as a newlywed apparently being stalked by Jack Watson's ex-convict. As the bodies started to pile up, the clue to the mystery was in the title.

ABOVE MIDDLE: Norman J. Warren was another maverick British director. The first of his two horror collaborations with David McGillivray was the 1976 film *Satan's Slave* (Brent Walker Video, 1982) starring Michael Gough. A more explicit "foreign version" of the film also exists.

ABOVE RIGHT: The second collaboration between Norman J. Warren and David McGillivray, *Terror* (United Entertainment, 1998) was about the cursed descendants of a family of witch-burners. Inspired by Dario Argento's *Suspiria* (1977), it was conceived as a "fun horror film."

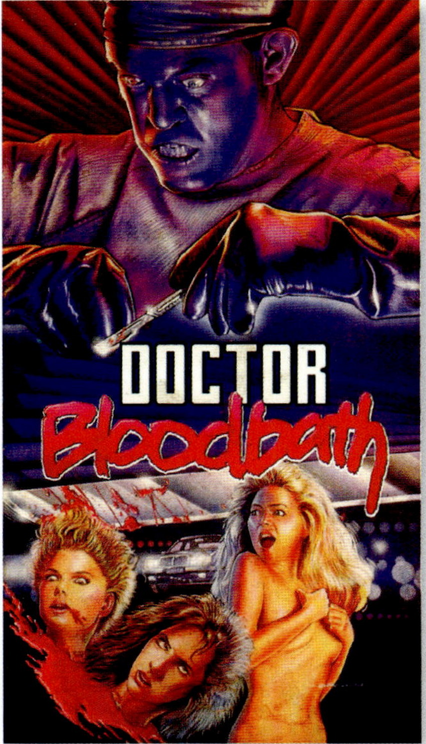

TOP LEFT: Pete Walker's proto-*giallo*, *Die Screaming Marianne* (Unicorn Video, 1986), was partly filmed in Portugal and starred Susan George as a nightclub dancer caught up in a fatal family feud to secure a large inheritance. This was Walker's first attempt at a horror-thriller after making a series of softcore sex movies.

TOP RIGHT: Tom Parkinson's surreal *Disciple of Death* (Unicorn Video, n.d.) was the fourth and final attempt by British radio disc jockey Mike Raven (Austin Churton Fairman) to turn himself into a star of horror movies. Despite looking like Vincent Price and appearing in films for both Hammer and Amicus, his career never took off.

BOTTOM LEFT: Antony Balch's bizarre horror-comedy *Horror Hospital* was released on video in America under the title *Doctor Bloodbath* (Bingo Video, 1988). Horror star Michael Gough hammed it up as a mad surgeon in a wheelchair who used his country sanitarium to conduct mind-controlling experiments on the guests.

BOTTOM RIGHT: *Night of the Laughing Dead* (Super Video, 1985) was the US video title for Peter Sykes's underrated 1973 horror-comedy *The House in Nightmare Park* (a.k.a. *Crazy House*), which starred veteran British comedian Frankie Howerd as a hammy stage actor trapped in an old dark house with a family of psychopaths.

OPPOSITE PAGE: Promotional flyer for *Bloody New Year* (Academy Entertainment, 1987), cowriter and director Norman J. Warren's overly ambitious horror movie shot on an island off the coast of Wales. A group of friends found themselves trapped in a haunted hotel that time-warped them back to New Year's Eve celebrations in 1959.

SHOULD OLD AQUAINTANCE BE FORGOT?
OR JUST BRUTALLY MURDERED.
BLOODY NEW YEAR
You've been invited to a very special New Year's Eve party. The Christmas tree's still up and you'll love the decorations. Just a few things you should know: your hosts have been dead for 30 years and they are the angriest, most demonic bunch of blood-thirsty ghouls you ever want to meet.
One more thing before you R.S.V.P.: whatever you do, don't dare come alone!
ORDER DATE: OCTOBER 6
STREET DATE: OCTOBER 22
Catalog #1091
Suggested Retail $79.95
90 minutes
Horror
ACADEMY ENTERTAINMENT PRESENTS BLOODY NEW YEAR starring SUZY AITCHISON COLIN HEYWOOD CATHERINE ROMAN NIKKI BROOKS MARK POWLEY JULIAN RONNIE Music by NICK MAGNUS Executive Producer MAXINE JULIUS
R RESTRICTED
Screenplay by FRAZER PEARCE Produced by HAYDEN PEARCE Directed by NORMAN J. WARREN
ACADEMY ENTERTAINMENT

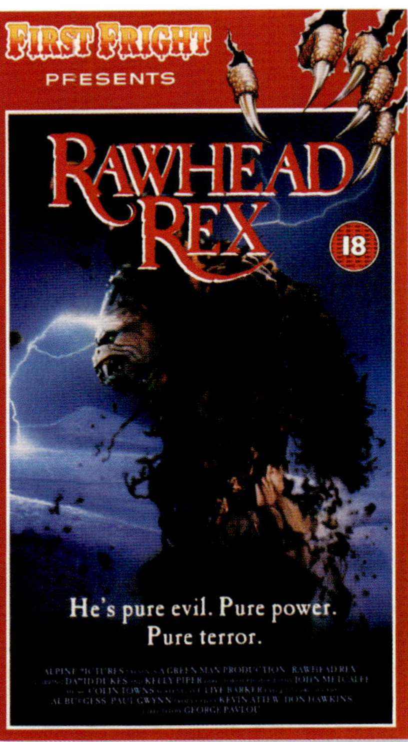

TOP LEFT: Before he became an acclaimed horror author and filmmaker, Clive Barker and a group of his Liverpool school friends (including Doug Bradley and Peter Atkins) made two amateur films in the 1970s that were finally released on video as *Clive Barker's Salome & The Forbidden* (Redemption, 1998) in a special "silver sleeve" edition that was limited to just 3,000 units.

BOTTOM: Japanese video sleeve for George Pavlou's low-budget 1985 debut *Underworld* (Tohokushinsha, n.d.), which was released by Charles Band's Empire Pictures as *Transmutations* in America. Coscripted by Clive Barker, the starry cast included Denholm Elliott, Steven Berkoff, Ingrid Pitt, Phil Davis, and Miranda Richardson. Barker reportedly hated it.

TOP RIGHT: Filmed in Ireland, George Pavlou's follow-up feature, *Rawhead Rex* (First Independent Films, 1991), was also released by Empire Pictures in the US and again featured a script by Clive Barker, this time based on his original story. With its rural setting and plot similarities to Tigon's *The Blood on Satan's Claw* (1971), it can now be considered part of the "folk horror" subgenre.

ABOVE LEFT: Disappointed with the two films he scripted for George Pavlou, Clive Barker made a deal with New World Pictures to write and direct *Hellraiser* (R&G Video/StarMaker Entertainment, 1994). Issued in America as a "Gold Series" VHS, this Collector's Edition anticipated the later DVD Extras format by also featuring a TV commercial preview and interviews with Barker and the cast.

TOP RIGHT: Scripted by Peter Atkins, Tony Randel's *Hellbound: Hellraiser II* (20:20 Vision, 1990) picked up right where the first film ended. This time Clive Barker coexecutive produced and came up with an original screen story for a sequel that put greater emphasis on the demonic Cenobites (led by Doug Bradley's "Pinhead"). The film exists in various versions around the world.

BOTTOM RIGHT: After the box-office success of *Hellraiser* (1987), Clive Barker's next screenwriting and directing credit was *Nightbreed* (Home Media Entertainment, 1990), based on his novel *Cabal*. Unfortunately, studio interference resulted in a diluted version of his ambitious vision for a sympathetic monster movie in which the villain was a human, played by David Cronenberg.

CHAPTER 5

SCI-FI SHOCKERS

"Science fiction films are not about science. They are about disaster, which is one of the oldest subjects of art."

Susan Sontag

"WHILST BATHING, THE TWO GIRLS NOTICE THAT THEY ARE BEING WATCHED. UNFORTUNATELY IT IS NOT ONE OF THE MEN . . . IT TURNS OUT TO BE A HORRIBLE MONSTER IN HUMANOID FORM. HE IS A HIDEOUS LOOKING CREATURE, WITH SOFT, RUBBERY, SPONGE-LIKE SKIN, THREE EYES AND A SET OF ANTENNAE BONES ON THE TOP OF HIS SKULL."

DAY THE WORLD ENDED VIDEO BOX BLURB (1989)

During the 1950s, science fiction movies boomed in the postatomic age.

While nuclear radiation caused giant behemoths to rise from beneath the waves, mankind reached out for the stars—and sometimes, terrifyingly, the stars reached *back* . . .

In those days the idea that you could watch and record movies in your own home seemed like something out of science fiction itself. And yet, within just a few decades, a videotape player/recorder could be found in most houses as the prices came down.

As with other genres, it was the low-budget or public domain science fiction titles that quickly found their way onto video first, but as the technology became more sophisticated, and distributors learned to enhance their releases with extras such as wide-screen, colorization, subtitles, trailers, and other bonus material, the major studios began to allow their bigger-budget productions to come to videotape for the first time.

One of the most notable home video releases was 20th Century Fox's *Star Wars* (1977), which eventually made its debut on tape in May 1982. However, due to concerns about video sales damaging the film's theatrical reissue ahead of the release of *Return of the Jedi* (1983), the *Star Wars* videocassette was initially limited to rental only for its first three months. When consumers began to inquire how they could buy copies of the tape, some dealers were more than happy to sell them a copy at up to $120 each under such spurious schemes as a "lifetime rental," thereby getting around Fox's embargo.

Not long afterwards, Paramount decided to market videocassettes of *Star Trek II: The Wrath of Khan* (1982) at the then unheard of sell-through price of just $39.95. The risk paid off—the release was a huge success that helped usher in the 1980s video boom, as prerecorded cassettes started to come within the financial reach of most families.

PREVIOUS SPREAD: *Robot Monster* (Dir: Phil Tucker, 1953).

THIS PAGE: *Day the World Ended* (Dir: Roger Corman, 1955).

TOP LEFT: Based on a treatment by H.G. Wells and adapted from his own novel, William Cameron Menzies's 1936 release *Things to Come* (Alpha Video Distributors, 1994) is considered to be the first major British science fiction film. This American public domain video release (it has since come back into copyright in the US) featured the heavily cut version available at the time.

TOP RIGHT: Released in 3-D by Astor Pictures in 1953, *Cat-Women of the Moon* (Rhino Home Video, 1991) was exactly what the title said: a space mission to the Moon discovered giant spiders and a race of telepathic cat-women in black tights who want to conquer the Earth. The music score was by future Oscar winner Elmer Bernstein (whose name was misspelled on the credits).

BOTTOM LEFT: Australian video cover for *Invasion of the Saucer Men* (Roadshow Home Video, n.d.), released by American International Pictures in 1957. The rights to Paul W. Fairman's story in *Amazing Stories* were purchased through collector and literary agent Forrest J Ackerman. Low-budget special effects maestro Paul Blaisdell created the flying saucer and big-brained aliens.

BOTTOM RIGHT: Australian video cover for *Fiend Without a Face* (Video Box Office, n.d.), released in 1958. A retired scientist created thought-projected monsters (achieved through stop-motion animation) that sucked out the brains and spinal cords of their victims. Forrest J Ackerman sold the film rights to the original *Weird Tales* story by Amelia Reynolds Long.

TOP: George Pal's 1953 production of *The War of the Worlds* (Paramount Pictures, 1996) was a contemporary reimagining of H.G. Wells's 1898 novel, with the action transposed to Southern California. Gene Barry and Ann Robinson attempted to evade the death-rays of invading Martian war machines, which hovered instead of walking on tripod legs as in the original book. It still won the Oscar for Best Visual Effects.

BOTTOM: Often considered to be one of the worst movies of all time, the twenty-five-year-old director of *Robot Monster* (Rhino Home Video, 1991) reportedly tried to commit suicide when it was released in 1953. Despite its miniscule budget and ludicrous-looking "Ro-Man" invader from the Moon, it was shot in dual-strip polarized 3-D (dubbed "Tru-Stereo") and featured another early music score composed by Elmer Bernstein.

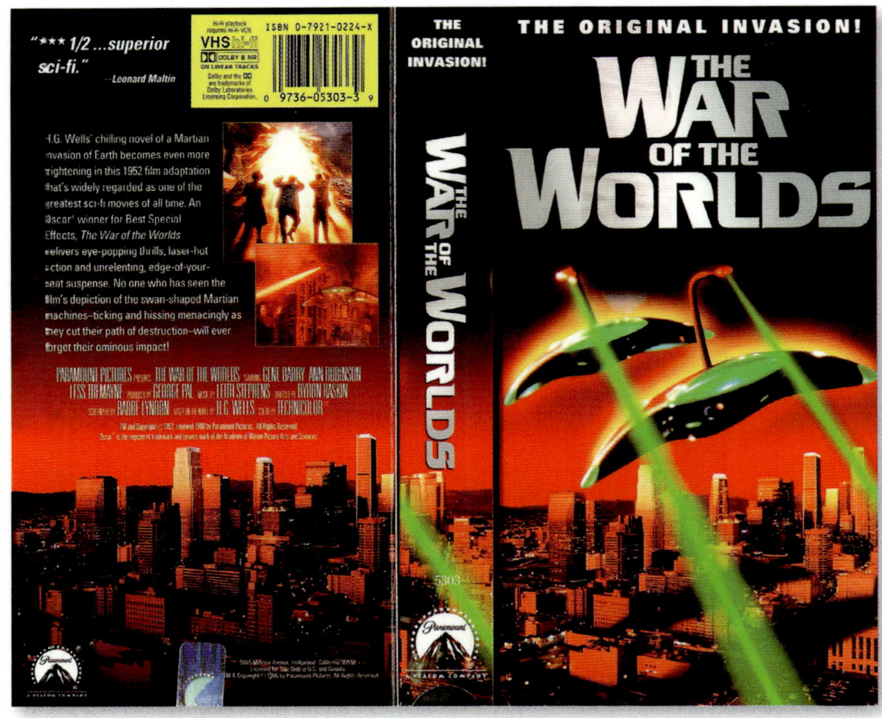

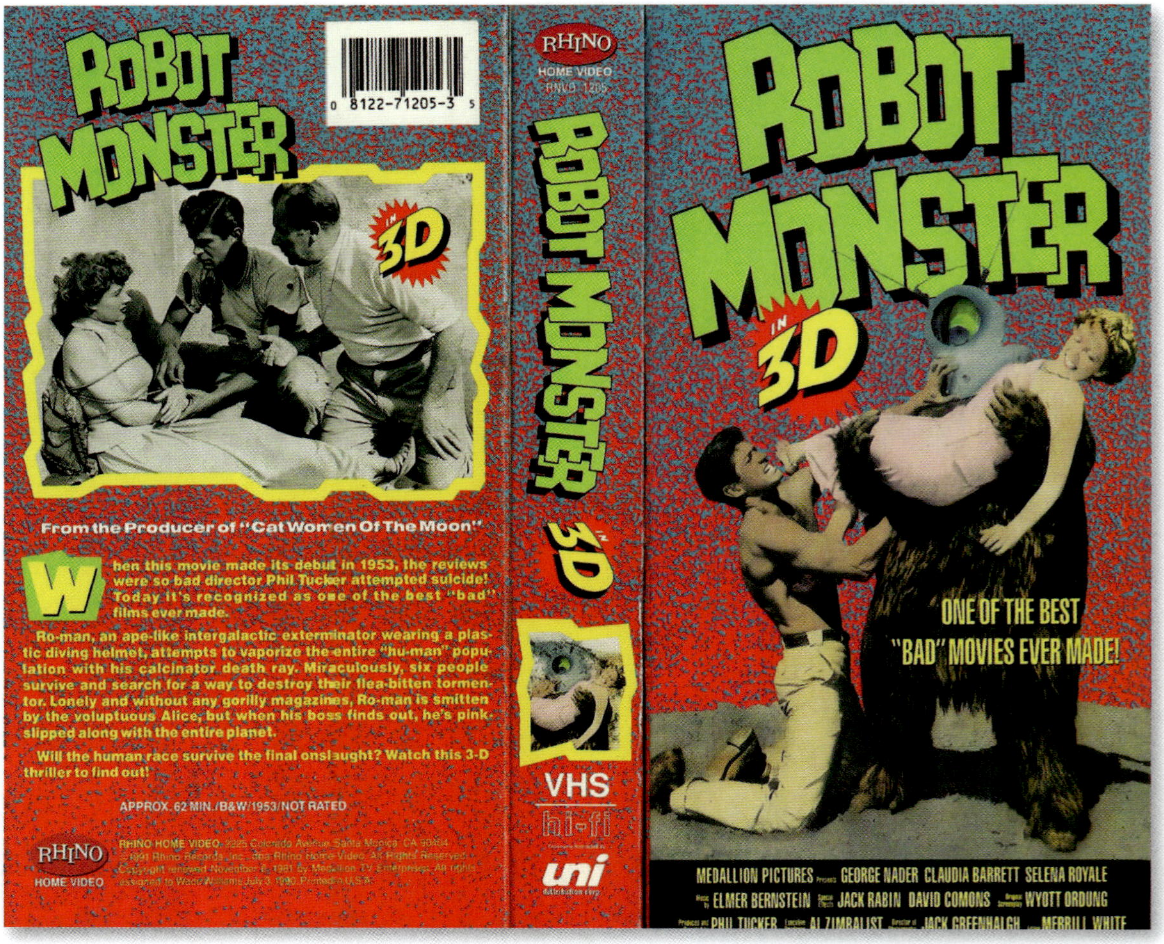

TOP LEFT: Based on an original screen treatment by Ray Bradbury, Jack Arnold's *It Came from Outer Space* (Good Times Home Video, 1987) was released in 3-D by Universal in 1953. Richard Carlson's amateur astronomer and Barbara Rush's schoolteacher discovered that local townsfolk were being abducted by benign aliens, who had accidentally crashed their spaceship on Earth.

BOTTOM LEFT: There was nothing benign about the extraterrestrials in Columbia Pictures' 1956 release, *Earth vs. the Flying Saucers* (Good Times Home Video, 1989). Scientist Hugh Marlowe and his new bride Joan Taylor had limited time to come up with an anti-magnetic weapon to stop hostile aliens from invading the Earth. The stop-motion special effects were created by Ray Harryhausen.

ABOVE RIGHT: The VHS "Double Feature" *Killers from Space/Day of the Triffids* (Good Times Home Video, 1986) paired two science fiction movies from 1954 and 1963, respectively. In the first, Peter Graves's dead nuclear scientist was revived by bug-eyed aliens, while Earth was invaded by giant walking plants in the second, based on the 1951 novel by John Wyndham.

TOP: Australian video box for the 1958 cult classic *Attack of the 50 Foot Woman* (CBS/Fox Video, 1994) which starred Alison Hayes as a woman who grew to gigantic size after an alien encounter and decided to revenge herself on her cheating husband. Director Nathan Juran insisted on being credited as "Nathan Hertz" because he was reportedly embarrassed by the film's low budget.

BOTTOM LEFT: Originally released in 1974, the West German-Austrian softcore sci-fi sex comedy *2069: A Sex Odyssey* (Imperial Video Corp., 1983) finally made it to American shores in a dubbed version three years later. Disguised as the French Olympic skiing team, five women from Venus arrived on Earth looking for male donors to help repopulate their all-female planet.

BOTTOM RIGHT: Canadian-born actress and *Playboy* Playmate of the Year Dorothy R. Stratten portrayed a blonde android from the thirty-first century in the 1980 comedy *Galaxina* (Guild Home Video, 1982). Two months after the movie was released, she was murdered by her estranged husband. The film included a clip from *First Spaceship on Venus* (1960), released by the same theatrical distributor.

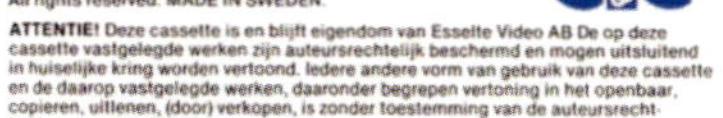

TOP: Swedish video box for Roger Vadim's 1968 comedy *Barbarella* (Esselte CIC Video, n.d.), in which the director's then-wife, Jane Fonda, portrayed the titular space adventurer from Jean-Claude Forest's popular French comic strip. Terry Southern's screenplay was reportedly rewritten by at least fourteen other writers, including Vadim, Tudor Gates, and an uncredited Charles B. Griffith.

BOTTOM LEFT: Roger Corman's original 1957 version was coscripted by Charles B. Griffith and Mark Hanna. In 1988, Jim Wynorski decided to remake *Not of This Earth* (MGM/UA Home Video, 1988) with the same (inflation-adjusted) budget and schedule. He cast former porn actress Traci Lords in her first mainstream role, as a nurse hired to take care of an alien needing blood transfusions.

BOTTOM RIGHT: Danish actress Brigitte Nielsen starred as an alien warrior princess who traveled to Earth to recover a mystical crystal so she could prevent Richard Moll's evil warlord from using its powers for himself in the direct-to-video release *Galaxis* (Osmosis Pictures/Turner Home Entertainment, 1995). The film was released under the alternate title *Terminal Force* in some overseas territories.

KNOCKOUT VIDEO FILM
DISTRIBUTORS
BIRMINGHAM

KNOCKOUT VIDEO

Flesh Eaters X

Absolutely nothing will prepare you for what you will SEE

Starring MARTIN KOSLECK
RITA MORLEY

TOP LEFT: Released in Europe in 1960, but not for another two years in the US (and then cut by nearly fifteen minutes), *First Spaceship on Venus* (Englewood Entertainment, 1998) was an East German-Polish coproduction starring French-Japanese actress Yoko Tani as a member of a space expedition looking for life on Venus. It was based on the first book by Polish author Stanislaw Lem.

BOTTOM LEFT: Mario Bava's stylish 1965 Italian-Spanish coproduction *Planet of the Vampires* (Orion Home Video, 1993) starred American actor Barry Sullivan as the commander of a team of astronauts who landed on a hostile planet. Released by American International Pictures in the US, it is now considered a primary influence on Ridley Scott's *Alien* (1979).

ABOVE RIGHT: Filmed around Long Island, New York in 1961 but not released until 1964, Jack Curtis's low-budget *The Flesh Eaters* (Knockout Video, 1981) gave a rare starring role to 1940s character actor Martin Kosleck. He played a renegade Nazi scientist who had created a hungry aquatic organism. The uncut version featured some scenes of graphic violence unusual for the time.

"A MASTERFUL, ALTOGETHER MEMORABLE EXCURSION INTO A FANTASTIC WORLD-TO-COME. *THE TIME MACHINE* IS 'ENGROSSING SCIENCE FICTION . . . AND LOTS OF FUN!' (*NY HERALD TRIBUNE*)"

***THE TIME MACHINE* VIDEO BOX BLURB (1984)**

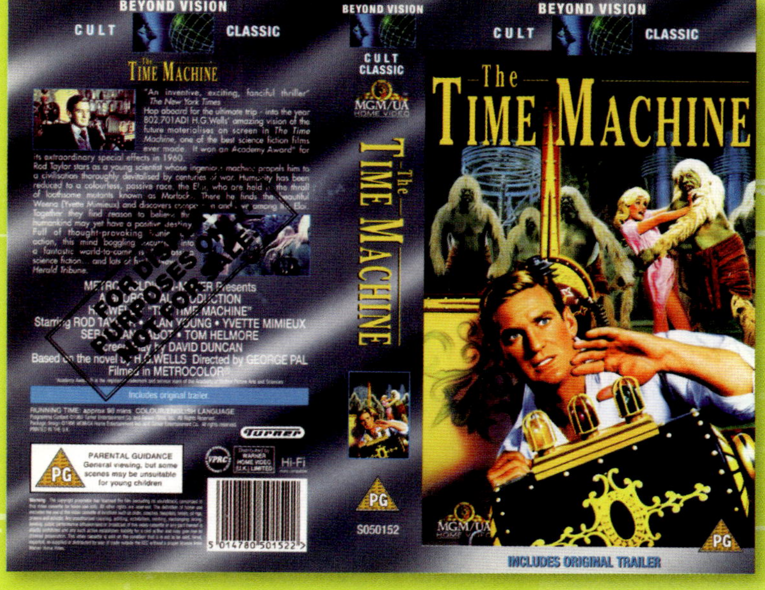

ABOVE: Based on the 1895 novella by H.G. Wells, George Pal's 1960 production of *The Time Machine* (MGM/UA Home Video, 1996) is now considered a classic of science fiction cinema. Rod Taylor starred as the Victorian time-traveler who ended up in the distant future, where he discovered that humankind had divided into the peaceful but naïve surface-dwelling Eloi (as exemplified by newcomer Yvette Mimieux's passive Weena), and the monstrous, subterranean Morlocks, who fed upon the Eloi. It won the Academy Award for Best Special Effects.

Ah . . . the VHS era! Don't we remember it fondly? Who cared back then that the tapes were often fuzzy and lacking in definition—a million miles away from the clarity of DVDs and Blu-rays? Who worried that most of the films were panned and scanned for the then-current Academy ratio? But the main thing for enthusiasts was the availability of a slew of films that we'd wanted to see for years (and uncut—initially; only porn movies were trimmed).

It was obvious to me that a revolution was underway, and I became the first video reviewer for both *Starburst* and *Shock Xpress* magazines. It wasn't just the horror titles that the tape revolution gave access to—we rediscovered some science fiction gems from the past. One film that enjoyed a crisp video transfer was George Pal's colorful *The Time Machine* (1960) with its beautifully designed retro-future time vehicle.

Finally we were given a chance to see on VHS Kurt Maetzig's elusive *First Spaceship on Venus* (1960), something of a "Europudding" (a film designed for multiple markets with actors from different countries—a phenomenon VHS alerted us to); it was still one of the most sophisticated of films about interplanetary voyages, with a vision of dead Venusian cities that owed something to the surrealist SF illustrator Richard Powers. Mario Bava's delirious—and equally surreal—*Planet of the Vampires* (1965) eventually became available for home viewing as well.

There were other neglected curios such as Jack Curtis's SF/horror hybrid *The Flesh Eaters* (1964). This bizarre outing featured some of the most gruesome effects audiences had seen, with victims being munched by the eponymous glowing creatures, before a gigantic amoeba-like monstrosity rises from the sea at the climax.

We now have Blu-rays and 4K discs, and censorship has relaxed considerably, but we can still remember affectionately how many rare and obscure treats the VHS era granted us.

Barry Forshaw

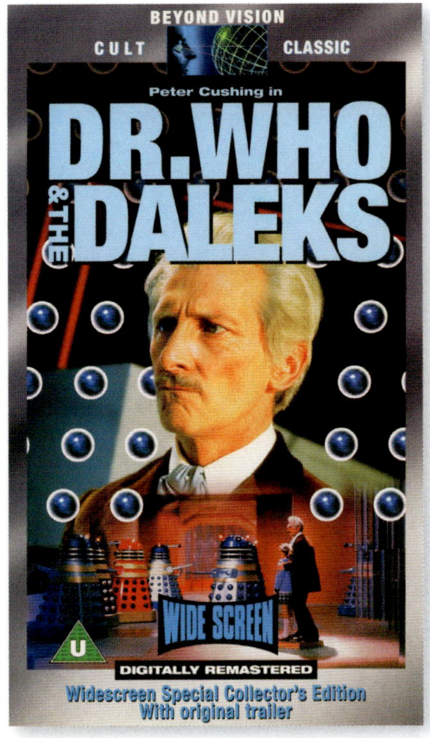

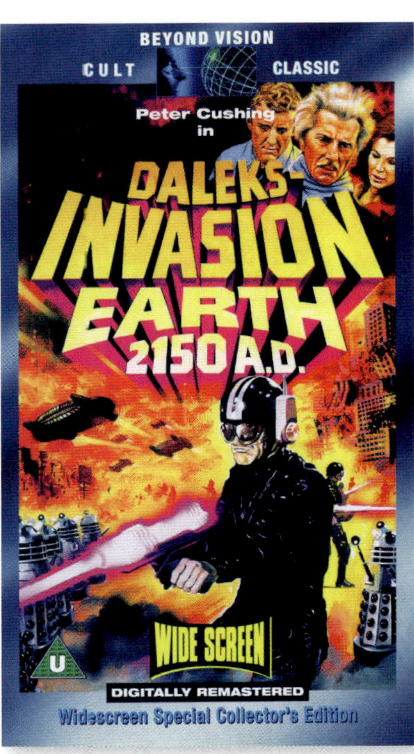

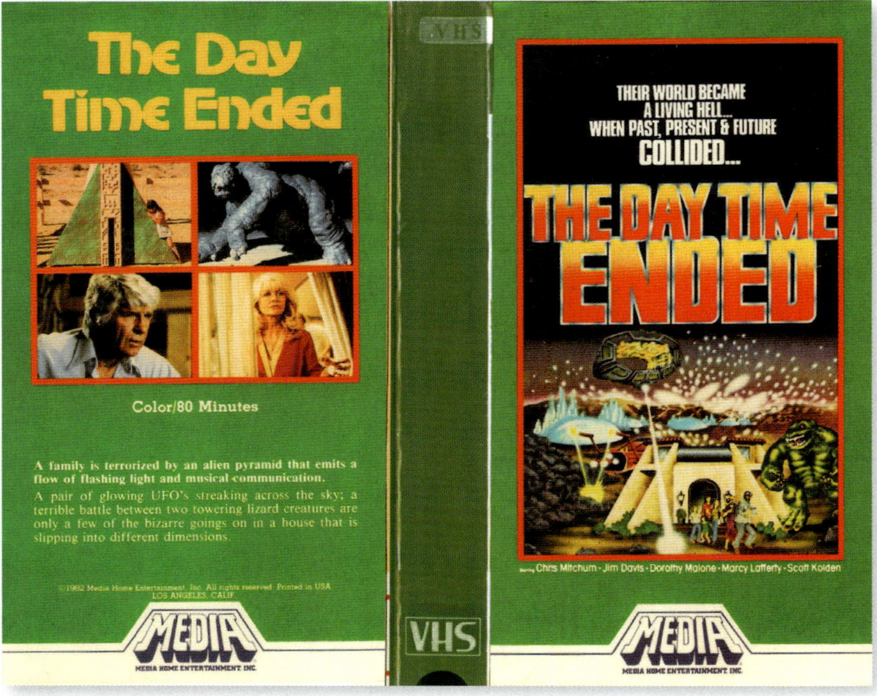

TOP LEFT: Two years after the TV show premiered on the BBC in 1963, Amicus producers Milton Subotsky and Max J. Rosenberg made *Dr. Who and the Daleks* (Warner Home Video, 1996), the first Doctor Who story to be filmed in color and wide-screen for the cinema. Peter Cushing was cast as the eponymous space and time traveler who, along with his two granddaughters and Roy Castle's hapless boyfriend, accidentally ended up in an alien war between the peace-loving Thals and a race of evil cyborgs called the Daleks.

TOP RIGHT: Although Peter Cushing returned as Dr. Who for the 1966 sequel, it was his evil cyborg adversaries who received top billing in *Daleks' Invasion Earth 2150 A.D.* (Warner Home Video, 1996). This time the eccentric time-traveler, together with his niece, granddaughter, and Bernard Cribbins's hapless police constable, were transported to a ravaged London in the year 2150, where they became involved in a conflict between the invading Daleks, their "Robomen" slaves, and the human resistance movement.

BOTTOM: Executive produced by Charles Band and directed by John "Bud" Cardos, *The Day Time Ended* (Media Home Entertainment, 1982) was a 1979 movie in which veteran performers Jim Davis and Dorothy Malone found themselves and their family trapped in a space/time warp where they encountered stop-motion aliens and monsters (created by David Allen, Randy Cook, and others), before they were all transported thousands of years into the future. In 1997 it was reissued in a "Collector's Edition" on Band's Cult Video label.

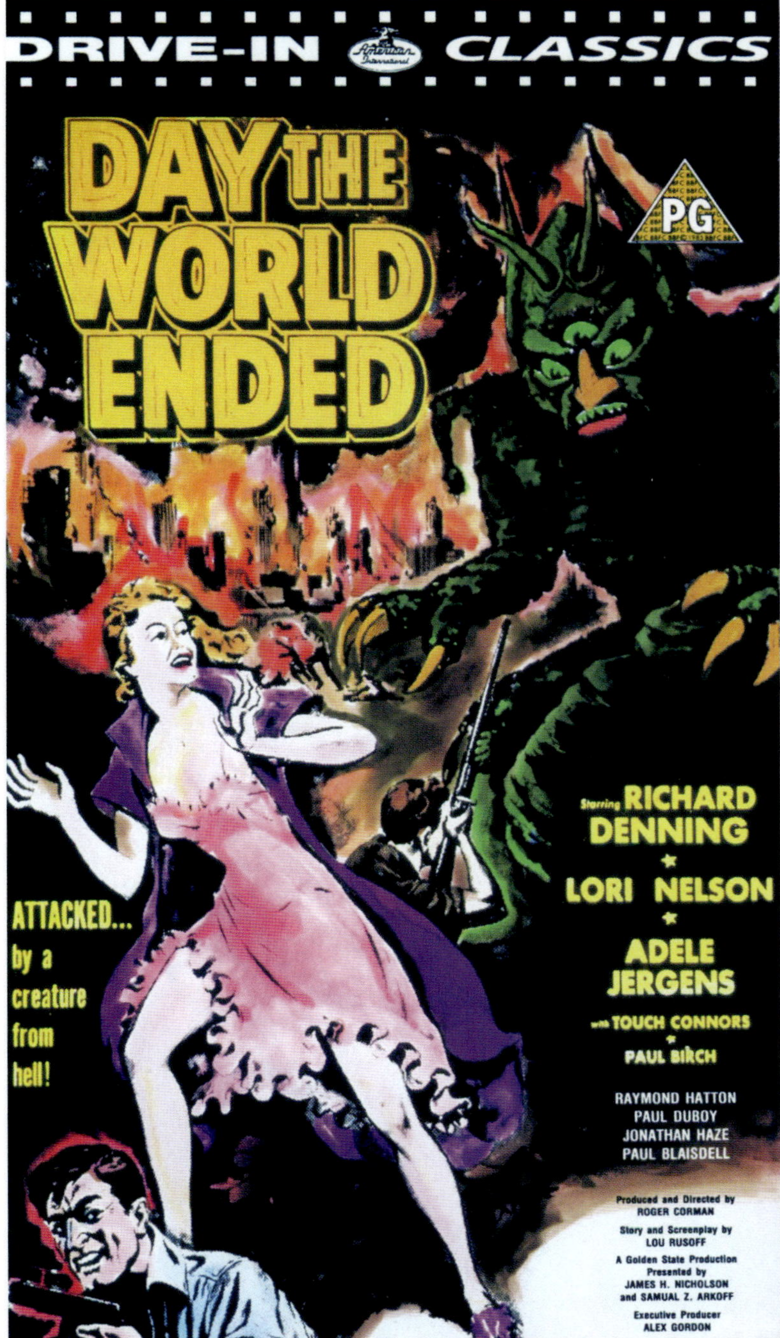

ABOVE LEFT: Originally distributed by American Releasing Corporation (later American International Pictures) in 1955, Roger Corman's *Day the World Ended* (Hendring, 1989) was set in a postapocalyptic world. A group of survivors in a sheltered canyon, led by Richard Denning's heroic geologist, struggled to survive against radioactive fallout, a mutated monster, and each other.

TOP RIGHT: *Radioactive Dreams* (Vestron Video, 1987) starred John Stockwell and Michael Dudikoff as Philip Hammer and Marlowe Chandler, two young men who had grown up in a fallout shelter reading old detective novels. Finally leaving their bunker after fifteen years to become postapocalyptic private eyes, they stumbled upon the launch keys to the last nuclear weapon.

BOTTOM RIGHT: Set in a flooded futuristic London of 2008, Rutger Hauer's maverick cop pursued a monstrous serial killer that tore out the hearts of its victims in *Split Second* (HBO Video, 1992). With an *Alien*-inspired creature created by future director Stephen Norrington and a strong cast (including Kim Cattrall and Michael J. Pollard), the original director quit due to the stress of filming.

TOP RIGHT: One of the first, and best, of the "big bug" movies of the 1950s, *Them!* (Warner Home Video, 1987) was released in 1954 and featured mutated giant ants created by atomic radiation and an exciting climax in the storm drains under Los Angeles. Later video releases restored the two-color opening title card, left over from when it was going to be shot in color and 3-D.

BOTTOM RIGHT & ABOVE LEFT: Like *Them!*, released the year before, Jack Arnold's *Tarantula* (MCA Universal Home Video, 1993) also featured an atmospheric desert setting, as a scientist's experiments into developing a radioactive growth nutrient caused rapid acromegaly in humans and turned the titular arachnid into a giant rampaging monster. Unlike the full-size prop ants in *Them!*, it used a combination of photographic effects, miniatures, and mattes to create the illusion of the giant creature, which was eventually incinerated by Air Force jets. Clint Eastwood appeared in an early uncredited role, and years later a clip from this film turned up in Don Siegel's *Coogan's Bluff* (1968), in which the actor was top-billed.

TOP LEFT & ABOVE RIGHT: Based on a story cowritten by Jack Arnold, like Universal-International's *Tarantula* (1955), John Sherwood's *The Monolith Monsters* (MCA Universal Home Video, 1994) was once again located in the desert, as a crashed meteorite exploded into pieces which, when exposed to water, grew to giant size, fragmented, and multiplied. The encroaching rock formations menaced a small town and turned those who came into contact with them to stone (an image featured prominently on the video box art). The special photographic effects were created by Clifford Stine, who began his career on *King Kong* (1933), while the film's opening meteorite crash used alternate takes from a scene in *It Came from Outer Space* (1953).

BOTTOM LEFT: Released in 1957, the same year as *The Monolith Monsters*, Kurt Neumann's *Kronos* (Englewood Entertainment, 1997) featured the eponymous alien machine, which increased in size as it absorbed its energy from power stations and a nuclear blast. The special effects were created by Jack Rabin, Irving Block, and Louis DeWitt, who also coproduced with Neumann.

TOP LEFT: Victor Mature, Carole Landis, and Lon Chaney, Jr. starred in *One Million B.C.* (Heron Communications/The Nostalgia Merchant, 1988), a 1940 drama about rival prehistoric tribes. The film's special effects (featuring photographically enlarged lizards and a stuntman in a dinosaur suit) were recycled in numerous other movies. D.W. Griffith had his name removed from the credits.

TOP RIGHT: Virgil W. Vogel's 1957 lost world adventure *The Land Unknown* (MCA/Universal Home Video, 1994) also used photographically enlarged lizards and a man in a suit to create its low-budget dinosaurs in black-and-white CinemaScope. It also threw in a giant carnivorous plant for good measure. Universal's VHS release included the film's original theatrical trailer.

BOTTOM LEFT: Originally conceived as a project by *King Kong*'s Willis H. O'Brien in the early 1940s, *The Valley of Gwangi* (Warner Home Video, 1991) became a 1969 collaboration between producer Charles H. Schneer and associate producer/animator Ray Harryhausen. Despite its excellent stop-motion effects, it was unjustly relegated by its distributor to double-feature status.

BOTTOM RIGHT: Bob Eggleton's box cover art for *Planet of Dinosaurs* (GoodTimes Home Video, 1994), which was released directly to video. Most of the budget for this independent 1978 science fiction movie went on the superb stop-motion dinosaurs (created by Douglas Beswick and others), including a homage to Ray Harryhausen's *The Beast from 20,000 Fathoms* (1953).

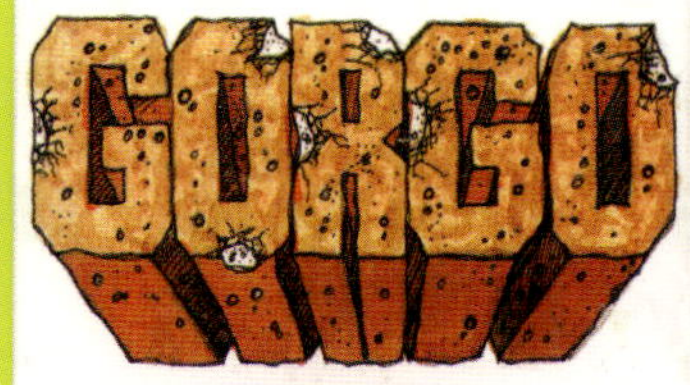

ABOVE LEFT: Director Eugène Lourié reworked his own *The Beast from 20,000 Fathoms* (1953) and *The Giant Behemoth* (1958) into the British monster-on-the-loose movie *Gorgo* (Memory Lane Video, 1984), released in 1961. A volcanic eruption off the Irish coast unleashed a giant prehistoric monster (another man-in-a-suit) that was captured and put on show in a London funfair.

ABOVE RIGHT: *Gorgo* (Star Classics, 1987) was novelized in paperback by Monarch Books in 1960, although the story was "sexed up" by American author "Carson Bingham" (Bruce Cassiday). The movie also became the basis for a twenty-three-issue run of comic books (1961–65) from Charlton Comics, along with spin-off titles, many of which were illustrated by Steve Ditko.

It was 1984—one year into being a first-time father, two years into first wife Marlene and I sharing a dire Vermont dirt-road rental abode, and one year into my penciling DC Comics' comic-book series *Saga of the Swamp Thing*—and our possessions were few, save for a barely legal car and what we'd each held on to from our respective college years. We couldn't afford to go out much, so we'd occasionally rent a VHS player and a handful of movies to watch.

Videocassettes were rare, expensive beasts, but something was happening. Instead of the $59.95 to $100 videocassettes the video shops offered for rental, local department stores began carrying racks of cheap videos for $20 or less. We'd give them a cursory look, but it wasn't until I spotted a green-and-gray slipsleeve promising Eugène Lourié's *Gorgo* (1961) could be mine that very moment—well, who needs to eat? I'd already paid the rent, so despite the fact we didn't own a VCR, however absurd the idea of owning something I couldn't watch, *Gorgo* was coming home with me!

Friends allowed us to watch this new acquisition on their home video set-up, and all were underwhelmed—except for me, of course. It was ugly, but it was still love, despite the crappy transfer, poor tracking, and the Technicolor faded to near black and white. Later in the 1980s, United Home Video offered a slightly superior clamshell edition (with far better cover art), which I rented, followed by same-ol' washed-out transfers from United Home Video (1987, with new airbrush-toned cover art), Star Classics (1987) and Alpha Video (1995).

It wasn't until the Roan Group's handsome letterboxed laserdisc release that Lourié's masterpiece remotely resembled the movie MGM released theatrically, but I'll forever harbor a mongrel love for that Memory Lane first-ever purchase.

Stephen R. Bissette

"WHEN AMERICAN REPORTER STEVE MARTIN (RAYMOND BURR) INVESTIGATES A SERIES OF MYSTERIOUS DISASTERS OFF THE COAST OF JAPAN, HE COMES FACE TO FACE WITH AN ANCIENT CREATURE SO POWERFUL AND SO TERRIFYING, IT CAN REDUCE TOKYO TO A SMOLDERING GRAVEYARD. NUCLEAR WEAPON TESTING RESURRECTED THIS RELIC FROM THE JURASSIC AGE, AND NOW IT'S RAMPAGING ACROSS JAPAN."

GODZILLA, KING OF THE MONSTERS! VIDEO BOX BLURB (1998)

JAPAN'S JOLLY GREEN GIANT

Originally released in 1954 by Toho Co. Ltd., Ishirō Honda's *Godzilla* (a.k.a. *Gojira*) was about a giant prehistoric monster awakened from the seabed by American nuclear testing. It proved to be a huge box-office success in its native Japan (and subsequently in overseas markets), and led to a series of multiple remakes and sequels that continues to this day.

The first Godzilla movie released on home video was *Godzilla, King of the Monsters!*, the 1956 "Americanized" version of the original film, heavily reedited, dubbed into English, and featuring new footage of actor Raymond Burr as a reporter covering the reptilian creature's destruction of Tokyo. Vestron Video simultaneously issued it in all home media formats (VHS, Betamax, and video disc) in 1983, and it has been released subsequently by various other companies, including Good Times Home Video and Paramount/Gateway.

Paramount Home Video also had the rights to a number of Godzilla sequels including such titles as *Mothra vs. Godzilla*, *Invasion of the Astro-Monster*, *Godzilla's Revenge*, and *Terror of Mechagodzilla*, while *Godzilla vs. Megalon* was mistakenly thought to be in the public domain, which resulted in many unauthorized versions being released on VHS. A number of other titles in the series appeared from such companies as Video Treasures, Westcoast Motion Pictures, New World Video, and Anchor Bay Entertainment.

All these early releases of the Godzilla films were the original dubbed American theatrical or TV versions, presented in panned-and-scanned prints, with cassette box art often aimed at children.

It was not until 1998, and the release of the first American *Godzilla* movie, that Toho's original Godzilla series would be brought together on home video by Simitar Entertainment, many of them in "Digitally Remastered" wide-screen transfers for the first time.

ABOVE LEFT: *Godzilla, King of the Monsters!* (Paramount/Gateway, 1992) was the 1956 American version of Ishirō Honda's 1954 original. It was cocredited to director Terry O. Morse, who shot additional footage of actor Raymond Burr. This is the film that was actually responsible for introducing Godzilla to a worldwide audience as Toho's original cut of the movie remained officially unavailable outside of Japan until 2004.

ABOVE RIGHT: In 1977, filmmaker Luigi Cozzi released a newly colorized version of the 1956 movie in Italy, adding extra stock footage to extend the running time and reprocessing the original soundtrack, creating a magnetic band eight-track stereophonic recording with new electronic music and sound effects. Enzo Nistri was hired to paint a new poster for the colorized version.

OPPOSITE PAGE, BELOW LEFT: Uncredited original video box artwork for *Godzilla, King of the Monsters!* (Paramount/Gateway, 1992), the heavily edited "Americanized" version. Raymond Burr reprised his role for the direct sequel *Godzilla 1985* (1985) which, like its predecessor, was reedited from the original Japanese version (released in 1984 as *The Return of Godzilla*) and featured additional footage for US audiences.

THIS PAGE: Proving the law of diminishing returns, during the 1960s and '70s Toho's original classic *kaiju* series steadily became more silly and childish with each subsequent sequel. Here is a selection of early video box art for *King Kong vs. Godzilla* (Good Times Home Video, 1987) [TOP LEFT]; *Ghidrah the Three-Headed Monster* (Video Treasures, 1988) [TOP RIGHT]; *Godzilla vs. the Sea Monster* (Video Treasures, 1989) [MIDDLE]; *Godzilla's Revenge* (Paramount/Gateway, 1992) [MIDDLE RIGHT]; *Godzilla vs. Gigan* (R&G Video/Starmaker Entertainment, 1992) [BOTTOM MIDDLE], and *Godzilla vs. Mechagodzilla* (New World Video, 1988) [BOTTOM RIGHT].

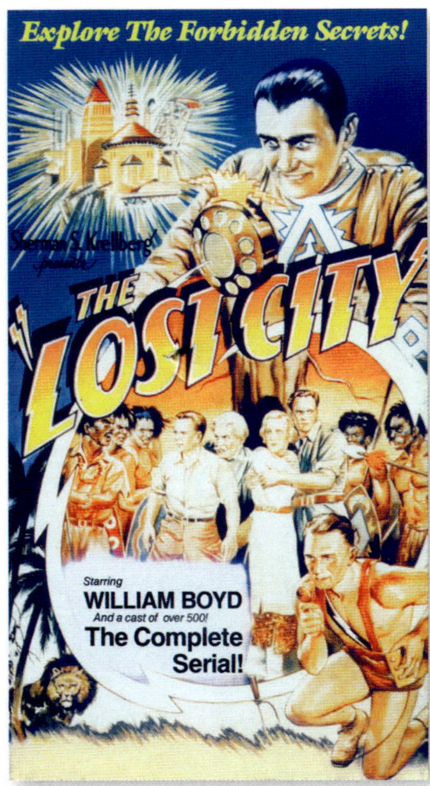

TOP LEFT: Second of four different feature films reedited from a twelve-chapter serial, *The Lost City* (GoodTimes Home Video, 1990) was independently produced by Sherman S. Krellberg in 1935. William "Stage" Boyd starred as crazed Lemurian scientist Zolok who, from his base in central Africa, electronically created natural disasters and turned the locals into zombie slaves.

TOP RIGHT: Republic Pictures' twelve-chapter super-science serial *Undersea Kingdom* (Republic Pictures Home Video, 1990) was first released in 1936 and thirty years later shown on TV as an edited-down feature film entitled *Sharad of Atlantis*. Lon Chaney, Jr. had a supporting role as the main henchman of the evil ruler of Atlantis, who plotted to conquer the surface world.

BOTTOM LEFT: Originally released by Republic Pictures in 1952 and edited down for TV in 1966 as the feature film *Retik the Moon Menace*, the public domain video of *Radar Men from the Moon Volume II* (United American Video, 1987) featured only episodes five to eight of the twelve-part serial about atomic-powered flying hero Commando Cody and his recurring battles with invaders from the Moon.

BOTTOM RIGHT: Australian VHS cover for *Planet Outlaws* (Hollywood House Video, n.d.), a reedited feature film version of Universal's twelve-part serial *Buck Rogers* (1939), released in 1953 by Sherman S. Krellberg. It included a new opening narration and additional footage of physicist Dr. Maurice Biot, "one of the leading aerodynamists in the world," talking about UFOs.

ABOVE LEFT: Chris Achilléos video cover for *City Beneath the Sea* (Warner Home Video, 1987), a 1971 made-for-TV pilot movie from Irwin Allen, who hoped to turn it into a regular series. Released theatrically in the UK as *One Hour to Doomsday*, Stuart Whitman starred as the commander of an underwater city who had to deal with a gold heist and a planetoid hurtling toward the Earth.

TOP RIGHT: A reworking of Gene Roddenberry's previous made-for-TV pilot movie *Genesis II* (1973), *Planet Earth* (Warner Home Video, 1987) starred John Saxon as a twentieth-century man revived from suspended animation in the postapocalyptic world of 2133, where he encountered a society dominated by women and a group of militaristic mutants. *Buck Rogers* did it better in 1939.

BOTTOM RIGHT: Chris Achilléos video cover for *Strange New World* (Warner Home Video, 1987), a third and final attempt at the same TV pilot movie in 1975, but this time without Gene Roddenberry's involvement. John Saxon again starred, this time as a different character revived from cryogenic suspension into the postapocalyptic year of 2174. It also was not developed into a weekly series.

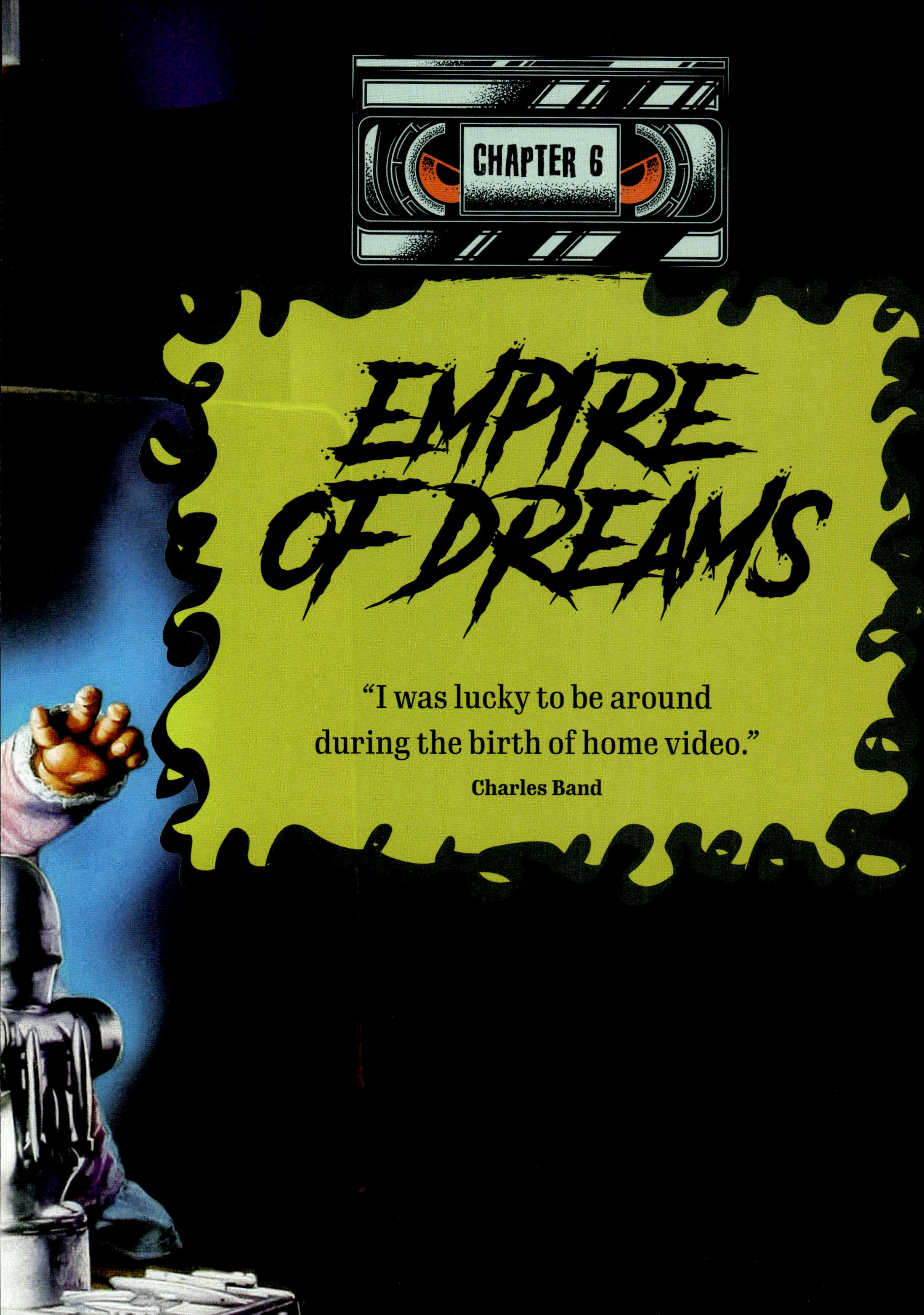

CHAPTER 6

EMPIRE OF DREAMS

"I was lucky to be around during the birth of home video."

Charles Band

"UNLIKE OTHER STUDIOS, AT EMPIRE THERE WAS NO SUCH THING AS DEVELOPMENT HELL. YOU'D TALK ABOUT AN IDEA, USUALLY INSPIRED BY A POSTER OR JUST A TITLE. AND TWO MONTHS LATER YOU WERE SHOOTING THE FILM."

STUART GORDON

Charles Robert Band was born in 1951 and grew up in Europe and Hollywood.

The son of Italian-born film director Albert Band (*I Bury the Living, Dracula's Dog*) and the brother of composer Richard Band, he began his career in the early 1970s, independently producing such low-budget B movies as *Mansion of the Doomed* (1976), *Crash!* (1976), *End of the World* (1977), *Laserblast* (1978), and *The Day Time Ended* (1979), employing the talents of many established actors, including Richard Basehart, Gloria Grahame, José Ferrer, John Carradine, Christopher Lee, Dean Jagger, Lew Ayres, Keenan Wynn, Roddy McDowall, Jim Davis, and Dorothy Malone.

Unhappy with the way his films were being distributed, in 1983 Band founded Empire Pictures which, at its height, would put out an average of two titles a month—one given a theatrical release and the other on home video.

Empire's first big hit came in 1985 with the opening of *Ghoulies*, which grossed more than $1 million during its first weekend in New York alone. As more and more successes followed, Band purchased the twelfth-century Castello di Giove in Italy as a base of European operations, along with the studio facility Dino de Laurentiis Cinematografica.

Production significantly increased, with various subsidiary companies being added, before Empire collapsed in 1988 due to financial difficulties. Band then created Full Moon Productions to make low-budget horror, science fiction, and fantasy movies, continuing to this day.

Full Moon initially teamed with Paramount Pictures and Pioneer Home Entertainment to release its direct-to-video product on VHS and LaserDisc, although the arrangement ended in 1994, following a disagreement over the actual budget of the H.P. Lovecraft adaptation *Lurking Fear*.

Charles Band was also one of the pioneers responsible for ushering in the home video boom with his companies Media Home Entertainment and Wizard Video—the latter being one of the first video distribution labels to release European horror product in the US from cult filmmakers such as Jesús Franco and Lucio Fulci.

PREVIOUS SPREAD: *Dollman vs. Demonic Toys* (Dir: Charles Band, 1993).

THIS PAGE: Charles Band.

TOP LEFT: Charles Band's horror movie debut as a producer, *Mansion of the Doomed* (Bingo Video, 1988) was filmed under the title *The Eyes of Dr. Chaney*. Directed by actor Michael Pataki, Richard Basehart's mad doctor attempted to transplant the eyes of his victims into his blind daughter. Under the title *Massacre Mansion* it was seized but not prosecuted as a "video nasty" in the UK.

TOP RIGHT: Christopher Lee later claimed that he was misled about the quality of Charles Band's 1977 science fiction movie *End of the World* (Cult Video/Amazing Fantasy Entertainment, 1997) when he agreed to star as an alien disguised as a priest. *Lolita* star Sue Lyon played the heroine, while the supporting cast included veterans Dean Jagger, Lew Ayres, and Macdonald Carey.

BOTTOM LEFT: Norwegian video cover for *Laserblast* (Video Screen, n.d.), Charles Band's overly ambitious 1978 science fiction movie in which Kim Milford's disenchanted teen discovered an alien laser cannon which he used to take revenge on his enemies. The two reptilian alien creatures were created by David Allen and others using stop-motion animation effects.

BOTTOM RIGHT: Chuck Connors portrayed the telekinetic owner of a roadside attraction who was surrounded by his creepy mannequins in cowriter/director David Schmoeller's 1979 debut feature *Tourist Trap* (Intervision Video, n.d.). Despite its violence, executive producer Charles Band's teen slasher received a PG rating in the US. An uncredited Linnea Quigley played a mannequin.

EMPIRE ENTERTAINMENT'S FIRST EDITION

ABOVE LEFT: 1986–87 was Empire Pictures' most productive period. Not only did it mark the company's biggest output of theatrical releases, but they also went into the 1987 American Film Market announcing nearly forty forthcoming releases. To promote this ambitious slate, in 1986 Empire produced a set of perforated stamps highlighting these new titles, many of which were never made.

TOP & BOTTOM RIGHT: Another way Empire Pictures promoted their package of new titles was with a pack of playing cards depicting the poster art for the company's "winning hand" of upcoming releases. The Jack of Diamonds depicted *Troll*, Empire's biggest box-office success of 1986, which grossed more than $2.5 million over its opening weekend on 959 screens.

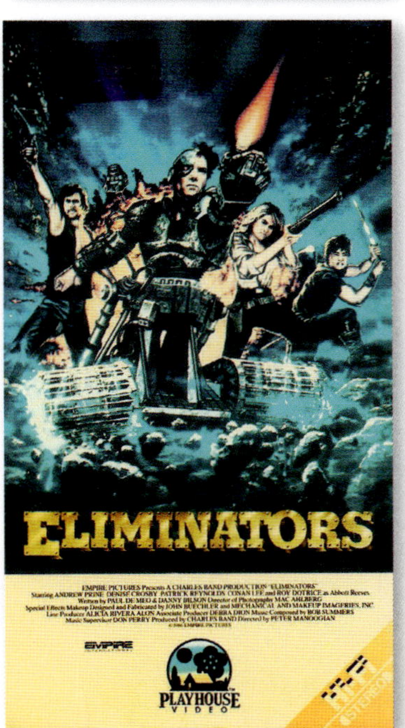

TOP LEFT: Japanese video cover for *The Dungeonmaster* (Vestron Video International, 1985), which was originally entitled *Ragewar* and had seven directors who each handled a different segment. A computer programmer transported to a fantasy world presided over by Richard Moll's evil sorcerer had to overcome a series of challenges with the help of his computerized wristband.

BOTTOM LEFT: Peter Manoogian's *Eliminators* (Playhouse Video, 1986) featured Roy Dotrice as an evil scientist who created a half-man, half-machine "Mandroid," which teamed up with a group of unlikely allies to avenge himself on his creator. Filmed in Spain, it was scripted by the writing team of Danny Bilson and Paul De Meo, who went on to bigger and better things.

ABOVE RIGHT: German actor Klaus Kinski starred as the creepy serial-killer son of a Nazi officer who trapped and tortured his female victims in *Crawlspace* (First Independent Films, 1991). Writer and director David Schmoeller had so much trouble working with the notoriously difficult actor that he later produced and directed the 1999 short film *Please Kill Mr. Kinski*.

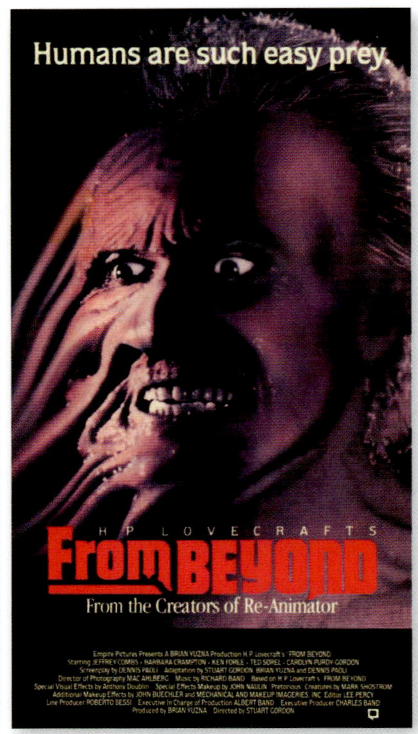

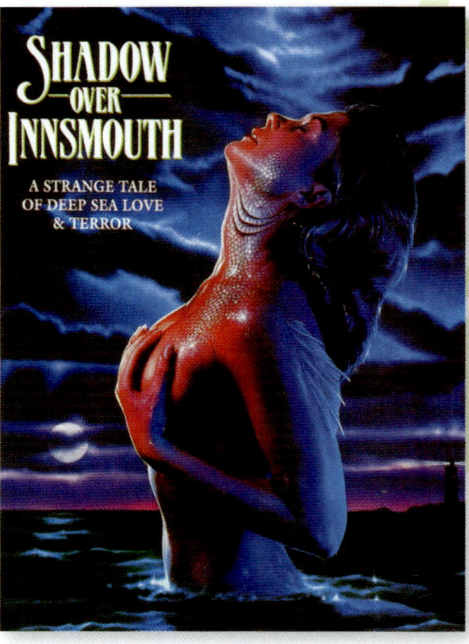

ABOVE LEFT: Initially conceived as a theatrical stage production and then a half-hour television pilot, *Re-Animator* (Vestron Video, 1986) was released to home video in its unrated theatrical version. An alternative R-rated cut included a number of scenes that had previously been removed from the original two-and-a-half hour assembly print for pacing purposes.

TOP RIGHT: Stuart Gordon was forced by the Motion Picture Association of America (MPAA) to trim multiple sequences before *From Beyond* (Vestron Video, 1987) was finally granted an R rating. Filmed in Italy and utilizing four special effects companies, according to producer Brian Yuzna the production ran out of money before the effects for the climax could be completed.

BOTTOM RIGHT: 1991 trade advertisement for *Shadow Over Innsmouth*, which Charles Band and Stuart Gordon attempted to get made for many years. With a script by Gordon's regular collaborator Dennis Paoli, comics artist Bernie Wrightson created the concept illustrations and Dick Smith designed some of the early makeup effects before the project was cancelled.

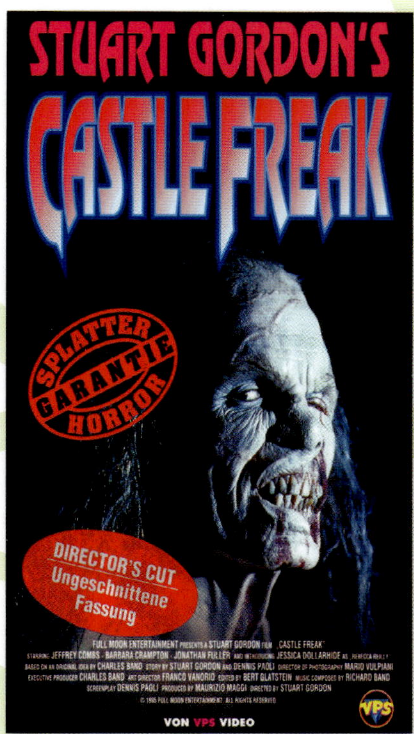

"HERBERT WEST HAS A SERIOUS PROBLEM—WILL HE BECOME THE FIRST IN A NEW BREED OF HEADHUNTERS OR ARE ALL HIS WOES COMING TO A HEAD?"

***RE-ANIMATOR* VIDEO BOX BLURB (1986)**

ABOVE: German video sleeve for the "Director's Cut" (containing two minutes' more explicit sex and gore) of Stuart Gordon's *Castle Freak* (VPS Video, 1995), filmed at executive producer Charles Band's castle in Italy. Despite "being based on an original idea" by Band, the script by Gordon and Dennis Paoli actually owed its inspiration to H.P. Lovecraft's story "The Outsider." Tate Steinsiek's direct-to-video 2020 remake was coproduced by original star Barbara Crampton.

LOW-BUDGET LOVECRAFTS

After his untimely death in 1937, pulp author Howard Phillips Lovecraft's stories were mostly ignored by the movies until the 1960s.

American International Pictures released *The Haunted Palace* in 1963, which was based on Lovecraft's novella "The Case of Charles Dexter Ward" but mostly credited to Edgar Allan Poe. AIP followed that with *Die, Monster, Die!* (1965), based on "The Colour Out of Space," and *The Dunwich Horror* (1970).

In 1984, fledgling producer Brian Yuzna and first-time director Stuart Gordon did a deal with Charles Band for Empire Pictures to facilitate production and distribute *Re-Animator*, loosely based on Lovecraft's obscure serial "Herbert West—Reanimator," first published in 1922.

A surprise hit at the Cannes Film Festival, and a critical success upon its release in 1985, *Re-Animator* easily became Empire's highest grossing movie at the time. However, following a protracted lawsuit, Yuzna eventually regained the rights to the property and went on to independently make two sequels, *Bride of Re-Animator* (1990) and *Beyond Re-Animator* (2003).

Following the success of *Re-Animator*, Yuzna, Gordon, scriptwriter Dennis Paoli, and stars Jeffrey Combs and Barbara Crampton were reunited at Empire's newly acquired Rome studios for yet another H.P. Lovecraft adaptation, *From Beyond*, which was based on a 1934 fanzine story. Unfortunately, when it was released in 1986, the movie was not the domestic hit its predecessor had been.

Charles Band himself took over the direction of his next Lovecraft adaptation. *The Evil Clergyman* was inspired by a fragment from a letter and was initially supposed to form part of an anthology movie called *Pulse Pounders* (1988), which was never released due to the collapse of Empire Pictures.

C. Courtney Joyner wrote and directed *Lurking Fear* (1994) for Band's Full Moon Entertainment, while Stuart Gordon, Dennis Paoli, Jeffrey Combs, and Barbara Crampton reunited the following year for *Castle Freak*, which was heavily influenced by Lovecraft's 1926 story "The Outsider." Both films were released directly to video, and the latter title was remade in 2020.

Since the 1980s, Band had been announcing that Stuart Gordon was going to film an adaptation of the author's seminal story "The Shadow Over Innsmouth." Although that never happened, he did manage to incorporate various elements from Lovecraft's fiction into the teen TV miniseries *The Resonator: Miskatonic U* (2021), *Beyond the Resonator* (2022), and *Curse of the Re-Animator* (2022).

It always started with art. An amazing painting of a monster fighting a hero, terrorizing a beautiful girl, blasting apart a city, or crawling back from the grave. The art was what made the boxes jump off the video shelves, and the movies inside had to make that rental worth it.

The art and the title were the keys to writing for Full Moon because those were your inspirational kick-starters, and then you ran from there.

Most of the work I did for Full Moon was installments in their franchises of *Puppet Master* or *Trancers*, and there were expectations. The fans were legion and devoted, and they knew the films—sometimes better than the filmmakers. We'd dive into the scripts, conscious of the continuity from other installments, but not always being able to tie-up plot elements, particularly if it was Jack Deth bouncing around the time quadrants.

With *Puppet Master III: Toulon's Revenge* (1991), Charlie Band told me his idea of doing a prequel to the first film. He wanted to go back to the origins of Toulon and the Nazis. I'd always loved those great World War II adventure films like *Where Eagles Dare*, and that was the style I set out to pay tribute to. Director David DeCoteau and I met, watched the movies, and fell into creative sync.

That was always the great thing about working for Full Moon—if you wanted to explore something different or fun, Charlie let you do it. You had to respect the budget, and those limitations could be difficult, but he let imaginations soar.

When I was offered *Doctor Mordrid* (1992), which Charlie codirected with his father Albert Band, we set out to make a comic-book movie with tight funds but unlimited inspiration from the great comics of the 1960s, especially those by Jack Kirby. For the box art, there was a beautiful painting of Jeffrey Combs, arms outstretched, commanding the magical elements of the universe, which was our guarantee to anyone who took our movie off the shelf that—if nothing else—there would be fun and imagination, because the creators loved the genre as much as anyone putting down their money to see it.

That was the Full Moon secret. We were all fans, who were lucky enough to be making movies.

C. Courtney Joyner

ABOVE LEFT: C. Courtney Joyner's first screenwriting credit for Empire Pictures was for Renny Harlin's US movie debut, *Prison* (New World Video, 1988). Kane Hodder's vengeance-seeking spirit, sent to the electric chair for a crime he didn't commit, returned thirty years later to wreak havoc on Lane Smith's new governor and the inmates led by Viggo Mortensen.

ABOVE MIDDLE: Written and directed by C. Courtney Joyner and filmed in Romania, *Lurking Fear* (Paramount Pictures, 1994) was loosely inspired by H.P. Lovecraft's 1923 serial story. This was the last Full Moon production to be released on videocassette by Paramount when a dispute over the movie's budget resulted in the two companies parting ways after five years.

ABOVE RIGHT: Polish video cover, inspired by Jack Kirby's concept art, for Full Moon's *Doctor Mordrid* (Imperial Entertainment, 1993). Scripted by C. Courtney Joyner, Jeffrey Combs starred as the eponymous wizard (bearing more than a passing resemblance to Marvel Comics' *Dr. Strange*) who was sent to Earth to prevent an evil sorcerer from opening the gates to Hell.

ABOVE LEFT: Produced and directed by Charles Band, *The Creeps* (Full Moon Pictures/Amazing Fantasy Entertainment, 1997) involved all the classic monsters—Dracula, Frankenstein's Monster, Mummy, and Wolfman—being resurrected from rare manuscripts, but in smaller-scale versions of themselves. It was later reissued under the title *Deformed Monsters*.

TOP & BOTTOM RIGHT: Executive producer Charles Band conceived a series of contemporary reimaginings of the classic movie monsters for a young adult audience under the "Filmonsters!" banner. Only David DeCoteau's *Frankenstein Reborn!* and Jeff Burr's *The Werewolf Reborn!* (both Full Moon Releasing, 1998) were actually made before the *Goosebumps*-inspired project was canceled, leaving proposed Dracula, Mummy, Invisible Man, and Creature from the Black Lagoon remakes stuck in the initial planning stages. A half-hour "Making of" video was produced in 1998, and in 2005 both movies were edited into the cut-down compilation *Frankenstein & the Werewolf Reborn!*

TOP LEFT: Dutch video cover for Luca Bercovici's low-budget *Ghoulies* (Vestron Video International, 1985), in which a young man inherited his late father's estate and conjured up the malicious demons of the title. Made the same year as Joe Dante's *Gremlins*, the movie grossed more than $35 million worldwide thanks to its "toilet" marketing campaign. Three sequels followed.

TOP RIGHT: Directed by Albert Band and filmed in Rome, *Ghoulies II* (Entertainment in Video, 1987) had little connection to the first movie as the diminutive demons took up residence in a carnival funhouse aptly named "Satan's Den." John Carl Buechler once again supervised the mechanical and makeup effects, while David Allen and his crew handled the stop-motion animation effects.

BOTTOM: In an effort to save Empire Pictures, which was struggling financially at the time, Charles Band sold the rights to the *Ghoulies* franchise to Vestron Video. This resulted in the direct-to-video *Ghoulies Go to College* (Vestron UK, 1990), directed by John Carl Buechler. It was followed by Jim Wynorski's *Ghoulies IV* (1994), which brought the quartet full circle.

TOP: Tim Thomerson starred as Jack Deth, a time-traveling future cop from the twenty-third century who arrived back to mid-1980s Los Angeles to hunt down a criminal mastermind who could turn people into mindless zombies in Charles Band's hugely inventive *Trancers* (Vestron Video, 1987), scripted by Danny Bilson and Paul De Meo. To date it has been followed by five sequels.

BOTTOM LEFT: Following an unreleased short film, Tim Thomerson returned as Jack Deth in Charles Band's direct-to-video sequel *Trancers II* (Paramount Pictures, 1991). This time Richard Lynch's evil organization was creating an army of mindless Trancers in 1991, and Deth's previously dead wife (Megan Ward) was sent back from the future to help him defeat the growing menace.

BOTTOM RIGHT: Tim Thomerson's Jack Deth was time-jacked back to the future by his formerly dead wife and sent on a mission to shut down Andrew Robinson's government-sponsored Trancer training program in writer/director C. Courtney Joyner's direct-to-video sequel *Trancers III* (Paramount Pictures, 1992). After three movies, this was Helen Hunt's last *Trancers* film.

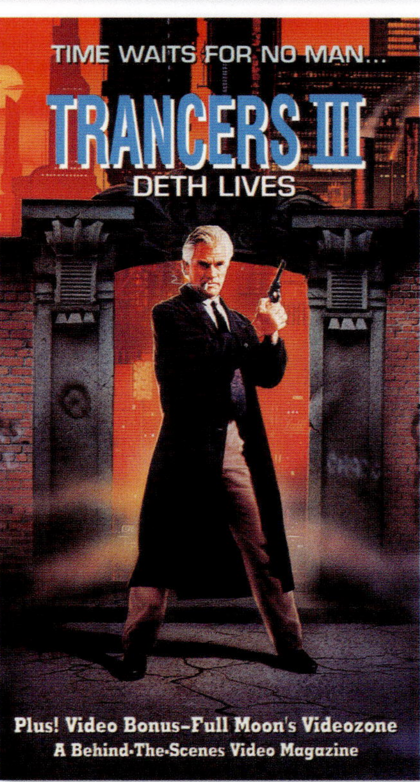

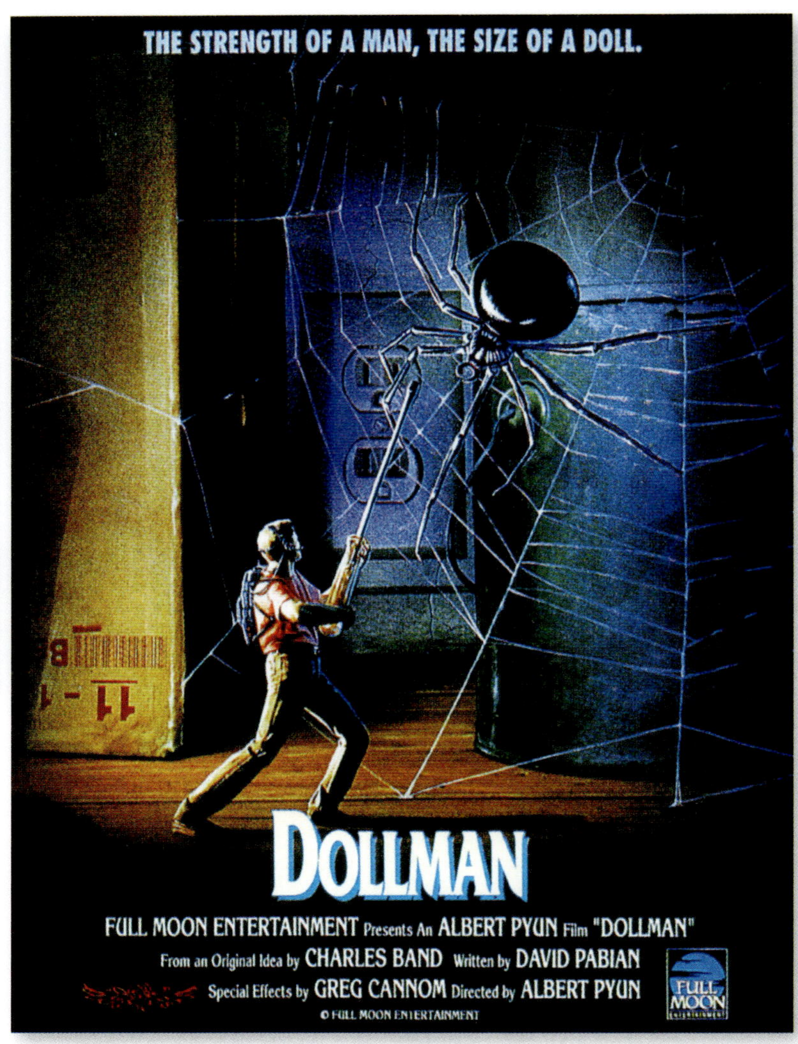

TOP LEFT: A group of people took shelter from a thunderstorm in an old mansion, where they encountered an elderly couple (veteran British actors Guy Rolfe and Hilary Mason) along with their murderous living toys in Stuart Gordon's *Dolls* (Vestron Video, 1988), scripted by Ed Naha and filmed in Italy. The dolls were created using animatronic puppets and stop-motion animation.

TOP RIGHT: The prepublicity artwork for Albert Pyun's *Dollman* (Paramount Home Entertainment, 1991) was obviously inspired by Richard Matheson's novel *The Shrinking Man*. Tim Thomerson's space cop Brick Bardo pursued his greatest enemy to Earth, where he turned out to be just thirteen inches high. Dollman next appeared in a post-credits cameo in *Bad Channels* (1992).

BOTTOM LEFT: Japanese video cover for Peter Manoogian's *Demonic Toys* (Full Moon Entertainment, 1992), about a group of people trapped in a locked warehouse by murderous toys brought to life by a demon looking to take over the body of an unborn child. Scripted by David S. Goyer, it was originally titled *Dangerous Toys* until a rock band with that name threatened to sue.

BOTTOM RIGHT: Videocassette and LaserDisc advertisement for Charles Band's *Dollman vs. Demonic Toys* (Paramount Home Video, 1993), which was a sequel to no less than three previous Full Moon movies—*Dollman*, *Demonic Toys*, and *Bad Channels*. Tim Thomerson returned as the diminutive detective Brick Bardo. *Puppet Master vs. Demonic Toys* was released in 2004.

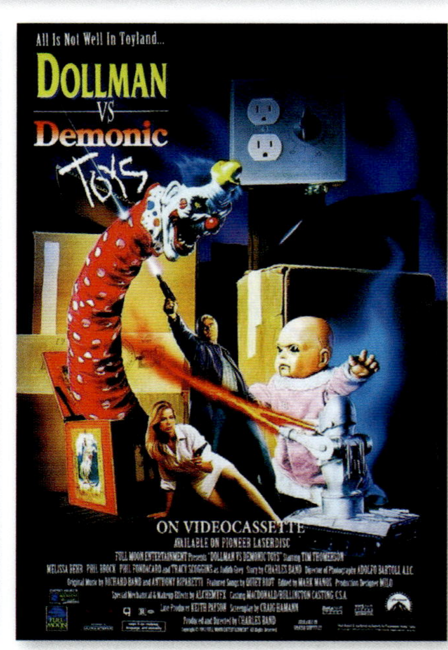

TOP LEFT: Japanese video cover for David Schmoeller's *Puppet Master* (Paramount Pictures/CIC Video, 1990), the first in Full Moon's hugely successful direct-to-video franchise. A former colleague used the Ancient Egyptian magic of puppeteer André Toulon (William Hickey) to reanimate various murderous puppets and exact revenge upon a group of psychics.

TOP RIGHT: German video cover for *Puppet Master II* (Paramount Pictures/CIC Video, 1991), a direct sequel directed by stop-motion animator David Allen. This time a group of paranormal investigators arrived at the hotel where the murders in the first movie occurred and fell victim to the homicidal living puppets and their undead creator André Toulon (Steve Welles).

BOTTOM LEFT: David DeCoteau's *Puppet Master III: Toulon's Revenge* (Paramount Home Video, 1991) was a prequel to the first film and set in 1941 Berlin, where children's puppeteer André Toulon (Guy Rolfe) used a magical formula to bring his carved creations to life. Unfortunately, Richard Lynch's evil Nazi wanted his secret to create an army of reanimated corpses.

BOTTOM RIGHT: Jeff Burr's convoluted *Puppet Master 4* (Paramount Home Video, 1993) had no less than five credited scriptwriters, as the spirit of André Toulon (a returning Guy Rolfe) used his living puppets to protect a group of friends staying at the original hotel from a trio of diminutive demons sent by an ancient Egyptian god. More sequels, prequels, and spin-offs followed.

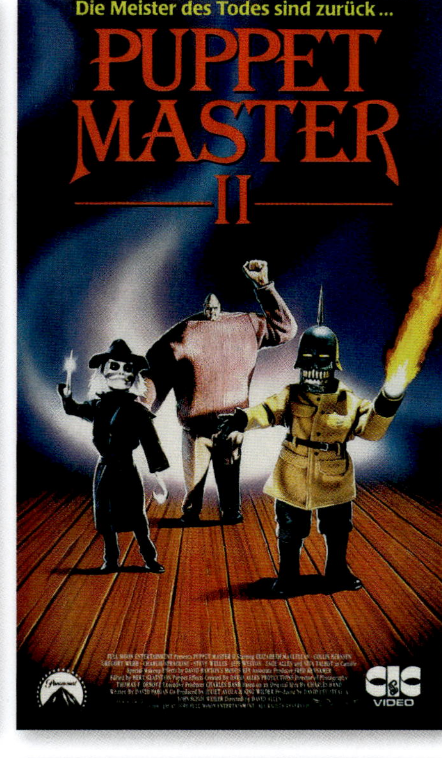

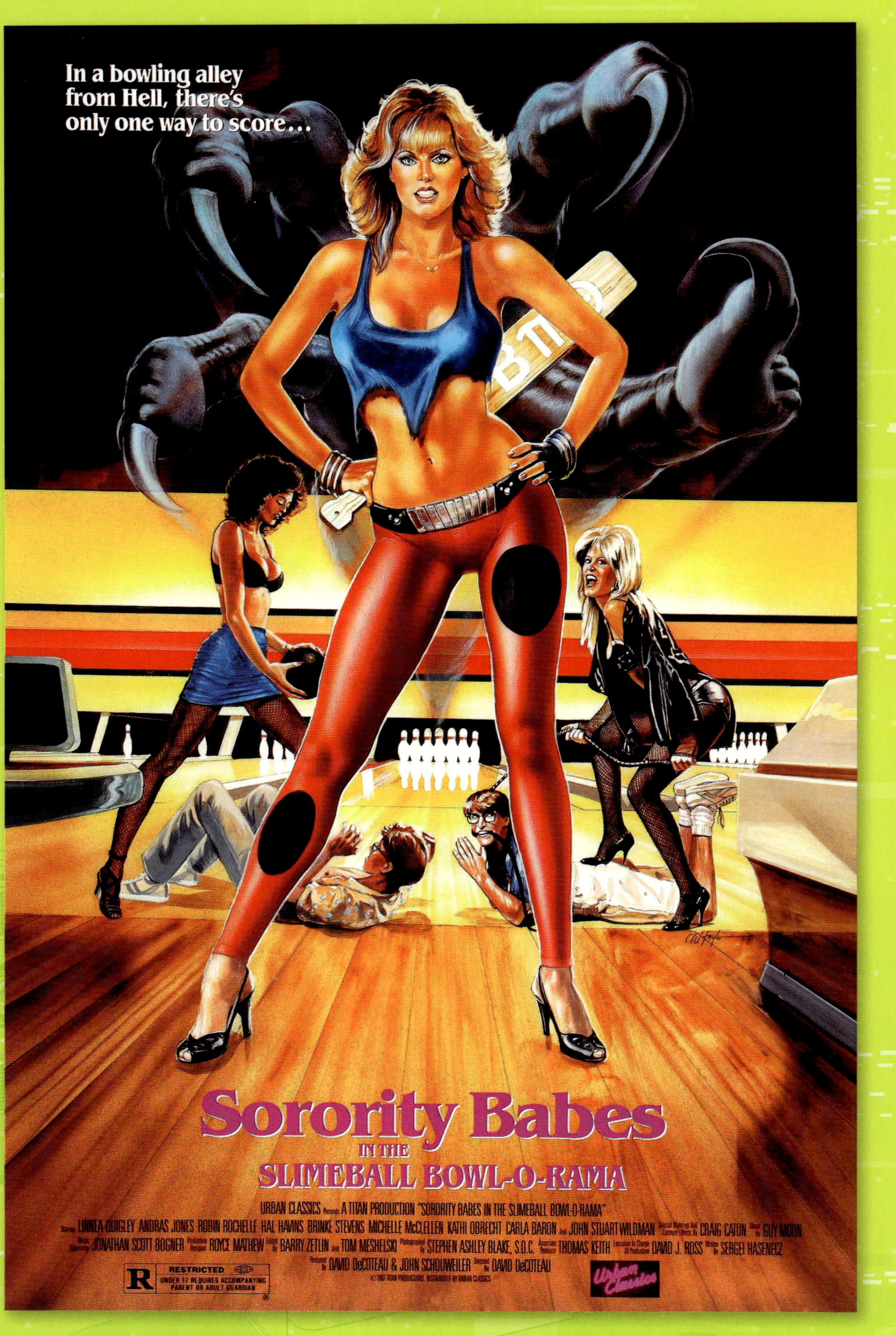
In a bowling alley
from Hell, there's
only one way to score…
Sorority Babes
IN THE
SLIMEBALL BOWL-O-RAMA
URBAN CLASSICS Presents A TITAN PRODUCTION "SORORITY BABES IN THE SLIMEBALL BOWL-O-RAMA"
Starring LINNEA QUIGLEY ANDRAS JONES ROBIN ROCHELLE HAL HAVINS BRINKE STEVENS MICHELLE McCLELLEN KATHI OBRECHT CARLA BARON And JOHN STUART WILDMAN Special Make-up And Creature Effects By CRAIG CATON Music By GUY MOON
Music Supervisor JONATHAN SCOTT BOGNER Production Designer ROYCE MATHEW Edited By BARRY ZETLIN And TOM MESHELSKI Photographed By STEPHEN ASHLEY BLAKE, S.O.C. Associate Producer THOMAS KEITH Executive In Charge Of Production DAVID J. ROSS Written By SERGEI HASENECZ
Produced By DAVID DeCOTEAU & JOHN SCHOUWEILER Directed By DAVID DeCOTEAU
R
RESTRICTED
UNDER 17 REQUIRES ACCOMPANYING PARENT OR ADULT GUARDIAN
Urban Classics

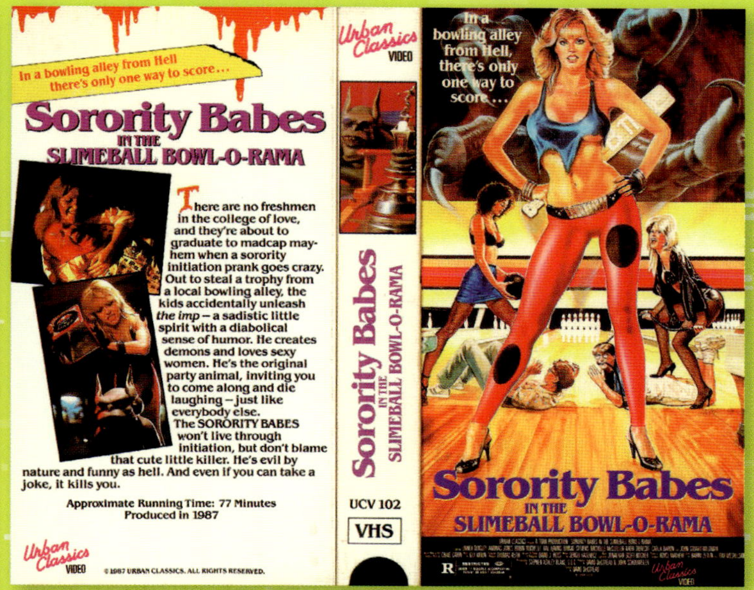

"WHAT IS THE DEADLY SECRET LOCKED BEHIND THE DOORS OF ZED'S TROPHY ROOM? . . . SHERLOCK HOLMES NEVER WORE OUTFITS LIKE THE SLAVE GIRLS FROM BEYOND INFINITY."

***SLAVE GIRLS FROM BEYOND INFINITY* VIDEO BOX BLURB (1995)**

My early movies, such as *The Slumber Party Massacre* (1982) and *Slave Girls from Beyond Infinity* (1987), were shot on 35mm film and shown in theaters. While it was a major thrill to see myself on the big screen, unfortunately most of those theaters were shabby downtown grindhouses where homeless drunks snored in the back row.

The advent of home video made it possible to watch movies in the safety and comfort of your own living room. It also became possible to watch the videotapes over and over till they wore out, or to freeze-frame on my naked butt in shower scenes (as I'm told many fans did).

I was in the right place at the right time to ride the massive VHS wave in the late 1980s and '90s. Indie filmmakers like Fred Olen Ray, David DeCoteau, Roger Corman, and Charles Band all started churning out low-budget quickies. Our target audience was primarily college-age males, so videos typically featured pretty girls, ample nudity, scary monsters, lots of gore, and lurid box covers to attract viewers.

Suddenly, I was working on a dozen new films each year. Video stores would often have an entire shelf dedicated to my many titles. I credit much of my success as an actress (and now as a director) to the video industry, and I still regard it with much fondness.

Brinke Stevens

ABOVE LEFT: Produced by Charles Band's micro-budget, mostly direct-to-video offshoot Urban Classics, Ken Dixon's *Slave Girls from Beyond Infinity* (Amazing Fantasy Entertainment, 1995) was based on Richard Connell's uncredited short story "The Most Dangerous Game." Elizabeth Kaitan and Cindy Beal's bikini-clad slave girls escaped their prison ship and crashed on a planet where their crazed host and his two android servants hunted humans for sport. Brinke Stevens played another interstellar castaway who was also pursued through the alien jungle.

ABOVE RIGHT & OPPOSITE PAGE: David DeCoteau's *Sorority Babes in the Slimeball Bowl-O-Rama* (Urban Classics Video, 1987) was another release from Charles Band's low-budget label. Scream Queens Linnea Quigley, Brinke Stevens, and Michelle Bauer were among those trapped in a bowling alley with a murderous, magical Imp that granted wishes. Stevens directed and costarred in Full Moon Features' 2022 sequel, *Sorority Babes in the Slime Bowl-O-Rama 2*.

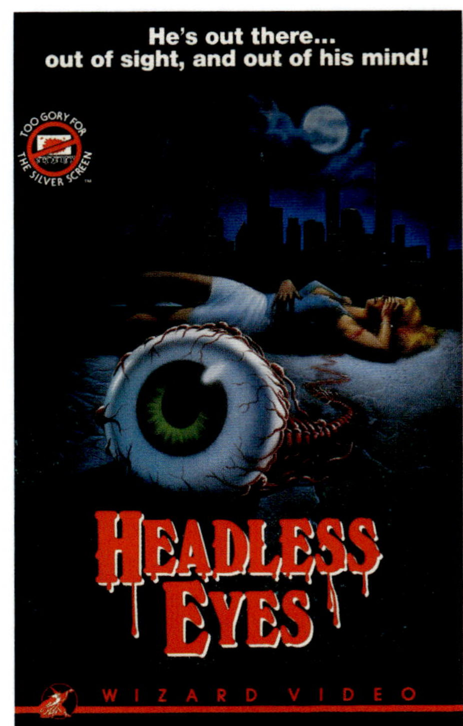

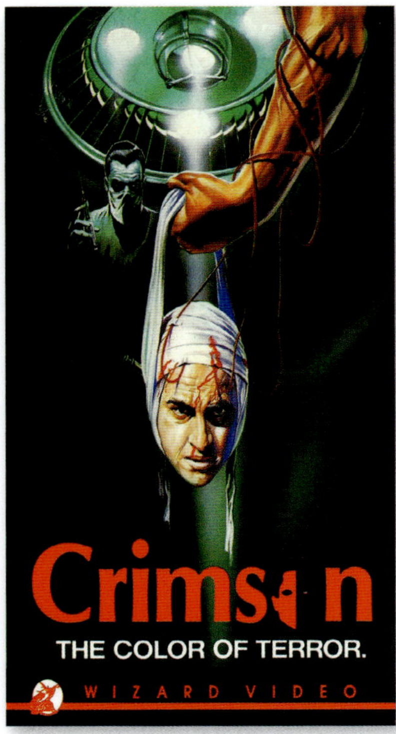

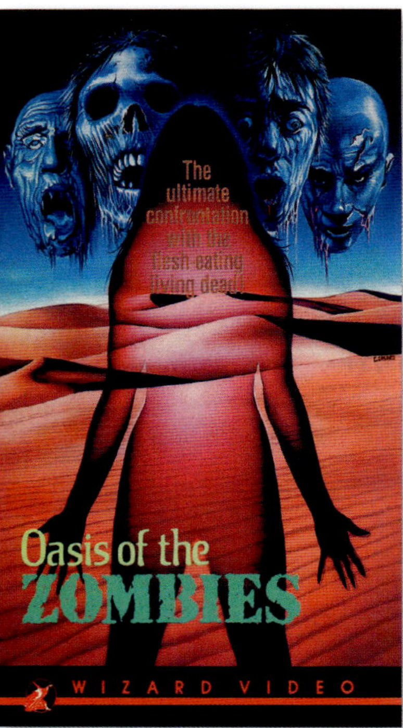

THIS PAGE: Alongside his other video distribution companies such as Force Video (1982–86) and Cult Video (1982–83), Charles Band's Wizard Video, founded in 1981, ushered in the new era of home entertainment. Much of Wizard's output was released in "big-box" format with eye-catching painted artwork, such as the lurid cover for Kent Bateman's 1971 New York grindhouse horror *The Headless Eyes* [TOP LEFT], about a crazed artist who cut out women's eyes with a spoon. Wizard's output covered all genres and tastes, and for the first time American audiences were exposed to the work of many European filmmakers who were still relatively unknown outside their own countries. Juan Fortuny's French-Spanish coproduction *Las ratas no duermen de noche* (1976) starred Paul Naschy and was released by Wizard as *Crimson* [TOP RIGHT]. Another film to get the retitling treatment was Riccardo Freda's 1981 Italian *giallo Murder Obsession* (a.k.a. *Murder Syndrome*), which appeared as simply *Fear* [BOTTOM LEFT]. Perhaps one of Wizard's biggest "discoveries" was Spanish director Jesús Franco, whose 1982 movie *Oasis of the Zombies* [BOTTOM RIGHT] was released by Wizard in the more common French version rather than the slightly longer Spanish cut of the film. Wizard Video lasted until 1987, when tastes began to change and the public started looking for quality over quantity. The brand was eventually revived in 2014 as part of Full Moon's subscription-based streaming service.

TOP: Although Wizard Video had previously released Jack Wood's low-budget occult movie *Equinox* (1970) under its original title, when they reissued it in their signature "big box" format with new sleeve art, it was retitled *The Beast* and given a different serial number. At least the distinctive artwork featured elements that were actually in the movie, which wasn't always the case with Wizard.

BOTTOM: Always looking for new business opportunities, Charles Band launched Wizard Video Games into the home video game market in March 1983. Wizard Video had already secured the rights to issue a game based on Tobe Hooper's *The Texas Chain Saw Massacre* (1974) from New Line Cinema, and after acquiring the gaming rights to John Carpenter's *Halloween* (1978), both cartridges were released for the Atari 2600 console. Unfortunately, following pressure from social groups over the games' perceived violent content, many retailers refused to stock them and sales were poor. Despite being announced, a further game based on the softcore SF comedy *Flesh Gordon* (1974) was never released.

OPPOSITE PAGE: For Charles Band it always began with the poster art. This was originally used in 1986 to promote an unproduced project entitled *Inhuman*, and was later repurposed to illustrate Stuart Gordon's adaptation of H.P. Lovecraft's *Shadow Over Innsmouth*, which also never happened. However, Gordon eventually got to incorporate elements of Lovecraft's story into his 2001 Spanish movie *Dagon* for other producers.

TOP LEFT: Filmed in 1988, *Pulse Pounders* was an anthology of three short movies that would have consisted of *H.P. Lovecraft's The Evil Clergyman*, *Trancers II: The Return of Jack Deth*, and *Dungeonmaster II: A Sorcerer's Nightmare*. It was not finished at the time due to Empire's collapse, but after a work print was discovered in 2011, the first two segments were released as short films.

BOTTOM LEFT & RIGHT: In development since the late 1960s, Charles Band and director David Allen repeatedly announced their stop-motion fantasy adventure *The Primevals* as forthcoming from Empire Pictures and Full Moon Entertainment. Filming took place in Romania in 1994, but the project was only completed in 2023—twenty-four years after Allen's untimely death.

CHAPTER 7

EURO EXPLOITATION

"In Europe an actor is an artist. In Hollywood, if he isn't working, he's a bum."

Anthony Quinn

"IN THOSE DAYS A FILM LIKE *THE HORRIBLE DR. HICHCOCK* WAS MADE ON A 10,000 DOLLAR BET. THE DIRECTOR, RICCARDO FREDA, DID A SCRIPT IN TWO DAYS WITH THE FINANCING IN A WEEK AFTER THAT. IT WAS A GAMBLE."

BARBARA STEELE

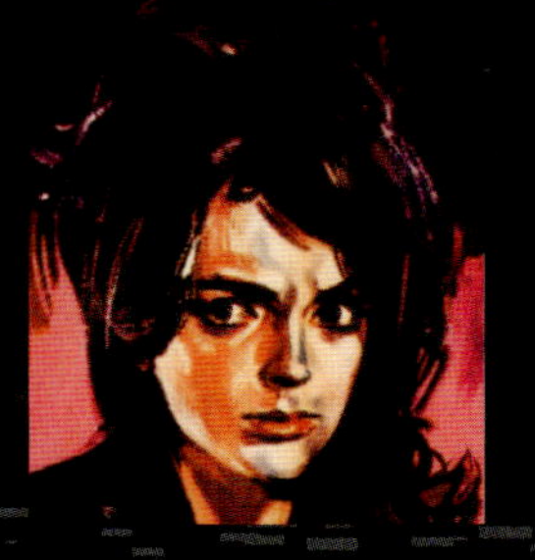

Around the same time that Hammer Films was reinventing the Gothic horror movie in Britain with its colorful reimaginings of Frankenstein and Dracula, and American International Pictures was doing the same thing with teenage versions of the characters aimed at the drive-in market,

in Europe—which arguably had been the birthplace of the horror movie during the silent era—there was a resurgence of interest in fantastic cinema after years of neglect.

Films such as Riccardo Freda's *The Devil's Commandment* (1957) from Italy, Victor Trivas's *The Head* (1959) from West Germany, George Franju's *Eyes Without a Face* (1959) from France, and Jesús Franco's *The Awful Dr. Orloff* (1962) from Spain helped spearhead this European revival.

Unfortunately, English-speaking audiences invariably saw these movies in horribly cropped and poorly dubbed versions, often extensively cut to appeal to the drive-in crowd and fill out the lower half of a double-bill.

A few distributors, including the aforementioned American International Pictures, made some effort to retain the integrity of the filmmakers' original vision (Mario Bava's *Black Sunday*, *Black Sabbath*, and *Planet of the Vampires*, for example, which nevertheless did all suffer from interference by AIP). Genres including Italy's peplum movies with musclemen such as Steve Reeves and Reg Park, or West Germany's *krimi* films inspired by the novels of British crime writer Edgar Wallace, frequently suffered much worse fates at the hands of smaller, fly-by-night distribution outfits, often looking for a quick sale to television.

All that changed with the videotape revolution. Despite many of those cut-and-dubbed versions flooding the video market in the early days of the medium, as additional material became available—especially from overseas—so viewers began to expect more for their rental fee.

Eventually, things began to improve. Those video distributors who were not simply out to make a fast buck began to source material directly from the countries it originated in. Titles only previously released in black and white were now in color, English subtitles replaced the haphazard dubbing, and badly cropped prints were finally seen in all their wide-screen wonder.

Thanks directly to the video boom, European fantastic cinema began to achieve the respect it always deserved, along with a whole new critical reevaluation as a result.

PREVIOUS SPREAD: *Black Sunday* (Dir: Mario Bava, 1960).

THIS PAGE: *The Ghost* (Dir: Riccardo Freda, 1963).

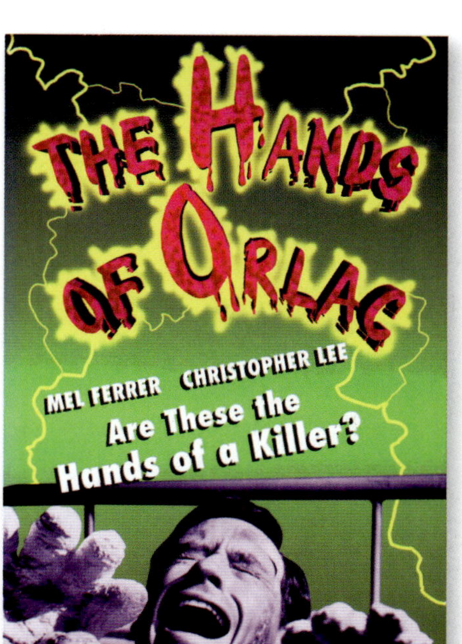

TOP LEFT: A British-French coproduction from 1960, Edmond T. Gréville's *The Hands of Orlac* (Acme Video, 1995) was the third movie based on the 1920 novel by Maurice Renard, about a pianist who received the transplanted hands of an executed murderer. Shot simultaneously in French and English, costars Mel Ferrer and Christopher Lee voiced their own roles in both versions.

TOP RIGHT: Roger Vadim's *Blood and Roses* (Paramount/Gateway, 1992) was a 1960 French-Italian coproduction that also starred Mel Ferrer. A modern-day retelling of J. Sheridan Le Fanu's 1872 novella "Carmilla," the director cast his wife, Danish actress Annette Vadim (Annette Susanne Strøyberg), as a young heiress who was apparently possessed by the spirit of her vampire ancestor.

BOTTOM LEFT: Issued as part of "Les fantastiques de Jean Rollin" video series in France, *Le frisson des vampires* (Film Office, 1996) showcased the director's third erotic vampire film, originally released in 1971. Shown in the US as *The Shiver of the Vampires*. A honeymooning couple found themselves spending the night in an old castle populated by the seductive undead.

BOTTOM RIGHT: French video cover for Jean Rollin's next film, *Requiem pour un vampire* (American Video, n.d.), which was filmed in 1972 and released in the US under various exploitation titles, including *Caged Virgins*. Two young girls (Marie-Pierre Castel and Mireille Dargent) stumbled upon a decrepit château, where they became the playthings of a centuries-old vampire.

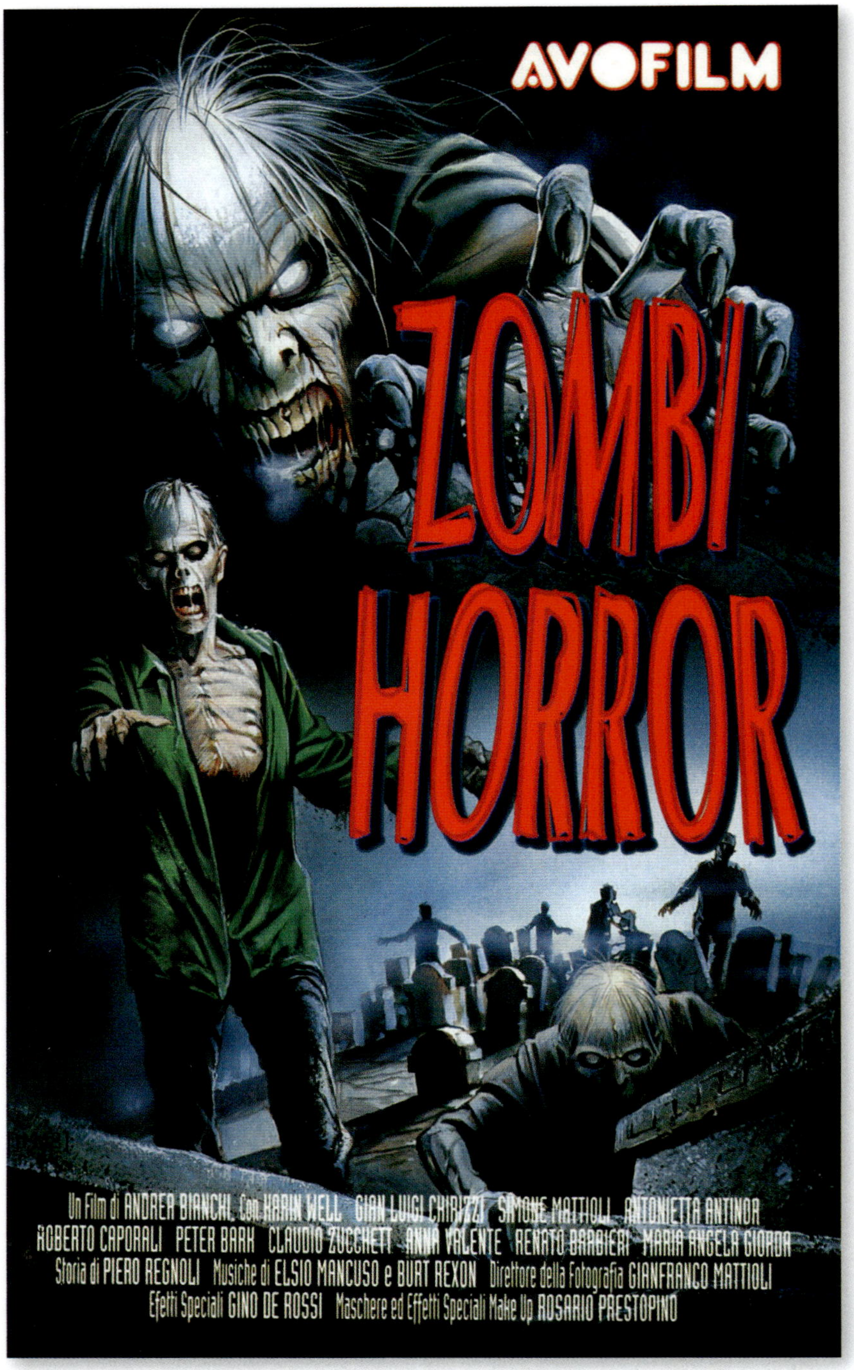

ABOVE LEFT: Italian video cover for Andrea Bianchi's *Zombi Horror* (Avofilm, 1995), which was released in the US as *Burial Ground: Nights of Terror*. After an archaeologist accidentally released a horde of hungry zombies from a stone crypt, a group of people took refuge in his old manor house, including a mother who had one of her breasts bitten off by her incestuous zombiefied son.

TOP RIGHT: Released under multiple titles, including *The Living Dead at the Manchester Morgue*, *Don't Open the Window*, and *Let Sleeping Corpses Lie*, Jorge Grau's 1974 Spanish-Italian production *The Living Dead* (AEE Video, 1991) was partly filmed in England, where an experimental ultra-sonic radiation machine, designed to kill insects, revived the dead.

BOTTOM RIGHT: Despite its US title, Pupi Avati's *Revenge of the Dead* (Lightning Video, 1985) was a more cerebral zombie movie, as Gabriele Lavia's novelist discovered from the ribbon on an old typewriter belonging to a deceased scientist that mysterious areas existed with the power to reanimate the dead. Originally titled *Zeder*, some video releases were heavily cut.

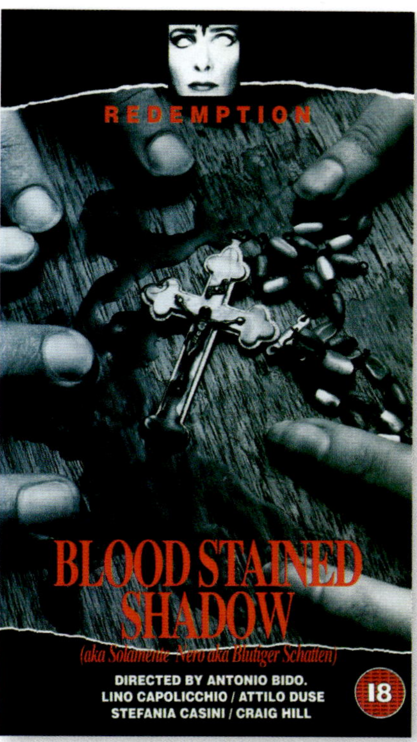

THIS PAGE: Founded in 1993 by controversial filmmaker Nigel Wingrove, Redemption Films was a UK-based video distribution company that specialized in releasing obscure European exploitation films by such neglected directors as Dario Argento, Mario Bava, Jesús Franco, Lucio Fulci, Jean Rollin, and others. The distinctive box designs by Wingrove and photographer Chris Bell featured often fetishistic black-and-white photos that symbolized the films, rather than stills or artwork from the movies themselves. As Wingrove explained, "With no money, I couldn't afford to advertise, so the sleeves had to, like book jackets, make people judge a film by its cover." The Redemption logo, of a woman's white, eyeless face, was actually Wingrove's former girlfriend, actress Eileen Daly. Among the titles they distributed throughout the decade were Antonio Bido's 1970s Argento-inspired *gialli, The Cat's Victims* [TOP LEFT] and *The Bloodstained Shadow* [TOP RIGHT]. Michele Soavi's 1987 debut *StageFright* [BOTTOM LEFT] was about a theater company being stalked by an escaped psychopath, while Bruno Mattei's *The Other Hell* [BOTTOM RIGHT] was a delirious slice of 1981 "nunsploitation" in which the sisters at an Italian convent were apparently possessed by the Devil. Redemption also expanded its list to include the work of non-European filmmakers and public domain classics such as *The Cabinet of Dr. Caligari, Nosferatu, Häxan, M, Vampyr, White Zombie,* and *The Vampire Bat.*

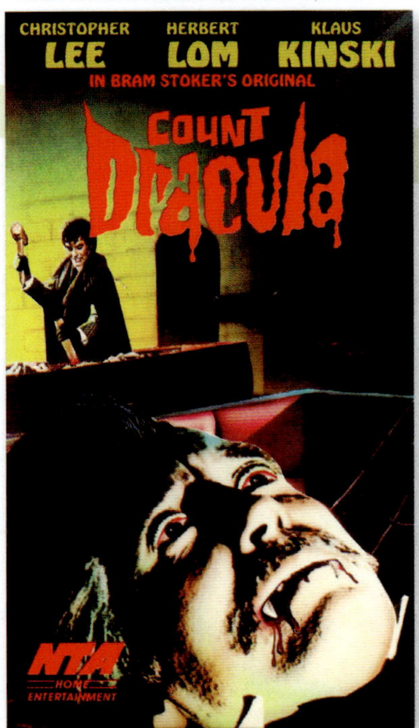

ABOVE LEFT: UK budget video of the underrated Italian-Spanish coproduction *Crypt of Horror* (SC Video, 1986), released in the US as *Terror in the Crypt* and *Crypt of the Vampire*. Filmed in 1964, it was yet another version of J. Sheridan Le Fanu's novella "Carmilla" and starred Christopher Lee as a Count who believed that his daughter was possessed by the spirit of her dead ancestor.

TOP RIGHT: French video cover for Antonio Margheriti's *La vierge de Nuremberg* (Lamcoz Productions, 1981), released as *Horror Castle* in the US in 1965. Christopher Lee played a disfigured servant who might have been the hooded killer stalking and torturing his female victims to death, although his voice was dubbed by another actor in the English-language version.

BOTTOM RIGHT: Disillusioned with playing the character in the Hammer sequels, Christopher Lee signed on for Jesús Franco's 1970 production of *Count Dracula* (NTA Home Entertainment, 1984) because it was supposed to be the "definitive" adaptation of Bram Stoker's novel. It was the first movie in which the character started out as an old man and grew younger as he fed on fresh blood.

THE EURO FILMS OF CHRISTOPHER LEE

British actor Sir Christopher Lee was of Italian descent. Fluent in English, Italian, French, Spanish, and German, and reasonably proficient in several other languages, he was just as comfortable making movies on the Continent as he was in his native UK.

Only a year after appearing in Hammer Films' *Horror of Dracula*, Lee turned up as another vampire in the Italian comedy *Uncle Was a Vampire* (1959), although his voice was dubbed for the English-language version (something that happened all too often). *The Hands of Orlac* (1960) was a UK-French coproduction, while *The Devil's Daffodil* (1961) and *Secrets of the Red Orchid* (1962) were two West German *krimi* movies, also featuring Klaus Kinski. Having previously appeared in Hammer's *The Hound of the Baskervilles* (1959), Lee finally played Sherlock Holmes himself in the West German-made *Sherlock Holmes and the Deadly Necklace* (1962) from the same director, Terence Fisher.

Mario Bava directed the actor in the 1961 *peplum*, *Hercules in the Haunted World* and the 1963 supernatural mystery *The Whip and the Body*, and his other Italian films from this period include *Kataris* (a.k.a. *Challenge the Devil*, 1963), *Horror Castle* (1963), *Crypt of the Vampire* (1964), and *The Castle of the Living Dead* (1964). *Psycho-Circus* (1966) was another *krimi* with Kinski, while *The Torture Chamber of Dr. Sadism* (1967), also from West Germany, was at least loosely based on a story by Edgar Allan Poe.

Jesús Franco's *The Bloody Judge*, *Count Dracula*, and *Eugenie* (all 1970), along with his two "Fu Manchu" films, were multinational coproductions, and *Cuadecuc, vampir* (1970) and *Umbracle* (1972) were a pair of experimental films from Spanish filmmaker and politician Pere Portabella.

Horror Express (1972) was a Spanish-UK production that teamed Christopher Lee and Peter Cushing with Telly Savalas, and Lee recreated his signature role one last time in the French comedy *Dracula and Son* (1976).

ABOVE LEFT: Christopher Lee starred as the corpse-like Count Frederic Regula, who needed a thirteenth female victim to attain immortality in Harald Reinl's stylish West German production *The Castle of the Walking Dead* (Saturn Productions, 1985), supposedly inspired by Edgar Allan Poe's story "The Pit and the Pendulum." It was originally released as *The Blood Demon* in the US by Hemisphere Pictures in 1969 on a double-bill with *Mad Doctor of Blood Island* (1968), and later reissued under the more exploitative title *The Torture Chamber of Dr. Sadism*.

ABOVE RIGHT: Eugenio Martin's *Horror Express* (Prism Entertainment, 1985) cast Christopher Lee and Peter Cushing as rival professors traveling on the Trans-Siberian Express with a million-year-old mind-sucking alien. Filmed mostly without sound, effects and dialogue were added later, with the two stars and Telly Savalas providing their own voices for the English-language version.

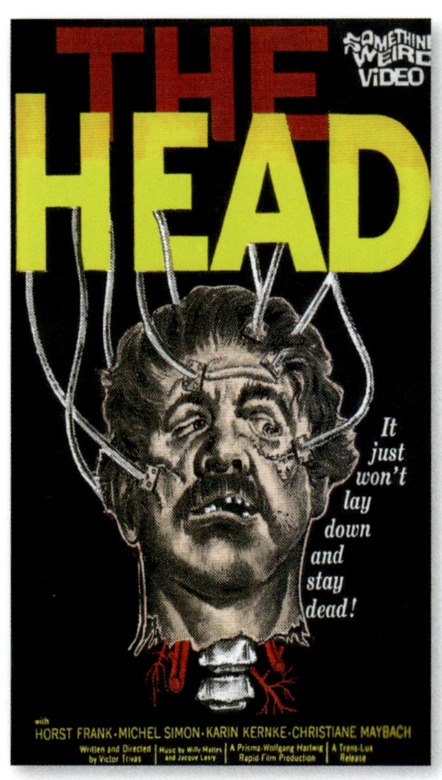

TOP LEFT: Filmed in 1959 as *Die Nackte und der Satan*, Victor Travis's *The Head* (Something Weird Video, 1993) is a West German production in which Horst Frank's mad scientist used a serum to keep the head of his colleague alive after he died and grafted the head of a beautiful hunchbacked nurse onto the body of a stripper. Filmed the same year as the similar *The Brain That Wouldn't Die*.

TOP RIGHT: Filmed in West Germany in 1970, Michael Armstrong's *Mark of the Devil* (Video Treasures/Anchor Bay Entertainment, 1997) was another movie inspired by *Witchfinder General* (1968). This US "Collector's Edition" featured the first presentation of the original uncut version, struck from a 35mm negative and presented in its original theatrical aspect ratio of 1.85:1.

BOTTOM: German video sleeve for Jörg Buttgereit's independent sequel *Nekromantik 2* (Jelinski + Buttgereit, 1991), in which a hospital nurse, played by Monika M. in her film debut, exhumed the corpse of a recent suicide and took it home to appease her necrophilic obsession. Controversially, the film was initially confiscated by Munich police for "glorifying violence."

TOP: Riccardo Freda's *The Horrible Dr. Hichcock* (Republic Pictures Home Video, 1986) was filmed in Italy in 1962 and starred British actress Barbara Steele as a woman who married a doctor (Robert Flemyng) with necrophilic desires. This was the cut version, originally released in the US in 1964 by Sigma III Corporation after American International Pictures turned it down.

BOTTOM LEFT: Italian video cover for Antonio Margheriti's 1964 film *I lunghi capelli della morte* (Video Ciak, 1985), which was released overseas under the title *The Long Hair of Death*. Recalling her role in Mario Bava's superior *Black Sunday* (1960), Barbara Steele was cast in two roles, as the murdered daughter of a woman burned at the stake for witchcraft and the stranger who avenges her.

BOTTOM RIGHT: Reissued on video as one of "Frank Henenlotter's Sexy Shockers from the Vaults," Massimo Pupillo's *Terror-Creatures from the Grave* (Something Weird Video, 1997) starred Barbara Steele as the widow of a spiritualist who had apparently come back from the dead for revenge. This includes a nude shot of Mirella Maravidi not seen in other versions of the film.

TOP LEFT: Mario Bava's psychological *giallo, Hatchet for the Honeymoon* (Home Media Entertainment, 1985), was about a serial killer who was haunted by the ghost of his wife while he murdered new brides with a cleaver. When the production ran out of money, star Stephen Forsyth refused to take part in any further shooting after not being paid for two weeks.

BOTTOM: Italian artist Arnaldo Putzu's stunning British video sleeve design for Mario Bava's proto-"slasher" film, *Blood Bath* (Hokushin Audio Visual, 1983). Banned in the UK when first submitted for theatrical release in 1972, this uncut version was added to that country's "video nasty" list, where it stayed. It reportedly has more alternative titles than any other movie.

TOP RIGHT: Originally released in 1977, Mario Bava's final movie, *Shock* (Videomedia/Vampix, 1981), was distributed in the US as *Beyond the Door II*, although it had no thematic connection with the first film. Daria Nicolodi moved into an old house with her new husband and young son, only to discover that it was haunted by the vengeful spirit of her abusive former husband.

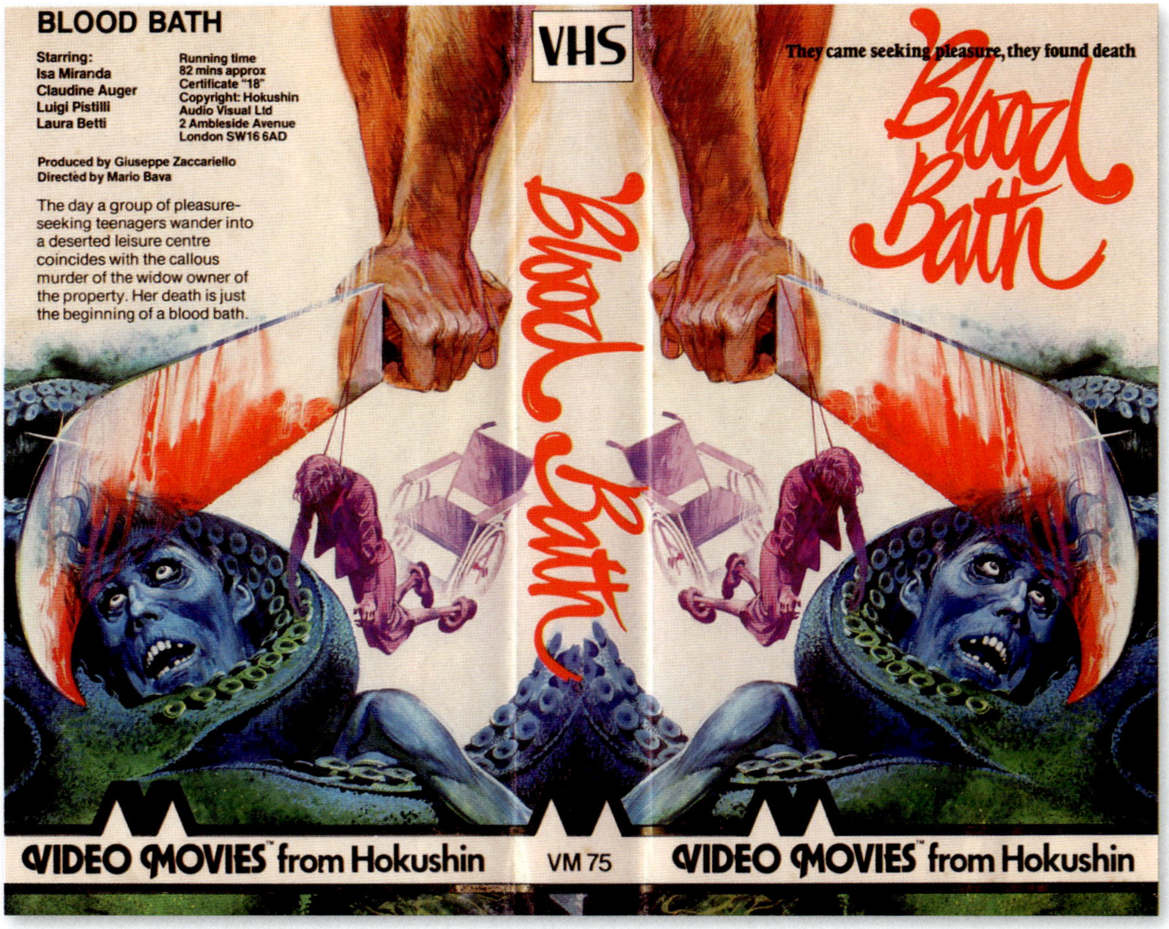

BLOOD BATH

Starring:
Isa Miranda
Claudine Auger
Luigi Pistilli
Laura Betti

Running time
82 mins approx
Certificate "18"
Copyright: Hokushin
Audio Visual Ltd
2 Ambleside Avenue
London SW16 6AD

Produced by Giuseppe Zaccariello
Directed by Mario Bava

The day a group of pleasure-seeking teenagers wander into a deserted leisure centre coincides with the callous murder of the widow owner of the property. Her death is just the beginning of a blood bath.

VHS

Blood Bath

They came seeking pleasure, they found death

Blood Bath

VIDEO MOVIES™ from Hokushin

VM 75

VIDEO MOVIES™ from Hokushin

TOP: Lucio Fulci's proto-*giallo*, *A Lizard in a Woman's Skin* (Video Independent Productions, n.d.) was set in London and starred Florinda Bolkan as a woman suspected of murder after she dreamed the killing. Stanley Baker was the police inspector on her trail. Carlo Rambaldi's fake disemboweled dogs were so realistic that Fulci nearly ended up in jail for animal cruelty.

BOTTOM LEFT: Dutch video cover for Lucio Fulci's best-known film, *Zombie 2* (European Video Corporation, 1981). Released just a year after George Romero's *Dawn of the Dead* (1978), this cheap Italian production arguably surpassed the success of that movie, although its high gore quotient (especially a nasty eye-impaling) got it banned as a "video nasty" in the UK.

BOTTOM RIGHT: Released in 1980, *City of the Living Dead* (Inter-Light Video, 1982) was the first part of Lucio Fulci's "Gates of Hell" trilogy and was followed by *The Beyond* (1981) and *The House by the Cemetery* (1981), all starring British actress Catriona MacColl. Loosely inspired by the fiction of H.P. Lovecraft, a journalist and psychic traveled to Dunwich to close a doorway to Hell.

Here in Italy, the golden age for *giallo* movies started in February 1971 as Dario Argento's *The Cat O'Nine Tails* became a box-office triumph. It lasted until the end of 1975 with another and even greater Argento box-office hit, *Deep Red*. After that, the *giallo* genre peak started slowly descending until it vanished, leaving only Argento as its unique and undisputed master and king.

When the VHS craze started many years later, *Deep Red* became a sales and rentals champ again here in Italy. However, when DVDs arrived, oddly, the movie was not released in that format by the company who owned the rights—seemingly because the new chairman thought it to be too violent and vulgar, and not worth considering.

Then, as requests for an Italian DVD of *Deep Red* increased, the managers of the main Italian wholesale dealer decided to import and market the British version, because it also featured the Italian-language soundtrack. In just over six months they sold more than 10,000 units. When this astounding fact spread among DVD markets and managers, the legal owner of the rights to *Deep Red* finally decided to issue it in Italy, to good business.

However, other Italian distributors continued to buy foreign editions of *Deep Red* because, while its official release featured only the movie with no extras, the British version contained many extras that pleased the Italian fans. This sales trend continues to this day.

The official Italian edition of *Deep Red* was created from the same old video master used many years before for its VHS release, while foreign releases feature brand new transfers and masters, forcing Italian fans to buy only these overseas versions.

The same keeps on happening today in the Italian Blu-ray/DVD market—not only with our *giallo* classics, but with every other kind of Italian movie. It's absurd, but this is the way it goes here.

Luigi Cozzi

"I WAS VERY INFLUENCED BY AMERICAN MOVIES . . . IN PARTICULAR THOSE PRODUCED BY VAL LEWTON."

DARIO ARGENTO

ABOVE LEFT: Norwegian video sleeve for Luigi Cozzi's *Starcrash* (In Video, 1982), credited under his usual pseudonym of "Lewis Coates." Released a year after *Star Wars*, Caroline Munro (dubbed by Candy Clark) portrayed space smuggler Stella Star, hired by Christopher Plummer's Emperor of the Galaxy to rescue his son (David Hasselhoff) and destroy Joe Spinnell's secret super-weapon.

ABOVE RIGHT: Released barely a year after *Alien* and the remake of *Invasion of the Body Snatchers*, Luigi Cozzi's *Alien Contamination* (Paragon Video Productions, 1982) combined elements of both those movies, as pulsating green eggs from Mars spread an acid-type substance that caused people to explode. As *Contamination*, this was seized but never prosecuted as a "video nasty" in the UK.

ABOVE LEFT: Dario Argento's influential directing debut, *The Bird with the Crystal Plumage* (United Home Video, 1986), starred Tony Musante as an American writer in Rome who became involved in a series of gruesome murders. Loosely inspired by Fredric Brown's 1949 novel *The Screaming Mimi*, this has been credited with popularizing the *giallo* ("yellow") film genre.

TOP RIGHT: The second of Dario Argento's "Animal Trilogy" (the third was *Four Flies on Grey Velvet*), *The Cat O'Nine Tails* (Warner Home Video, 1987) was based on a story cowritten by Luigi Cozzi. An investigative journalist (James Franciscus) and a blind former reporter (Karl Malden) investigated a series of murders committed around a genetic medical institute.

BOTTOM RIGHT: Norwegian video cover for Dario Argento's *Deep Red* (JEL Video, 1979), which starred David Hemmings as an English jazz musician in Rome who became involved in the murder of a psychic medium by a killer wearing black leather gloves. Luigi Cozzi's memorabilia shop in Rome is named Profondo Rosso, after the original Italian title of this *giallo* thriller.

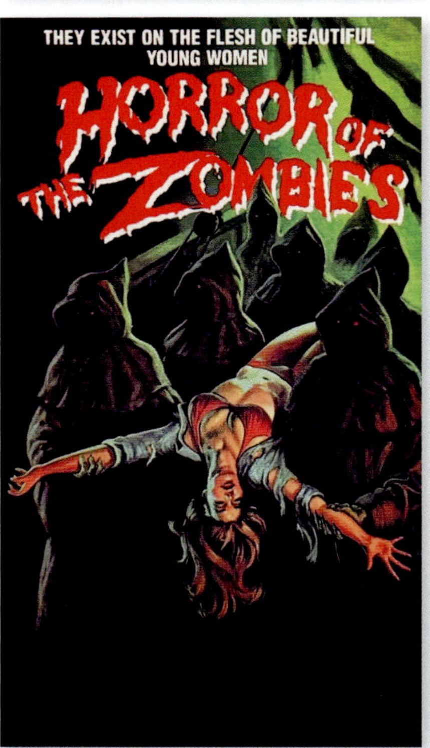

THIS PAGE: Spanish film director Amando de Ossorio is best known for his "Blind Dead" tetralogy, made between 1972–75. The series is loosely linked by the concept of a cult of zombified medieval Templar Knights who found their victims through sound and sucked their blood. This striking South Korean video cover [TOP LEFT] is for the first film in the sequence, *Tombs of the Blind Dead* (Dong Yang Productions, 1984). It was shot in Spain and Portugal, and a bizarrely reedited and dubbed version was released in the US as *Revenge from Planet Ape* to cash in on the popularity of the *Planet of the Apes* movies! Despite this, the film's success helped kick-start the Spanish horror film boom of the early 1970s and *Return of the Evil Dead* (Bingo Video, 1988) [TOP RIGHT] quickly followed the next year. This time the undead Templar Knights wrought revenge on the village that originally put them to death. *Horror of the Zombies* (VidAmerica/World's Worse Videos, 1988) [BOTTOM LEFT] was released in 1974. Better known under the title *The Ghost Galleon*, the Devil-worshipping Knights menaced some swimsuit models during a photo shoot at sea. Ossorio's fourth and final entry in the sequence was *Night of the Seagulls* (Archer Video, 1982) [BOTTOM RIGHT], as another coastal village found itself menaced by the mummified Knights, who rose from the sea every seven years to demand the sacrifice of seven young maidens. An unofficial, fifth "Blind Dead" film, *La cruz del diablo*, was made in 1975 by British director John Gilling from an original script written by Paul Naschy. It was never officially released outside Spanish-speaking countries.

TOP LEFT: Spanish video cover for Santos Alcocer's *El Coleccionista de cadáveres* (Divisa Ediciones, 1999), which was filmed in 1967 but not released until the early 1970s under the title *Cauldron of Blood*. In one of his last roles, Boris Karloff played a blind sculptor who was unaware that the skeletons he used in his art were the victims of his deranged wife (Viveca Lindfors).

TOP RIGHT: Swedish video cover for Eugenio Martin's *A Candle for the Devil* (Red Baron Videodivisionen, n.d.), which is better known under the title *It Happened at Nightmare Inn*. Aurora Bautista and Esperanza Roy played repressed sisters who murdered female guests at their small Spanish hotel when they did not live up to their high moral standards and religious beliefs.

BOTTOM LEFT: Almost a century after it was written, the early 1970s saw a revival of cinematic interest in J. Sheridan Le Fanu's vampire novella "Carmilla." While Hammer Films made *The Vampire Lovers* in 1970, two years later Vicente Aranda's stylish Spanish production *The Blood Spattered Bride* (Mountain Video, 1980) starred Alexandra Bastedo as the seductive succubus.

BOTTOM RIGHT: Like Hammer Films' *Countess Dracula* (1971), Jorge Grau's *The Legend of Blood Castle* (Consolidated Video Corporation, n.d.) was another variation on the Countess Elizabeth Bathory legend, as Lucia Bosè's aging noblewoman bathed in the blood of young virgins to regain her youth. The nude scenes were covered up for the Spanish version, released in 1973.

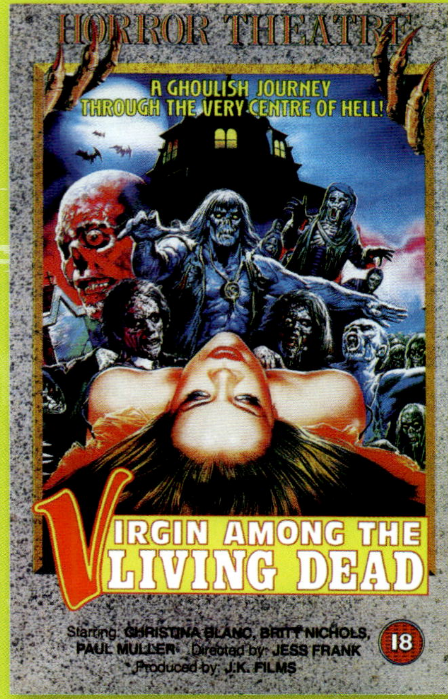

ABOVE LEFT: Preliminary Spanish video box artwork for Jesús Franco's seminal 1973 movie *A Virgin Among the Living Dead* (Hobby Video, 1987), in which Christina von Blanc's heroine returned to her ancestral castle only to discover that all her relatives (including her uncle, played by Howard Vernon) were dead, cursed by Anne Libert's Queen of the Night. In the end, she joined them.

TOP RIGHT: Described as one of the most butchered European films of all time, *A Virgin Among the Living Dead* (Careyvision, 1985) was distributed on home media in various versions for decades under different titles. In 1981, sequences shot by Jean Rollin for *Zombie Lake* were added, while Pierre Quérut filmed new porno inserts for a version featuring Alice Arno.

BOTTOM RIGHT: Spanish video box cover for Jesús Franco's *La tumba de los muertos vivientes* (Divisa Ediciones, 1999), released overseas as *Oasis of the Zombies*. This 1982 movie, about four college students searching for a hidden shipment of gold guarded by Nazi zombies, was shot in both French and Spanish versions with a partially different cast and an alternate music score.

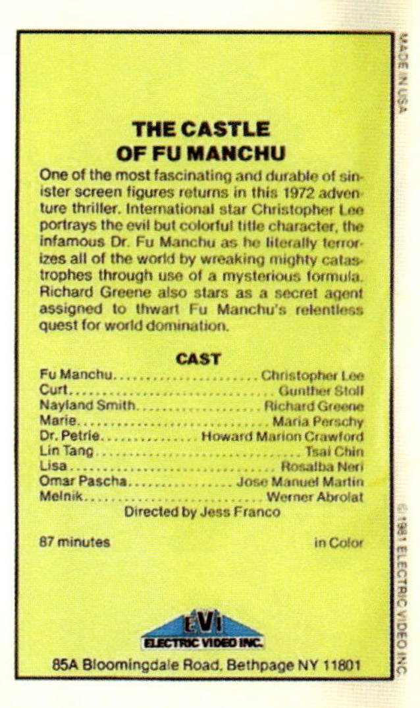

Believe it or not, I never saw a Mario Bava film theatrically until *Beyond the Door II*, nor a Dario Argento film until *Suspiria*. Yet, as a kid, I never missed a EuroCult movie that played on local television. It was there that my appreciations for Bava, Freda, Franco, Argento, Naschy, Vohrer, and others began. I particularly enjoyed seeing Christopher Lee show up in peculiar films like *The Castle of the Living Dead*. Still, on TV, they were all cropped, cut, dubbed, shown with commercial breaks.

So, in the early days of VHS, I gladly forked over $59.95 to see Argento's *Inferno*, or to see *Mill of the Stone Women* again (for the first time in color), after a thirty-year wait. I had to, because Ohio rental stores only stocked mainstream titles. I never saw *Five Dolls for an August Moon* until VHS, and *Rabid Dogs* was considered lost until it enticed me (and many others) to join the DVD revolution. Argento's movies were butchered here in America, so it was thrilling to import full-strength variants on Japanese LaserDiscs.

One night in 1987, Donna and I needed milk for the morning. Supermarkets were closed, so we went to a convenience store we'd passed numerous times without ever going in. As Donna was buying the milk, I wandered into their back room "Video Vault," expecting to find the usual humdrum offerings. Instead, I stood gaping at my wildest dreams come true: Wizard Video! Monterey Home Video! All Seasons Entertainment! Private Screenings! It was my first exposure to Andy Milligan, H.G. Lewis, and Jess Franco on video, and it's where my Franco fever began.

What I learned from the movies rented from that room altered my writing and put me on the path to founding *Video Watchdog* magazine.
Tim Lucas

"ROGER CORMAN HELPED ME IMMEASURABLY WHEN I WAS MAKING *VENUS IN FURS* AND *JUSTINE DE SADE*, TWO FILMS WITH HIGH PRODUCTION VALUES."
JESUS FRANCO

ABOVE LEFT: Jesús Franco directed both *The Blood of Fu Manchu* and *The Castle of Fu Manchu* (Electric Video Inc., 1981), the fourth and fifth entries respectively in producer Harry Alan Towers's diminishing series based on the books by Sax Rohmer. Filmed in Spain and Turkey in 1968, Christopher Lee returned for a final time as the insidious devil doctor plotting to rule the world.

ABOVE RIGHT: Towards the end of his career, Jesús Franco was reduced to making erotic shot-on-video movies such as *Lust for Frankenstein* (Shock-O-Rama Cinema, 2001), which starred the director's partner and long-time collaborator, Lina Romay, as the lesbian granddaughter of Dr. Frankenstein, who created a sex-starved creature played by American "Scream Queen" Michelle Bauer.

TOP LEFT: Filmed in 1968, but not released in the US until 1971 as *Frankenstein's Bloody Terror, La marca del Hombre Lobo* (Cine Español, 1997) was the first of thirteen films to star Spanish horror star Paul Naschy (Jacinto Molina Álvarez) as reluctant werewolf Waldemar Daninsky. Naschy, who also scripted, often cited *Frankenstein Meets the Wolf Man* (1943) as a seminal inspiration.

BOTTOM LEFT: Released theatrically in the US as *The Werewolf vs. the Vampire Woman* and on video as *Blood Moon* (Ariel International Releasing, 1987), this 1971 Spanish-West German coproduction marked the fourth appearance by Paul Naschy as "El Hombre Lobo." A huge box-office success in Spain, it helped kick-start the European horror film boom of the 1970s.

ABOVE RIGHT: Paul Naschy's next appearance as Waldemar Daninsky was in *Fury of the Wolfman* (Alpha Video, 1991), which was actually filmed in 1970 but not released in Spain until five years later. A troubled production, with the director reportedly turning up drunk on the set, the short running time was padded out with extra scenes of a different actor wearing the werewolf makeup.

ABOVE LEFT: Spanish video cover for Paul Naschy's sixth outing as Daninsky, *Dr. Jekyll y el Hombre Lobo* (Divisa Ediciones, 1999). In fact, the actor portrayed two other roles in the film, that of "El Hombre Lobo" and a bestial Mr. Hyde, after consulting the grandson of Dr. Jekyll (Jack Taylor) about finding a cure to his lycanthropic affliction. The Spanish version covered up the nude scenes.

TOP RIGHT: Paul Naschy's seventh outing as Waldemar Daninsky, *Curse of the Devil* (United American Video/Gemstone Entertainment, 1989) was a 1973 Spanish-Mexican coproduction that set up an entirely new origin for "El Hombre Lobo." This was not unusual for a series that often featured unconnected or contradictory plots, while frequent retitlings only added to the confusion.

BOTTOM RIGHT: Paul Naschy's eighth Daninsky film, *Night of the Howling Beast* (Super Video, 1984), was also released as *The Werewolf and the Yeti*. It yet again featured a new origin for the character, now a renowned adventurer, who after being bitten by a pair of cannibalistic women in Tibet was transformed into "El Hombre Lobo." It was banned as a "video nasty" in the UK.

CHAPTER 8
FOREIGN FRIGHTS
“Cinema is a worldwide phenomenon.”
Wim Wenders

"TAKE A BIZARRE JOURNEY TO A REMOTE ISLAND OF TERROR WHERE VOODOO AND LSD MESMERIZE THE SOUL . . . THIS SKIN CRAWLING THRILLER IS TOO REAL TO BE IMAGINED AND WILL HAUNT YOU LONG AFTER IT'S OVER."

***SNAKE PEOPLE* VIDEO BOX BLURB (1989)**

When the home video boom took off in the 1980s and '90s, it wasn't just in the US and UK. Like a zombie apocalypse plague, it quickly spread around the entire world.

In the early 1970s, the Dutch multinational company Philips introduced one of the first videocassette recording (VCR) machines aimed at households in the UK, mainland Europe, Australia, and South Africa, although their top-loading format was soon eclipsed by more sophisticated equipment developed and marketed by such Japanese and Korean companies as Sony, Matsushita, and Samsung.

Sony's superior Betamax format was eventually eclipsed by JVC's VHS (Video Home System), reputedly due to its longer playing time and a greater availability of pornographic movies in that format.

Another problem facing both the manufacturers and consumers was that different countries used different analog broadcast formats. Releasing a movie at the same time throughout the world could be prohibitively expensive so, to protect copyrights and their home markets, countries such as the US, Japan, and some of the Southeast Asian territories marketed their video players in NTSC (National Television Standards Committee); most of Europe and Asia used the PAL (Phase Alternate Line) format; while France, Russia, and some territories of Africa were in SECAM (Sequential Color And Memory).

For the dedicated videotape collector this proved to be a problem, as you could not play back a tape recorded in one format on a machine of a different format. As a result, a huge underground industry grew up where video equipment could be "fixed" to become "region-free."

This now allowed collectors to buy tapes from different countries and watch them in the comfort of their own homes, wherever they lived. As a result, foreign movies that had once been considered rare or even "lost," suddenly became available to a much wider audience.

Many of these films were not in English, or even subtitled, but that didn't matter when you could finally watch a title that before the advent of video had been completely out of the reach of the casual consumer. This was especially true of movies from Southeast Asia or India, which were virtually unknown in the western world.

Another bonus of this greater interaction between various countries was that some filmmakers—especially those moving into the medium-budget "direct-to-video" market—realized they could make their movies much cheaper abroad, leading to an explosion of coproductions between different continents aimed specifically at the burgeoning home video audience.

PREVIOUS SPREAD: *The Vampire Doll* (Dir: Michio Yamamoto, 1970).

THIS PAGE: *Snake People* (Dir: Juan Ibáñez and Jack Hill, 1971).

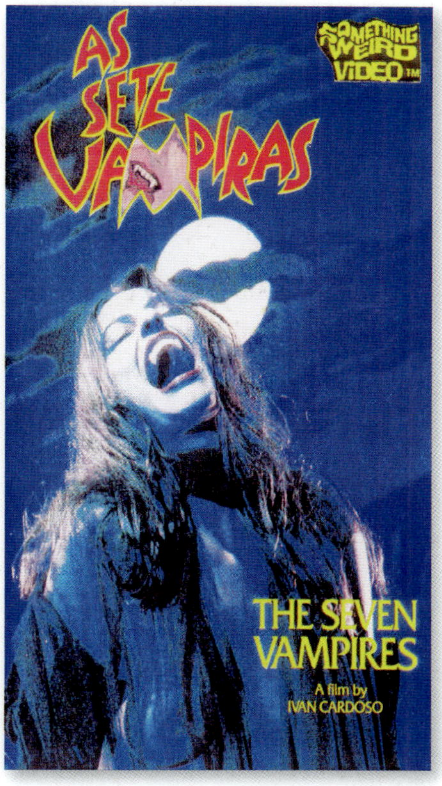

TOP LEFT: Reynold Brown's original poster artwork graced the video box cover for Sidney W. Pink's English-language version of the giant monster movie *Reptilicus* (Orion Home Video, 1994). The original Danish version was directed by Poul Bang and released in 1961, while American International Pictures extensively reedited the film for its US release the following year.

TOP RIGHT: Released in Taiwan in 1977 as *She shan gu nu*, Kuo-Hsiung Liu's obscure *Succubare* (VCR, 1984) was about a remote village in Northwest China ruled by four beautiful but wicked princesses who cursed any of the local men who tried to escape them. Unfortunately, the movie featured numerous scenes of animal cruelty that would probably get it banned today.

BOTTOM LEFT: Dutch video cover for Liliek Sudjio's *The Queen of Black Magic* (Variety Video, n.d.), which was originally released in Indonesia in 1981 as *Ratu ilmu hitam*. A young woman thrown over a cliff for being a witch was nursed back to health so she could get revenge on her persecutors. Also known as *Black Magic 3* in the US, it was loosely remade in 2019.

BOTTOM RIGHT: Ivan Cardoso's 1986 Brazilian horror–comedy *The Seven Vampires* (Something Weird Video, 1994) starred Nicole Puzzi as a reclusive dance instructor whose appearance in the titular nightclub ballet was plagued by a series of strange murders. Partly inspired by the 1986 movie *The Little Shop of Horrors*, it was originally released in Portuguese as *As Sete Vampiras*.

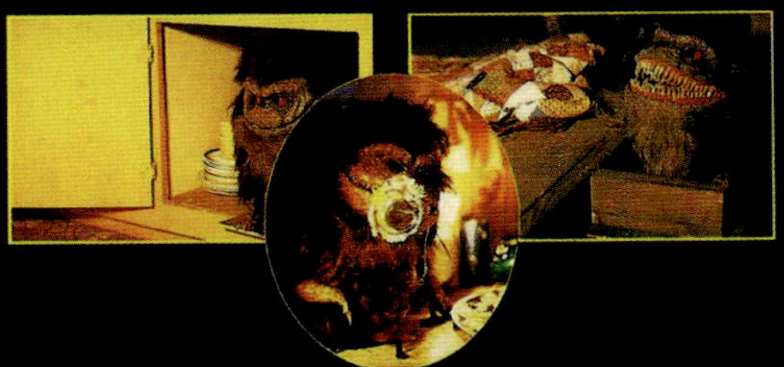

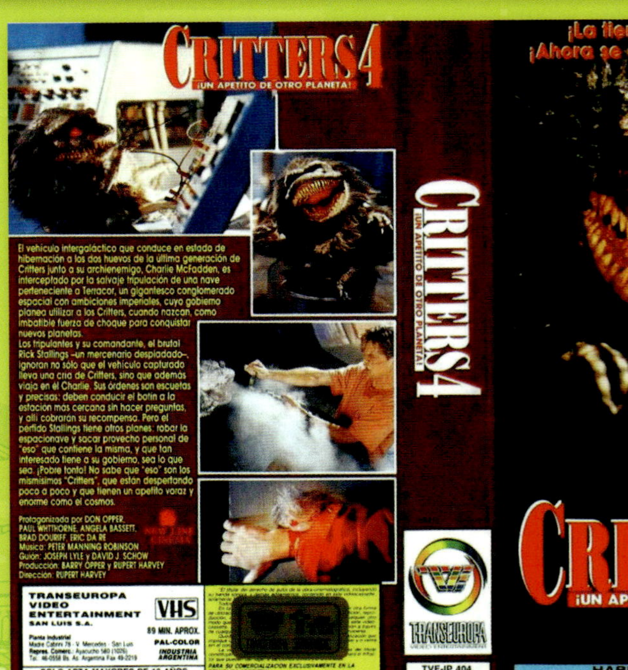

TOP: Brazilian video sleeve for Kristine Peterson's direct-to-video *Critters 3* (América Vídeo Filmes, 1992). Scripted by David J. Schow, it was the third film in the successful comedy science fiction franchise about hungry fur ball aliens that had begun in 1986. Don Opper reprised his role from the previous two movies, and a sixteen-year-old Leonardo DiCaprio made his feature film debut.

BOTTOM: Argentinean video sleeve for Rupert Harvey's direct-to-video sequel *Critters 4* (Transeuropa Video Entertainment, n.d.), which was filmed back-to-back with the previous installment. Coscripted by David J. Schow and Joseph Lyle, it was set on a space station in 2045. Don Opper returned to a cast that included Angela Bassett and Brad Dourif.

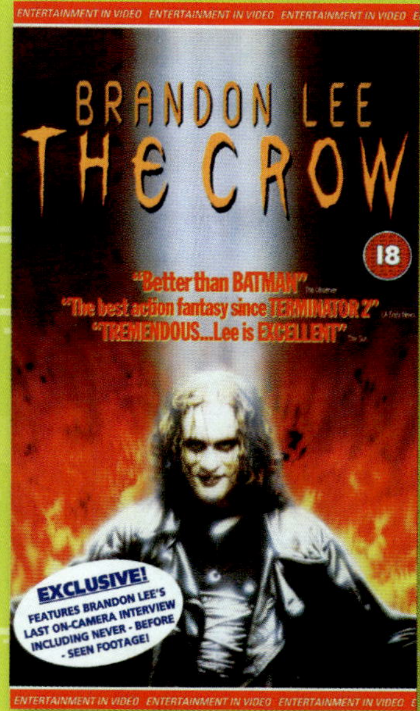

"A DEPRAVED SHOCKER OF INTENSE TERROR FROM THE GRUESOME BEGINNING TO THE BLOODY FINISH."

***LEATHERFACE: TEXAS CHAINSAW MASSACRE III* VIDEO SLEEVE BLURB (1990)**

Back in the hand-to-mouth days I had a side hustle repairing VHS tapes for two Hollywood emporia, in order to gain free access to inventory. Along with my own picks I would take home shopping bags full of malfunctional cassettes, which I diligently resurrected. Mostly.

This required a forensic knowledge of how those tapes functioned. I could spot a victim of "customer abuse" in seconds.

The tapes needing the most severe attention, of course, were porn.

I was later able to adapt a popular—and most likely apocryphal—urban video myth in order to send certain "X" certificate tapes to my British friends during the age of "video nasties." The story held that a "mystery guest" would rent popular mainstream movies like *On Golden Pond* or *Out of Africa*, say. By placing Scotch tape over the erasure tab, this bold cinema pirate could then emplace his own onanistic "special features" a few minutes into the movie's runtime.

Thus did I discover that I could mail a dub of *The Texas Chain Saw Massacre* to the UK if the dub started fifteen minutes into a clamshell copy of *Sleeping Beauty*. (Customs officials, being harried and overworked to begin with, would never play the tape past the first few moments, if at all.)

All of this contributed to my peculiar romance with the VHS medium, now largely disdained. Vulnerable to magnetics, were tapes—outpaced by digital clarity, messy, fragile, clunky, cumbersome. They took up too much shelf space. Today, their box art alone is the source of a vibrant and thriving nostalgia.

Time and tastes marched on. One of the final boxloads of tapes I repaired actually contained a rental copy of my own first movie—*Leatherface: Texas Chainsaw Massacre III*, just to bring it all full circle. I fixed it just to get it back into the retail rental rotation.

David J. Schow

ABOVE LEFT: Australian video sleeve for Jeff Burr's troubled sequel *Leatherface: Texas Chainsaw Massacre III* (RCA Columbia Pictures/Hoyts Video, 1991), the third entry in the franchise that started in 1974. It marked David J. Schow's feature film debut as a scriptwriter. R.A. Mihailoff was the third actor to portray the titular Texas psycho, while Viggo Mortensen had a supporting role. It was originally given an X rating in the US and refused classification in the UK.

ABOVE RIGHT: David J. Schow and John Shirley coscripted Alex Proyas's 1994 movie *The Crow* (Entertainment in Video, n.d.), which was based on James O'Barr's 1980s comic-book series. An extra on the videotape was the last-ever on-camera interview with star Brandon Lee, who was tragically killed in an accident on set before filming was completed. This resulted in uncredited script rewrites and the actor being digitally inserted into scenes that had not been filmed at the time of his death.

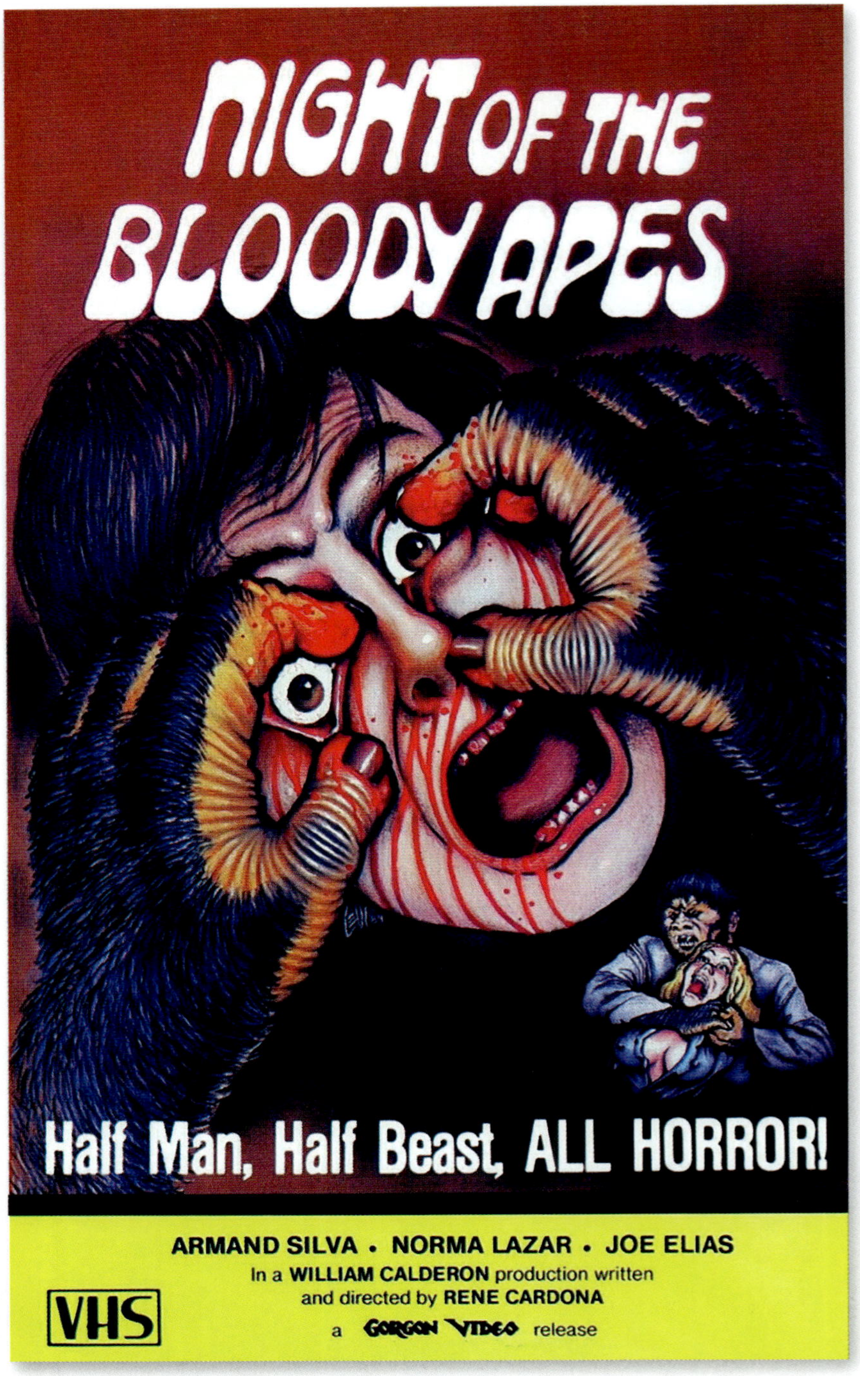

NIGHT OF THE BLOODY APES

Half Man, Half Beast, ALL HORROR!

ARMAND SILVA • NORMA LAZAR • JOE ELIAS

In a WILLIAM CALDERON production written and directed by RENE CARDONA

VHS

a GORGON VIDEO release

TOP LEFT: Made in Mexico in 1958, Rafael Baledón's *El hombre y el monstruo* (Madera Cinevideo, 1985) starred Enrique Rambal as a pianist who had sold his soul to the Devil to become the best in the world. However, whenever he played a cursed concerto he transformed into a hairy monster. Cowriter Abel Salazar played the concert promoter who revealed his secret.

BOTTOM LEFT: Julián Soler's 1972 Mexican version of Robert Louis Stevenson's 1886 novella *Strange Case of Dr Jekyll and Mr Hyde, El hombre y la bestia* (Eagle Video of the Americas, n.d.), starred Enrique Lizalde as Dr. Enrique Duval, who transformed into a murderous ape-like brute after drinking a potion until he was shot to death by his fiancée (Sasha Montenegro).

ABOVE RIGHT: The English-language version of René Cardona's gory 1969 Mexican movie *La Horripilante bestia humana* was released in 1972 as *Night of the Bloody Apes* (Gorgon Video, n.d.). José Elías Moreno's mad scientist transplanted a gorilla's heart into his dying son and turned him into an ape-monster. The 1983 UK video release was successfully banned as a "video nasty."

THIS PAGE: In the spring of 1968, an uncredited Jack Hill directed Boris Karloff in Los Angeles, shooting sequences with the ailing actor for four Mexican horror movies in a package deal with producer Luis Enrique Vergara. The films were subsequently completed in Mexico by director Juan Ibáñez. However, due to Vergara's unexpected death in 1970, the release of the four titles was delayed due to inheritance rights under Mexican law. They all eventually appeared from a variety of budget home video labels under a bewildering number of different titles. *La muerte viviente* (The Living Dead) was released in some Spanish-language theaters in the US only, before a dubbed print went straight to television as *Isle of the Snake People* in 1971. It also appeared as *Cult of the Dead* and *Snake People* (Gemstone Entertainment, 1989) [TOP LEFT]. *Invasion siniestra* was released as *The Incredible Invasion* and *Alien Terror* (Rhino Home Video, 1998) [TOP RIGHT], while *La camara del terror* was better known as *Fear Chamber, The Torture Zone,* and *The Chamber of Fear* (Unicorn Video, n.d.) [BOTTOM LEFT]. Supposedly based on a story by Edgar Allan Poe, *Serenata macabre* was the fourth and final film of the Karloff quartet to be released, three years after the actor's death. It turned up on various video labels as *Macabre Serenade, House of Evil,* and *Dance of Death* (MPI Home Video, 1989) [BOTTOM RIGHT].

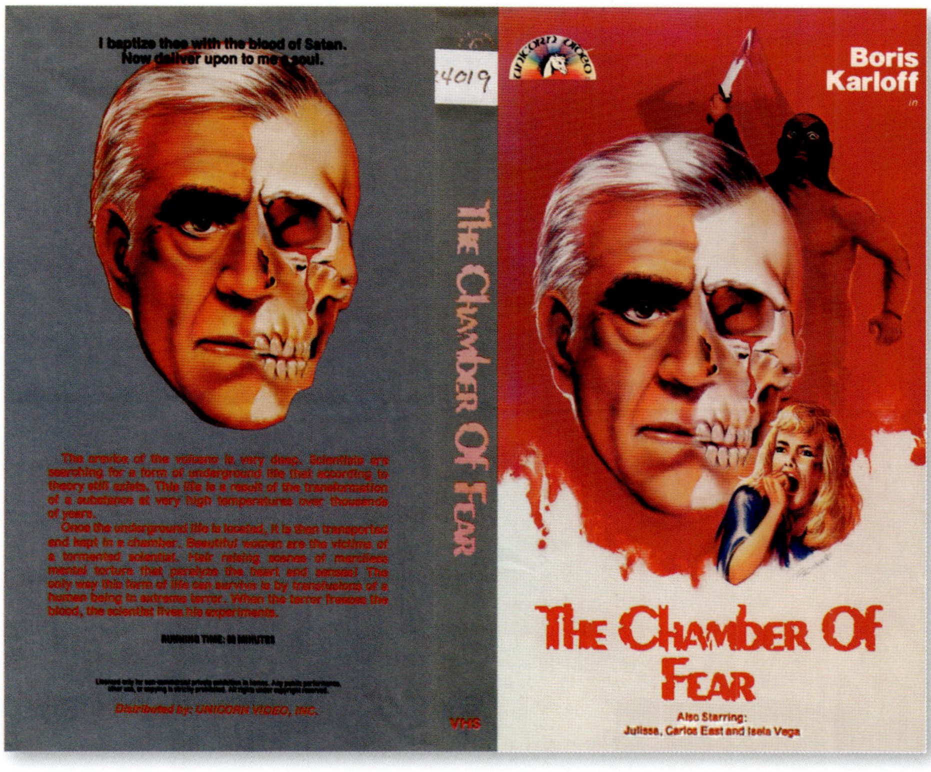

TOP LEFT: Colin Eggleston's 1978 film *Long Weekend* (Trans World Entertainment, 1986) marked the feature debut of scriptwriter Everett De Roche. Considered to be one of the first eco-horror movies, a bickering couple on a weekend camping trip to a remote Australian beach found themselves under attack from nature itself as revenge for the environmental damage they caused.

BOTTOM LEFT: Arch Nicholson's *Dark Age* (Charter Entertainment, 1988) was based on Grahame Webb's 1980 novel *Numunwari*. A giant crocodile, that possibly had mystic significance, brought terror to an Aboriginal community in Australia's Northwest Territory. Barely shown in its native country at the time, it is now considered an early example of "Ozploitation."

ABOVE RIGHT: Arch Nicholson had previously worked as second unit director on music video director Russell Mulcahy's 1984 feature debut *Razorback* (Warner Home Video, 1989). Scripted by Everett De Roche and based on the 1981 novel of the same name by Peter Brennan, it was about a giant wild boar that killed and devoured people in the Australian outback.

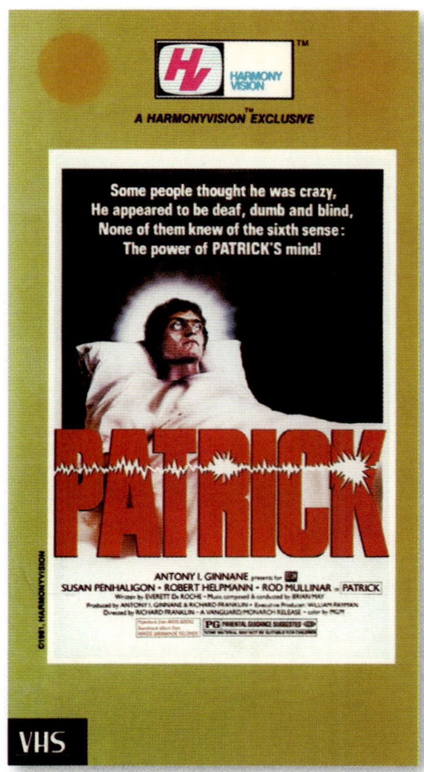

TOP: Terry Bourne's Australian horror–Western *Inn of the Damned* (Paragon Video Productions, 1985) starred American actor Alex Cord as a bounty hunter investigating a series of murders that occurred around a remote inn run by an elderly couple played by Dame Judith Anderson and Joseph Fürst. Filmed in 1973, it wasn't released in Australia until two years later.

BOTTOM LEFT: Richard Franklin's *Patrick* (Harmony Vision, 1981) was Everett De Roche's second produced script. British actress Susan Penhaligon starred as a private nurse looking after the titular comatose patient (Robert Thompson) who used his psychokinetic powers to stalk her. It was followed by an unconnected Italian "sequel" in 1980 and an Australian remake in 2013.

BOTTOM RIGHT: Peter Jackson's low-budget zombie comedy was released in 1992 in its native New Zealand and other markets as *Braindead*. However, due to Adam Simon's near-identical *Brain Dead* (1990), the title was changed in the US to *Dead-Alive* (Vidmark Entertainment, 1993). Forrest J Ackerman had a cameo as a tourist carrying a copy of *Famous Monsters of Filmland*.

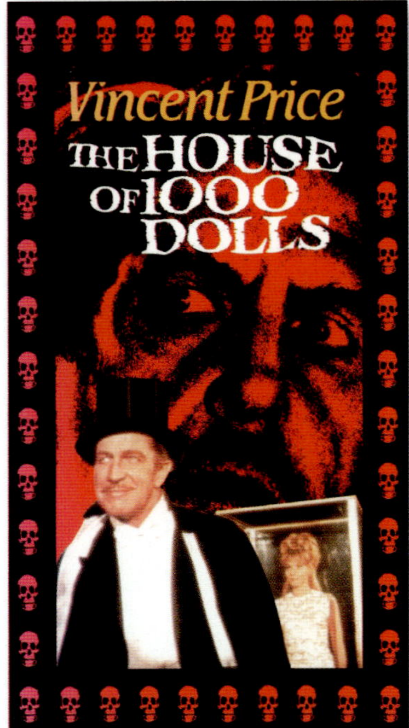

TOP LEFT: Harry Alan Towers's *House of 1000 Dolls* (HBO Home Video, n.d.) was a German-Spanish coproduction released by American International Pictures in the US. Vincent Price and Martha Hyer starred as a pair of white slavers who kidnapped young women under the guise of their nightclub magic act. It exists in alternative versions with different amounts of female nudity.

BOTTOM LEFT: Jesús Franco's *The Blood of Fu Manchu* (1968), the fourth in Harry Alan Towers's series of five Fu Manchu movies starring Christopher Lee, was filmed on location in Spain and Brazil and released in the US under a variety of different titles, including *Kiss and Kill*, *Against All Odds*, and *Kiss of Death* (JTC, 1992). It was still a stinker, no matter what it was called.

ABOVE RIGHT: Among the many high-profile actors that producer Harry Alan Towers was somehow able to convince to be in his productions was Oliver Reed, who starred as an otherworldly priest-king in *Gor* (Warner Home Video, 1987). It was the first of two films shot back-to-back in South Africa that were based on a series of sexy science-fantasy novels by John Norman.

THE DARK TOWERS

British film producer Harry Alan Towers was a consummate dealmaker.

Born in London in 1920, his company Towers of London initially syndicated radio programs around the world before moving into television production in the mid-1950s.

Following a scandal in 1961, when he jumped bail after being charged with operating a vice ring from a New York hotel, Towers returned to Europe, where he started producing feature films (many of which were also scripted under his regular pseudonym "Peter Welbeck").

For Towers it was always about putting the deal together—even if that sometimes meant that a movie had to be shot as a coproduction in different countries due to budgetary constraints.

Probably best known for his series of five *Fu Manchu* movies (1965–69) starring Christopher Lee as Sax Rohmer's evil devil doctor, these were filmed in various locations, including Ireland, Britain, Hong Kong, Spain, and Brazil.

Vincent Price starred alongside Towers's wife, Austrian actress Maria Rohm, in *House of 1,000 Dolls* (1967), which was also shot in Spain. Jack Palance headlined a version of H.G. Wells's *The Shape of Things to Come* (1979), filmed in Canada, while Anthony Perkins played both Dr. Jekyll and Mr. Hyde in *Edge of Sanity* (1989), which was produced in Hungary.

Hungary was also the location for Towers's 1989 version of *The Phantom of the Opera* starring Robert Englund in the title role, and he made three separate versions of Agatha Christie's whodunit *Ten Little Indians/And Then There Were None* set in England (1965), Iran (1974), and South Africa (1989).

During the 1980s and '90s Towers cashed in on the home video boom with such titles as *Howling IV: The Original Nightmare* (1988), *The Masque of the Red Death* (1989), *Buried Alive* (1989), *Night Terrors* (1993), and the Stephen King adaptation *The Mangler* (1995), which were all filmed in different locations around the world.

Harry Alan Towers died in Canada in 2009, aged eighty-eight. At the time he was trying to put together a deal with the Sax Rohmer estate for a sixth Fu Manchu movie, *The Children of Fu Manchu*.

ABOVE LEFT: Produced by Harry Alan Towers on location in South Africa and released directly to video, *Howling IV: The Original Nightmare* (International Video Entertainment, 1988) was the fourth and most faithful entry in the series of movies inspired by Gary Brandner's 1977 novel. Following principal photography, the film was taken away from director John Hough.

ABOVE MIDDLE: Polish video cover for Gérard Kikoïne's *Buried Alive* (Magic Pictures/Vision, 1993), which Harry Alan Towers also produced in South Africa. Supposedly based on the works of Edgar Allan Poe, it was actually a "slasher" thriller set in a facility for juvenile delinquent girls. It was also the final film made by veteran John Carradine prior to his death, and is dedicated to his memory.

ABOVE RIGHT: There were two versions of Edgar Allan Poe's *The Masque of the Red Death* (RCA/Columbia Pictures Home Video, 1991) released in 1989, one produced by Roger Corman and this one coproduced by Harry Alan Towers in South Africa back-to-back with his version of *The House of Usher*. Neither was a patch on Corman's 1964 original starring Vincent Price.

TOP LEFT: Kazuo "Gaira" Komizu is a director/screenwriter best known for his shot-on-video "torture porn" movies, known as *ero-guro* (erotic grotesque) in his native Japan. *Shojo no harawata*, better known as *Entrails of a Virgin* (Nikkatsu Video, 1986), is one of these *pinku eiga* (pink films), about a photographic model who was raped by the mud demon that killed all her companions.

BOTTOM LEFT: Kazuo "Gaira" Komizu's follow-up, *Bijo no harawata*, or *Entrails of a Beautiful Woman* (Nikkatsu Video, 1986), was about a murdered woman whose body melded with that of a dead gangster to return from the grave as a hermaphrodite zombie seeking revenge. During the 1980s, low quality VHS copies of these titles were regularly traded on the US collectors' market.

ABOVE RIGHT: During the early 1970s, Japanese director Michio Yamamoto directed three vampire films for Toho that became known as the "Bloodthirsty Trilogy." This consisted of *The Vampire Doll* (1970), *Lake of Dracula* (1971) and, in 1974, *Evil of Dracula* (Paramount/Gateway, 1994), which was released in its native country as *Chi o suu bara* (The Bloodthirsty Rose).

ABOVE LEFT: Filmed in Japan in English in 1959 by codirectors George Breakston and Kenneth G. Crane, and not released in the US for another three years, *The Manster* (The Al Taylor Company/ Walterscheid Productions, 1990) starred Peter Dyneley as an American foreign news correspondent who found a second head growing from his shoulder thanks to a mad scientist.

TOP RIGHT: Released in Japan in 1955, Ishirō Honda's *Jû jin yuki otoko* was about the search for an Abominable Snowman. Heavily edited, the 1957 American version, retitled *Half Human* (Rhino Home Video, 1990), replaced the original music score and included new scenes directed by Kenneth G. Crane featuring seasoned US actors John Carradine and Morris Ankrum.

BOTTOM RIGHT: Veteran actor James Craig's obnoxious mad scientist moved to Japan to create a hybrid Venus Flytrap monster in Norm Thomson's obscure 1968 movie *The Revenge of Dr. X* (Regal Video, 1985). Originally titled *Body of the Prey* and apparently based on an old script by Edward D. Wood, Jr., the credits on the videotape belong to *The Mad Doctor of Blood Island* (1969).

ABOVE LEFT: Produced by Roger Corman, Fred Gallo's *Dracula Rising* (New Horizons Home Video, 1993) was shot in Bulgaria and released directly to video. Zahari Vatahov's Vlad the Impaler time-traveled to the twentieth century and into the body of blond Christopher Atkins to reconnect with his reincarnated love (Stacey Travis), now an American art restorer.

TOP RIGHT: Full Moon Entertainment's direct-to-video *Subspecies* (Paramount Home Video, 1991) was the first American movie to be shot in Romania after the collapse of Communism in that country. It was the first of five (so far) movies, all directed by Ted Nicolaou, which starred Anders Hove as the undead Radu Vladislas attempting to gain control over the mystical Bloodstone.

BOTTOM RIGHT: Presented by Wes Craven and coscripted by his son Jonathan, The Kushner-Locke Company's direct-to-video *Mind Ripper* (WarnerVision Films, 1995) was shot in Bulgaria.

OPPOSITE PAGE: *Last Gasp* (WarnerVision Films, 1995) was produced simultaneously with *Mind Ripper* by Kushner-Locke in Romania.

ROBERT PATRICK JOANNA PACULA
PRAY YOU NEVER HEAR THE
LAST GASP
THE KUSHNER-LOCKE COMPANY IN ASSOCIATION WITH ATLANTIC GROUP FILMS PRESENT A KUSHNER-LOCKE PRODUCTION LAST GASP
ROBERT PATRICK JOANNA PACULA MIMI CRAVEN VYTO RUGINIS EDITOR ANDREW DOERFER DIRECTOR OF PHOTOGRAPHY ADAM KANE
PRODUCERS STANLEY ISAACS PHIL MITTLEMAN CO-EXECUTIVE PRODUCER LAWRENCE MORTORFF EXECUTIVE PRODUCERS PETER LOCKE
DONALD KUSHNER SCREENPLAY BY DAVID N. TWOHY STORY BY DAVID N. TWOHY AND STANLEY ISAACS DIRECTED BY SCOTT McGINNIS
KUSHNER-LOCKE INTERNATIONAL
©1994 THE KUSHNER-LOCKE COMPANY AND ATLANTIC GROUP FILMS. ALL RIGHTS RESERVED.
CREDITS NOT CONTRACTUAL. ©1994 KUSHNER-LOCKE INTERNATIONAL. ALL RIGHTS RESERVED

THIS SPREAD: From the late 1980s until the mid-2000s, entrepreneurs set up mobile "video clubs" in Ghana, West Africa. With a TV monitor, VHS playback equipment and a portable diesel generator they would travel the country, organizing impromptu screenings of videotapes in towns and villages with little or no electricity. Unable to afford printing, local artists were employed to hand-paint advertising posters on oversized canvases made up of sewn-together flour sacks. As many of these posters were created before the artist saw the movie, there was often a tendency to embellish the paintings, especially when it came to depictions of sex and violence, in an attempt to sell more tickets.

ABOVE LEFT: Ghanaian poster for *Hellraiser* (Manso Video Mamobi, n.d.) by Greater Accra Region artist Heavy J that incorporated imagery from the first three sequels scripted by Peter Atkins.

TOP RIGHT: *Hellbound: Hellraiser II* (Warsti Video Teshie, n.d.) poster painted on a repurposed flour sack by artist Papa Warsti for the coastal town of Teshie in the Greater Accra Region.

BOTTOM RIGHT: Joe Mensah's hand-painted poster for *Hellaiser III: Hell on Earth* (Pal Mal Video Club Tudu, 1993) for the Accra suburb of Tudu. Doug Bradley's Pinhead consuming one of his victims seemed to be a recurring motif.

ABOVE LEFT: Detail of a hand-painted poster on flour sacks by Ghanaian artist Leonardo that used the same image of Doug Bradley's Cenobite from *Hellaiser III: Hell on Earth* chewing on an unfortunate victim.

ABOVE MIDDLE: Poster for *Fist of the North Star* (Zapp Video Club, n.d.), coscripted by Peter Atkins and director Tony Randel, which was also painted by Leonardo for a screening behind the Glory Land Hotel in Odorkor, Accra.

ABOVE RIGHT: One-of-a-kind hand-painted Ghanaian flour-sack poster for a local video club screening of Jack Sholder's 1999 sequel *Wishmaster 2: Evil Never Dies* (n.d.), which was based on characters created by Peter Atkins.

My generation of Monster Kids had to rely on *Famous Monsters of Filmland* magazine and late-night local TV for our Classic Horror fix. The movies themselves were not at our beck and call, to be watched whenever we wanted. The only exceptions were the Super 8 "digests" that we could buy—at *exorbitant* prices—from an occasional High Street retailer or from catalogs.

And then God created videotapes.

I was late to the party, but not so late that the Betamax/VHS wars were over. The fighting was still on, and I picked the losing side. Although I have fond memories of an uncut and ultra-wide-screen ex-rental Betamax of Argento's *Deep Red* (found in a charity shop in North Wales), it was only when I finally converted to VHS that I could begin anything resembling a collection.

It was a few years later—when retail had replaced rental as an easy go-to—that I first beheld the full splendor of an entire Universal movie in an attractive case that could be taken home. That could be mine. They were all there—*Dracula, The Invisible Man, The Mummy, The Wolf Man, Frankenstein* and his Bride (and his Son, and his Ghost, and his House)—and there were even things we'd never dreamed we'd get to see, let alone own, like the Spanish *Drácula*, a thing from myth and rumor, shot on the same sets as the Tod Browning, but—it was whispered—with better atmosphere and better performances. They were half-right. The cobwebs and Lupita Tovar were fantastic, but Carlos Villarías's Count was really no match for Bela's. Didn't matter. Whether individual movies were good, bad, or indifferent, what mattered was that they were there.

Later, I was lucky enough to have my own movies come out on VHS, and it was an undeniable thrill to hold them in my hand and relish the box art. But I'd be lying if I didn't admit a little part of me was sad that I couldn't also have a Castle Films 8mm silent *Hellbound* or *Wishmaster* in guaranteed-to-fade color.

Peter Atkins

TOP: Veteran horror actor John Carradine traveled to Manila in the Philippines in 1978 to star as the undead leader of three seductive female vampires in Cirio H. Santiago's lowbrow comedy *Vampire Hookers*. It was subsequently released on video under various titles, including *Sensuous Vampires*, *Night of the Bloodsuckers*, *Cemetery Girls*, and *Twice Bitten* (Ariel Films/CBS, n.d.).

BOTTOM LEFT: Ton Friesen's art for the Dutch video sleeve cover of *Brides of Blood* (PolyGram Video, 1982), a 1968 Filipino horror movie directed by Eddie Romero and Gerardo de Leon. It starred American actor John Ashley as a member of a scientific group investigating radioactive mutations on a tropical island. It was the first in what became known as the "Blood Island Trilogy."

BOTTOM RIGHT: John Ashley was back for Eddie Romero and Gerardo de Leon's unconnected 1969 sequel *The Mad Doctor of Blood Island*, which was also released on home video under its TV title *Tomb of the Living Dead* (Horror Time Video, n.d.). This time Ronald Remy's mad scientist was attempting to create human/plant mutants using chlorophyll blood.

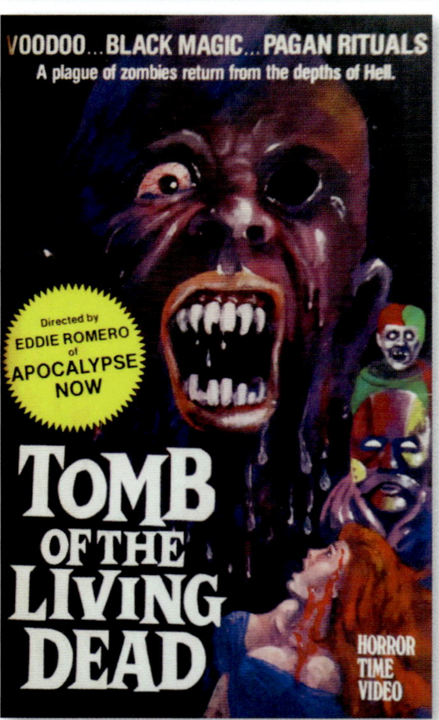

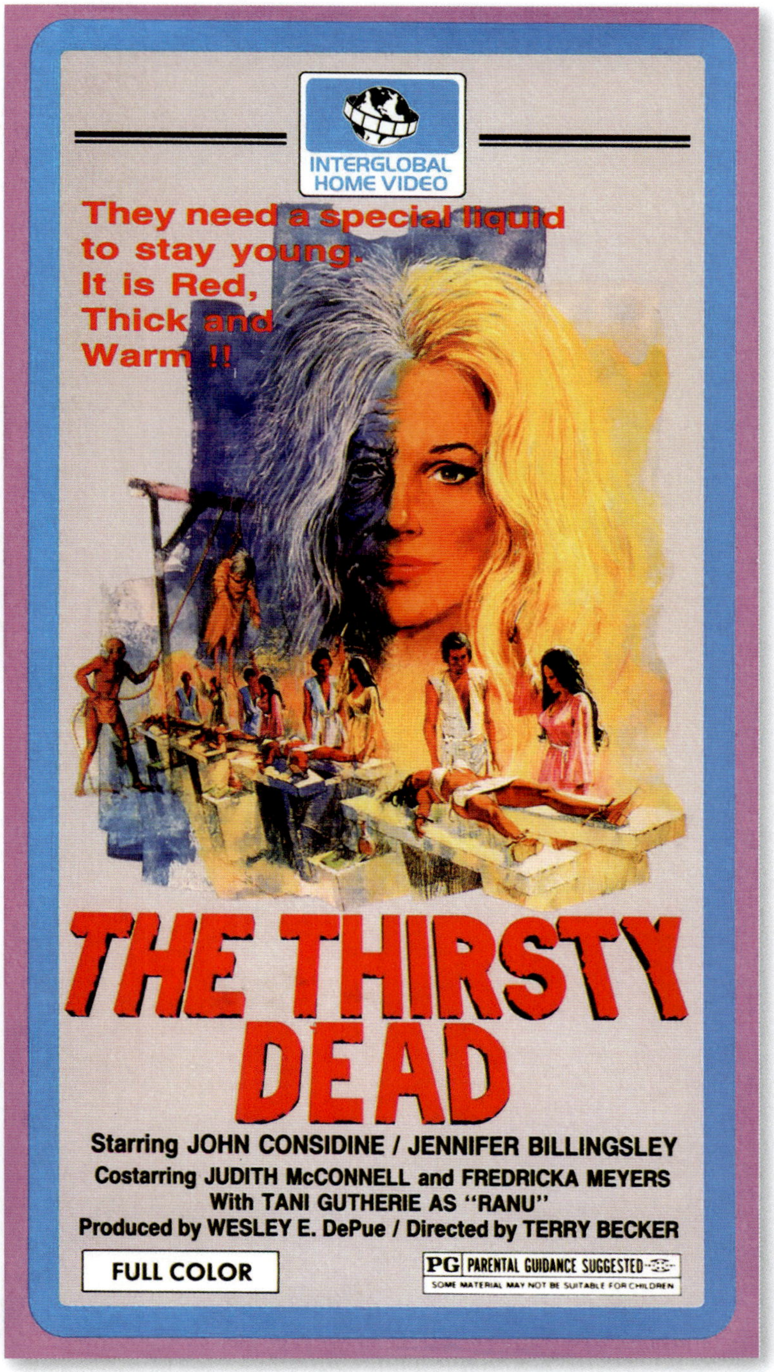

TOP LEFT: The third in the Filipino "Blood Island Trilogy," Eddie Romero's 1970 release *Beast of Blood* was a direct sequel to the previous movie in the sequence. Retitled *Blood Devils* (Apple Video Film Distributors, n.d.) in the UK, John Ashley's doctor hero returned to Blood Island and once again encountered the evil Dr. Lorca (now played by Eddie Garcia) and his chlorophyll monsters.

BOTTOM LEFT: John Ashley enjoyed working in the Philippines so much that he moved there and set up his own production company in partnership with director Eddie Romero. However, instead of using their usual distributor, Hemisphere Pictures, their 1971 collaboration *The Beast of the Yellow Night* (United Home Video, 1986), was released in the US by Roger Corman's New World Pictures.

ABOVE RIGHT: Canadian video box cover for Terry Becker's 1974 Filipino movie *The Thirsty Dead* (InterGlobal Home Video, 1987), in which Jennifer Billingsley's heroine and three other young women were kidnapped off the streets of Manila by a secret jungle cult that wanted their blood to retain a state of eternal youth. It was also released on home video under the title *Blood Hunt*.

CHAPTER 9
"VIDEO NASTIES"
"Video nasties are the product of diseased minds."
Lord Coggan, former Archbishop of Canterbury

"IT WILL LEAVE YOU WONDERING IF DEEP INSIDE US ALL, THERE MAY LURK THE CANNIBAL."

ANTHROPOPHAGOUS: THE BEAST VIDEO BOX BLURB (1983)

In Britain in the early 1980s there was no law governing the production and distribution of videocassettes. As a result, there was no age restriction on renting tapes and, unlike theatrical movie releases, no censorship laws to decide what they could or could not contain.

Soon the nascent video industry in the UK was awash with fly-by-night companies buying up the rights to mostly low-budget product—invariably horror and exploitation titles—and flooding the market with them.

Packaged in eye-catching, lurid, and often blatantly misleading covers to attract the casual renter, it was not long before a campaign was launched to protect the country's impressionable youth.

Fueled in much the same way as the backlash against horror comics was in the 1950s, a combination of self-appointed "moral guardians," special-interest groups, a hysterical press, and a right-wing government combined forces to change the situation.

These tapes, quickly dubbed by the British media as "video nasties" (a term that remains in use today), were soon being seized and destroyed in raids by police forces all over the country. Because of the practice of changing the titles of films for their video release, there was sometimes confusion about which movies were actually being targeted under the 1959 Obscene Publications Act. This often led to the farcical situation of some confiscated titles that had previously been legally certified for release in the UK being put on lists and then taken off again. In the end, just thirty-nine titles were considered prosecutable by the Director of Public Prosecutions (DPP), and this became the definitive "video nasty" list.

To put an end to this moral panic, Parliament passed the Video Recordings Act 1984, which stipulated that all videos had to be precensored for the British market. It was followed three years later by the introduction of the Video Packaging Review Committee, which put a final nail in the coffin of those often outrageous and gory video sleeve designs.

PREVIOUS SPREAD: *The House by the Cemetery* (Dir: Lucio Fulci, 1981).

THIS PAGE: *Cannibal Holocaust* (Dir: Ruggero Deodato, 1980).

WIN A MILLION Page 30

DAILY EXPRESS

Thursday November 24 1983 • 18p • TV Pages 24 and 25

THE VOICE OF BRITAIN

Union faces High Court over big fine revolt

MPs STUNNED BY SURVEY'S SHOCKING REVELATIONS

Four children in ten watch video nasties

Six-year-olds are

Mirror Comment

The evil of video violence

VIOLENT, sadistic and perverted video films are as great a danger to a child's mind as any infectious disease is to the body.

Yet children are being exposed to them every day.

High Street retailers so obsessed with profit that they have the films on their shelves plumb the depths of greed.

Yet these obscenities can be bought or hired in any town.

Adults who allow children to watch bestial sex, the dismemberment of bodies, cannibalism and torture in the privacy of the home have scaled the heights of depravity.

Yet it is happening in countless homes every night.

It would not be difficult to make these video horrors illegal and the Commons has set about doing it.

Devastating

But that's not the end of it. These films are not just the product of some corrupt continental.

British writers have written them. British actors and actresses have played in them. British producers have produced them. British shopkeepers have sold them.

And British parents have bought them.

It is no use any parent pleading: "The kids watch them while we are out."

If the films weren't in the house in the first place, the kids wouldn't be able to watch them.

The punishment for those involved in making and marketing the video horrors ought to be devastating.

But those who buy and hire them must share the guilt.

TOP LEFT: Astra Video was forced to quickly amend its trade advertisement for the 1982 release of Herschell Gordon Lewis's *Blood Feast* (1963) and the obviously fake *Snuff* (1975) by putting a "censored" sticker over the blood-spattered breasts of a victim and withdrawing the latter film completely following a public outcry over its proposed video release in the UK.

BOTTOM LEFT: Typically hysterical headline on the front of the November 24, 1983 edition of the right-wing newspaper the *Daily Express*, which claimed that "The boom in video nasties is turning Britain's children into a generation of ghouls, haunted by nightmares" and "children who once marveled at Mickey Mouse are now hooked on horror" while their parents remained unaware.

ABOVE RIGHT: Even populist newspapers such as the *Daily Mirror* got in on the act with a particularly alarmist editorial in its November 25, 1983 edition that berated parents for letting their children watch "violent, sadistic, and perverted video films" and demanded that "the punishment for those involved in making and marketing the video horrors ought to be devastating."

ABOVE LEFT: Despite starring an often-naked Ursula Andress and Stacy Keach, Sergio Martino's Italian-made *Prisoner of the Cannibal God* (Hokushin, 1981) was banned on video for a time in the UK for its scenes of real animal cruelty. Ironically, it was the same print that in 1978 had been released in the country theatrically after it had been heavily cut for the same reason.

TOP RIGHT: Credited as being coscripted by Jesús Franco, the French-Spanish coproduction *Cannibal Terror* (Modern Films, 1981) was banned in Britain simply because of its title. It was dropped from the Director of Public Prosecutions' list of successfully prosecuted videos in 1985, and an uncut version was eventually released in the UK in 2003.

BOTTOM RIGHT: Umberto Lenzi's *Deep River Savages* (Derann, 1982) was originally refused a certificate when submitted for theatrical distribution in the UK in 1975. The uncut video version was soon added to the DPP's banned list, but was dropped before it could make the final thirty-nine. It is widely considered to have started the European "cannibal" subgenre.

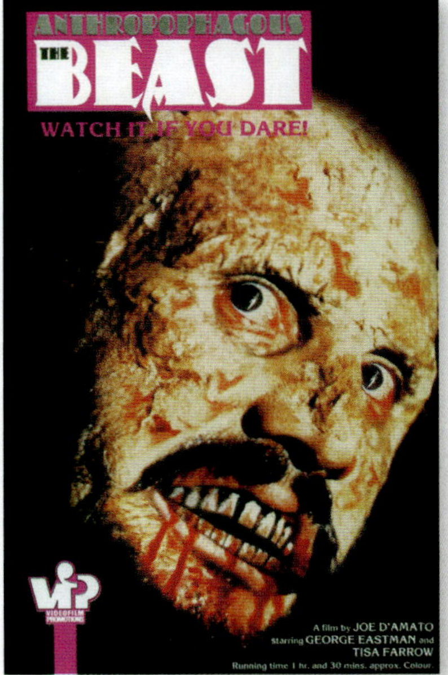

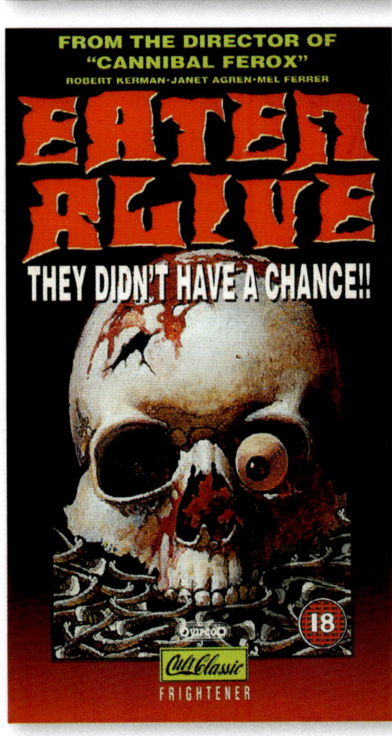

EATEN ALIVE!

The Ultimate Terror Movie...

Cannibal Holocaust

Available at all good video dealers VHS, BETA and VCC formats

GO VIDEO LIMITED

P.O. BOX 4BT, 35-37 WARDOUR ST., LONDON W1A 4BT TEL: 01-734 7195/6 TELEX: 922488

TOP LEFT: Joe D'Amato's gruesome *Anthropophagous: The Beast* (Video Film Promotions, 1983) featured a group of tourists being stalked on a remote island by a disfigured cannibal killer (George Eastman). Although it was banned in the UK, a heavily censored version was subsequently released by another company. It sold very poorly and is now a collector's item.

BOTTOM LEFT: Despite coming from the director of the infamous *Cannibal Ferox* (1981), Umberto Lenzi's *Eaten Alive!* (VIPCO, 1992) somehow managed to avoid ending up on the DPP's list. This was probably because the 1982 video was the original UK theatrical version, which had already been cut by nearly six minutes. A further second was missing from video reissues.

ABOVE RIGHT: Trade advertisement for Ruggero Deodato's "found footage" *Cannibal Holocaust* (Go Video, 1982), which had been precensored for its video debut but was still banned in Britain following moral outrage from Mary Whitehouse's "clean-up campaign" group, the National Viewers' and Listeners' Association, and the right-wing tabloid newspaper the *Daily Mail*.

"UNCENSORED HORROR VIDEO CASSETTES, AVAILABLE TO ANYBODY OF ANY AGE, HAVE ARRIVED IN BRITAIN'S HIGH STREETS . . . FAR REMOVED FROM THE SUSPENSE OF THE TRADITIONAL HORROR FILM, DWELLING ON MURDER, MULTIPLE RAPE, BUTCHERY, SADO-MASOCHISM, MUTILATION OF WOMEN, CANNIBALISM AND NAZI ATROCITIES."

"HOW HIGH STREET HORROR IS INVADING THE HOME" BY PETER CHIPPINDALE, *THE SUNDAY TIMES* (MAY 23, 1982)

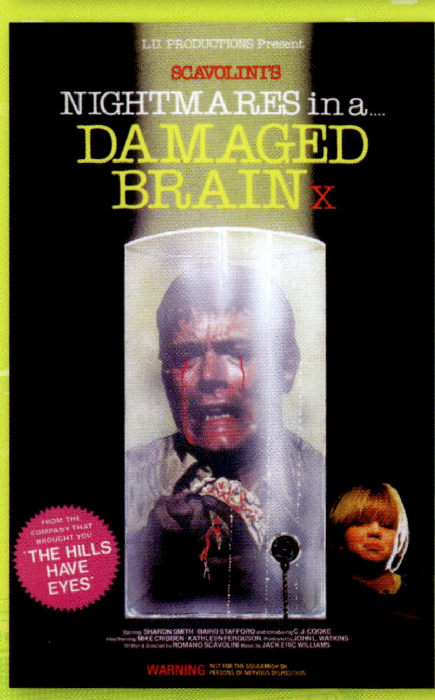

Ah, that nasty thrill! For a while there was nothing quite like it. After decades of crudely cut British releases—*Zombie Flesh Eaters* in which no flesh was eaten, Bava's *Blood Bath* where our censor had emptied the bath—you could take the complete versions home to watch.

Such open availability didn't last long.

A Manchester trade fair featured a brain in a jar to advertise *Nightmares in a Damaged Brain*, a spectacle that offended the journalist Peter Chippindale, or so he professed. His *Sunday Times* article was the spark that set censorship raging, and the uncut tapes rapidly went into hiding to elude police raids on the omnipresent video libraries. This offered aficionados a new delight—collecting the banned tapes.

Some of us set out to amass the entire list, a prodigious task. Quite a few titles proved hard to track down, and sometimes their inclusion in the list was puzzling. *The Werewolf and the Yeti* offered a flaying scene our censor would have balked at then, although not now, and perhaps the portrayal (not by any means endorsement) of racism in *Fight For Your Life* (an excellent reworking of *The Desperate Hours*) offended someone, but what was the issue with *Butcher, Baker, Nightmare Maker*?

Most of the media purveyed the view that all the listed films were equally deplorable, a menace from which the country must be protected. In my film review spot on BBC Radio Merseyside I tried to counteract this sort of propaganda, not least the local office of Trading Standards' bids to characterize collectors swapping videos as criminal rings (although copied tapes could be criminally close to unwatchable).

It was a fun time while it lasted, if no fun for the distributors and retailers who suffered prosecution. Perhaps we shouldn't feel too nostalgic about it, or too evolved. Censorship will always be with us, and only its targets change.

Ramsey Campbell

TOP: *Butcher, Baker, Nightmare Maker* (Atlantis Video Productions, 1983) was directed by William Asher, whose credits included TV's *Bewitched* and several "Beach Party" movies.

BOTTOM: The uncut version of *Nightmares in a Damaged Brain* (LU Productions, 1982) was successfully prosecuted for obscenity in the UK and its distributor given a six-month jail sentence.

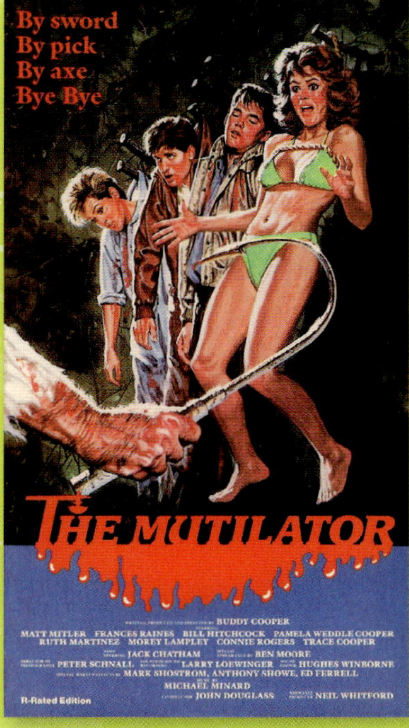

ABOVE LEFT: During the 1980s, video box art often depicted scantily clad women in mortal jeopardy. *Mardi Gras Massacre* (Gold Star/Derann, 1982), about a ritual serial killer stalking his victims in New Orleans, is a good example of this blatantly exploitative marketing trend. Advertised as being an "American Splatter Movie," it was quickly banned in the UK.

TOP RIGHT: Filmed in 1984 as *Fall Break*, a group of high school students on vacation at a beachside summer house were sliced and diced by the deranged father of one of the friends in Buddy Cooper's *The Mutilator* (Vestron Video, 1985). Released in both unrated and R-rated versions in the US, a slightly trimmed "Extreme Version!" was released on video in the UK in 2000.

BOTTOM RIGHT: Jesús Franco's 1980 entry in the cannibal subgenre, *Devil Hunter*, appeared on video in the US as *Manhunter* (Trans World Entertainment, 1986) with particularly salacious box art. An uncut video release in the UK was quickly added to the DPP's list of "video nasties" and is now a much sought-after item, commanding a high price among collectors.

TOP: Rosie Holotik's young psychiatric nurse discovered that the inmates had taken over the asylum in *Don't Look in the Basement* (Gorgon Video/MPI, n.d.), the directorial debut of Texas filmmaker S.F. Brownrigg. It was filmed in 1973 as *The Forgotten*, and despite being cut for release in the UK it still ended up on the "video nasties" list for a while.

BOTTOM LEFT: Filmed in 1979 under the working title *The Hollywood Strangler, Don't Answer the Phone!* (Jaguar Video, 1981) was Robert Hammer's only directing credit. Nicholas Worth played the disturbed former Vietnam vet who strangled his scantily clad victims. The UK video release was the edited theatrical version, which probably saved it from prosecution.

BOTTOM RIGHT: A psychotic young man obsessed with fire burned chained-up women alive with a flamethrower in James Ellison's shot-in-New Jersey *Don't Go in the House* (Arcade Video, 1982), filmed as *The Burning* in 1979. When the UK distributor agreed to replace the uncensored video with the cut "X" certificate version it was taken off the "video nasties" list.

TOP LEFT: Filmed in Utah by exploitation director James Bryan to cash in on the success of *Friday the 13th, Don't Go in the Woods* (Video Releasing Organization, 1982) featured various people ignoring that advice and being hacked to pieces by a backwoods maniac (Tom Drury). The movie's high gore quotient was enough to get it banned in the UK until 2007.

TOP RIGHT: A pair of prehistoric siblings cursed with eternal life feasted on the entrails of young people out for a stroll in contemporary Los Angeles in Lawrence David Foldes's *Don't Go Near the Park* (Home Video Productions, 1983). Eventually dropped from the DPP's banned list, it is only notable for featuring "Scream Queen" Linnea Quigley in her first horror film role.

BOTTOM: Filmed in 1974 as *Don't Hang Up* by independent Texas regional filmmaker S.F. Brownrigg and released to video as *Don't Open the Door* (Video Form Pictures, n.d.), a young woman (Susan Bracken) found herself trapped in a house with a homicidal maniac. Despite being advertised as "Not for the squeamish!!!" somehow this proto-slasher escaped prosecution in the UK.

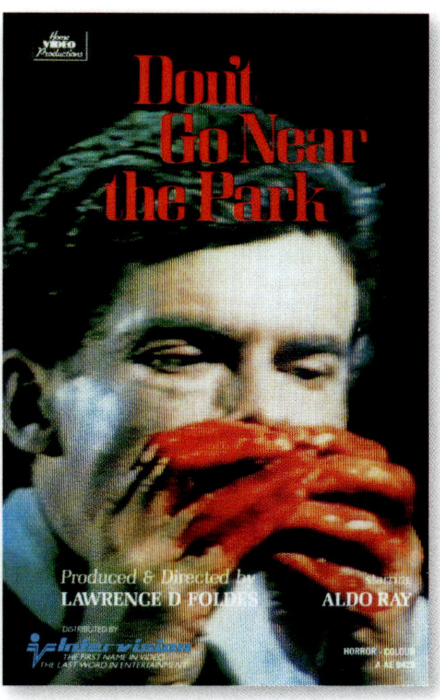

"FRAULEIN KRAST, A SADISTIC BIOLOGIST, CONCENTRATES HER EFFORTS ON THE WOMENFOLK WITH REFINED TORTURES AND HUMILIATION, LEAVING THEM AT THE MERCY OF A SEX-CRAZED HALF-MAN, HALF-BEAST SHE HAS CREATED WITH EXPERIMENTAL INJECTIONS . . ."

THE BEAST IN HEAT VIDEO BOX BLURB (1982)

NASTY NAZIS

One of the more bizarre subgenres to fall under the "video nasties" banner is generally referred to as "Nasty Nazi" movies.

Mostly produced in Italy during the 1970s, these films were basically exploitation versions of the old "prisoner of war" films that were popular after World War II, but with added sex and sadism.

With so many to choose from, it is perhaps surprising that only four titles eventually found their way on to the Director of Public Prosecutions' now-infamous list of thirty-nine releases that could be prosecuted under the terms of the Obscene Publications Act.

The oldest of these films was Market Video's *Love Camp 7* (1969) that, unlike its companions, was actually made in the US by exploitation director R.L. Frost (David Kayne), who was also known for the cult favorites *House on Bare Mountain* (1962) and *The Thing with Two Heads* (1972).

Cesare Canevari's *The Gestapo's Last Orgy* (*L'ultima orgia del III Reich*, 1976) was initially released to rental stores by Video Film Promotions in a version that was already missing more than ten minutes of footage and had a warning sticker on the back of the sleeve. That didn't stop it being banned though, and despite still not being available in the UK to this day, it was later released on DVD in the US under the title *Caligula Reincarnated as Hitler*.

From the same year, *SS Experiment Camp* (*Lager SSadis Kastrat Kommandantur*) was another Italian production, directed by Sergio Garrone. Although Go Video decided to cover up the topless woman's breasts on its advertising, it was still found guilty under the Obscene Publications Act and banned in the UK until 2016.

Perhaps the most infamous, as well as the most obscure of this quartet of "Naziploitation" films is *The Beast in Heat* (*La bestia in calore*, 1977), directed and coscripted by Luigi Batzella under the pseudonym "Ivan Katansky." Copies of the rare JVI videocassette can change hands for more than $500 among die-hard collectors.

ABOVE: The graphic advertising in the trade press for the VHS release of *SS Experiment Camp* (Go Video, 1982) was one of the things that sparked off the "video nasty" debate in Britain. Set towards the end of World War II, Giorgio Cerioni's sadistic Colonel von Kleiben used genetic experiments on female prisoners in an attempt to preserve the purity of a new Aryan race.

TOP LEFT: The American-made *Love Camp 7* (Market Video, 1983) basically started the whole subgenre of "Nasty Nazi" movies. It starred Maria Lease and Kathy Williams as two WAC lieutenants who went undercover in a prison camp and ended up being tortured, abused, and humiliated by their Nazi captors. Originally acquired by Abbey Video, it was reissued by Market before being banned.

BOTTOM LEFT: Nazi swastikas were featured prominently on video box art for "Naziploitation" movies, and *The Gestapo's Last Orgy* (Video Film Promotions, 1983) was no exception. Told in flashback, Daniela Levy's Jewish prisoner of war recalled the abuse and humiliation she endured at the hands of the Commandant and his soldiers.

ABOVE RIGHT: Macha Magall's sadistic SS endo-geneticist, Dr. Ellen Kratsch, created a hairy, sexually driven hybrid (Salvatore Baccaro) to abuse and torture nude female prisoners in *The Beast in Heat* (JVI, 1982). It was perhaps no wonder that it ended up on the DPP's list of banned films. Also known as *Horrifying Experiments of the SS Last Days*, among other titles.

TOP LEFT: When *The Beast in Heat* (1977) was released on video in the US as *SS Experiment Camp 2* (Mogul Communications, 1987) it featured much better video sleeve art.

TOP RIGHT: Bruno Mattei's *SS Girls* (Media Home Entertainment, 1981) involved a group of prostitutes whose mission was to uncover a plot against the Führer.

BOTTOM: Japanese video sleeve for Don Edmonds's 1975 *Ilsa: She Wolf of the SS* (TCC Video, n.d.). This slice of Canadian sexploitation (shot on the leftover sets from the TV series *Hogan's Heroes*) starred Dyanne Thorne as the sex-crazed warden of a Nazi prison camp conducting experiments on the female prisoners. It was rejected twice for certification in the UK.

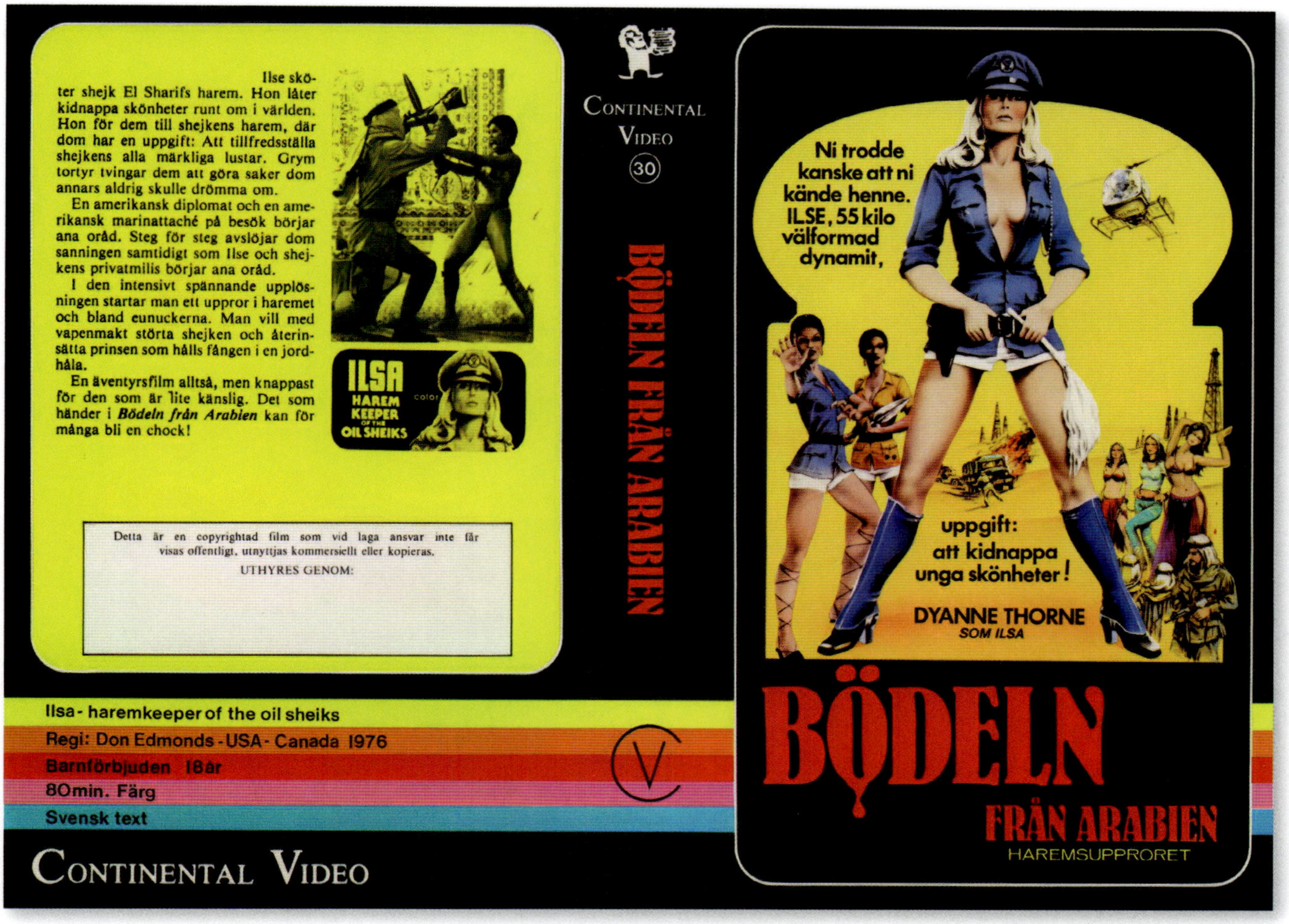

Ilse sköter shejk El Sharifs harem. Hon låter kidnappa skönheter runt om i världen. Hon för dem till shejkens harem, där dom har en uppgift: Att tillfredsställa shejkens alla märkliga lustar. Grym tortyr tvingar dem att göra saker dom annars aldrig skulle drömma om.
En amerikansk diplomat och en amerikansk marinattaché på besök börjar ana oråd. Steg för steg avslöjar dom sanningen samtidigt som Ilse och shejkens privatmilis börjar ana oråd.
I den intensivt spännande upplösningen startar man ett uppror i haremet och bland eunuckerna. Man vill med vapenmakt störta shejken och återinsätta prinsen som hålls fången i en jordhåla.
En äventyrsfilm alltså, men knappast för den som är lite känslig. Det som händer i Bödeln från Arabien kan för många bli en chock!
ILSA HAREM KEEPER OF THE OIL SHEIKS
Detta är en copyrightad film som vid laga ansvar inte får visas offentligt, utnyttjas kommersiellt eller kopieras.
UTHYRES GENOM:
Ilsa - haremkeeper of the oil sheiks
Regi: Don Edmonds - USA - Canada 1976
Barnförbjuden 18år
80min. Färg
Svensk text
Continental Video
Continental Video 30
BÖDELN FRÅN ARABIEN
Ni trodde kanske att ni kände henne. ILSE, 55 kilo välformad dynamit,
uppgift: att kidnappa unga skönheter!
DYANNE THORNE SOM ILSA
BÖDELN FRÅN ARABIEN
HAREMSUPPRORET

VHS
ILSE huntigeren fra Sibirien
ILSE HUN TIGEREN FRA SIBIRIEN
DYANNE THORNE as 'ILSA, the TIGRESS of SIBERIA'
FARVER
Video Copenhagen
EDB 309
UDLEJNINGSKASSETTE / UDLEJER:

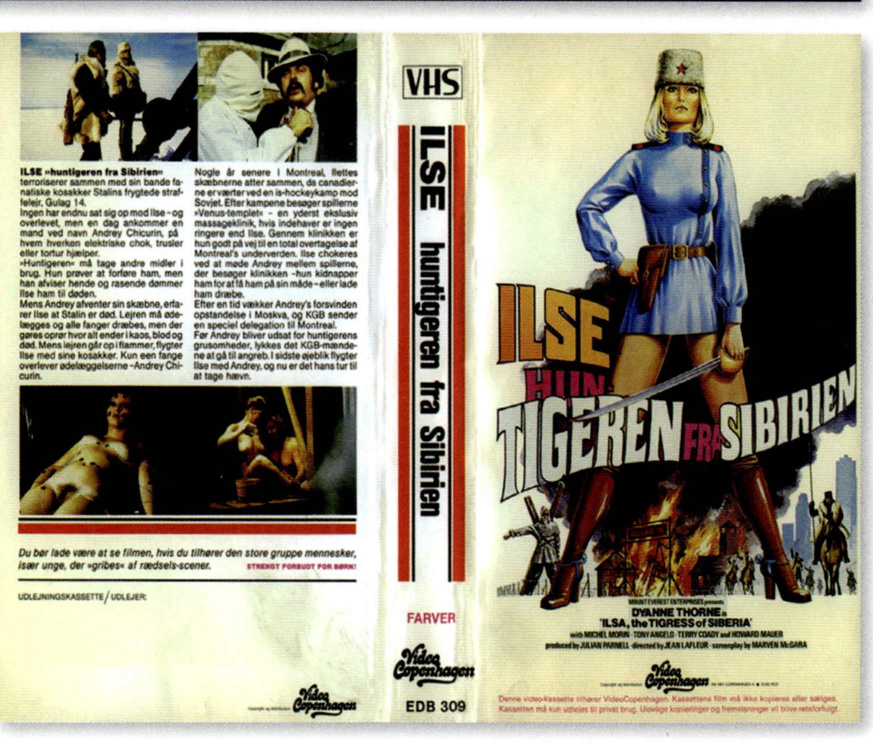

TOP: Swedish video sleeve for Don Edmonds's *Ilsa: Harem Keeper of the Oil Sheiks* (Continental Video, n.d.) which found Dyanne Thorne's former Nazi (who died at the end of the previous film) working for an Arab white-slave trader. Despite the sex and violence in this 1976 sequel being toned down, it was still refused a cinema certification in the UK, before finally being passed uncut in 2013.

BOTTOM: Dutch video sleeve for Jean LaFleur's *Ilsa, the Tigress of Siberia* (Video Copenhagen, 1983). After starring in the knock-off *Wanda, the Wicked Warden* (1977) for Jesús Franco, Dyanne Thorne returned the same year for this third and final official entry in the series as the ageless Ilsa, who was now marked for revenge by the sole survivor of a brutal Stalinist Gulag.

"ADULTS WHO ALLOW CHILDREN TO WATCH BESTIAL SEX, THE DISMEMBERMENT OF BODIES, CANNIBALISM AND TORTURE IN THE PRIVACY OF THE HOME HAVE SCALED THE HEIGHTS OF DEPRAVITY."

"THE EVIL OF VIDEO VIOLENCE." *DAILY MIRROR* EDITORIAL (NOVEMBER 25, 1983)

ABOVE LEFT: Released in UK cinemas in 1980 in a version missing almost two minutes, when it came out on video in a "Strong Uncut Version!!" a year later, Lucio Fulci's *Zombie Flesh Easters* (VIPCO, 1981) was quickly banned. Eventually reissued on video again just over a decade later, it was still the edited theatrical version.

ABOVE RIGHT: Video sleeve for Antonio Margheriti's *Cannibal Apocalypse* (Replay Video, 1982), which was released uncut in the UK but soon held up as an example of a "video nasty." When British police reportedly attempted to seize copies of the video, they ended up confiscating tapes of *Apocalypse Now* by mistake.

By 1982, the video industry had mushroomed, and the thriving rental sector was hungry for product. The major studios were slow to get in on the act, and so an unrestricted gold rush of the obscure, the unrated, the independent, and the unwatchable flooded the shelves of converted corner shops.

Stories began to appear in the press about the fact that gruesome horror films had bypassed the then-British Board of Film Censorship (which had no remit over video) to come out uncertified.

After a rash of "what-are-we-going-to-do-about it" articles in newspapers, panic spread through the video industry at the specter of police raids, expensive prosecutions, and *Fahrenheit 451*-style mass burning of videocassettes.

Of course, the police couldn't be as *au fait* with the Z-movie scene as anyone actually interested in the subject, which lead to absurdities like copies of *Apocalypse Now* (1979) being mistaken for *Cannibal Apocalypse* (1980), understandable confusions between Tobe Hooper's nasty *Death Trap* (1976) and Sidney Lumet's respectable *Deathtrap* (1982), and idiocies like the mistaking of Sam Fuller's *The Big Red One* (1980) for a porno movie!

Broadly, the position of the campaigners was that the video nasties were responsible for crime, violence, insanity, drug use, and rape. However, when the Video Recordings Act got rid of the nasties and crime, violence, etc. did not disappear from society, they concluded not that they were wrong, but that the Act hadn't done the job well enough, opening the way for a campaign for even more restrictions, not merely on video—citing the mild horror of *Child's Play 3* (1991) as a substitute for the long-gone grue of the Nazi cannibal zombie films—but on television, in the cinema, on the Internet.

And in your head . . .

Kim Newman

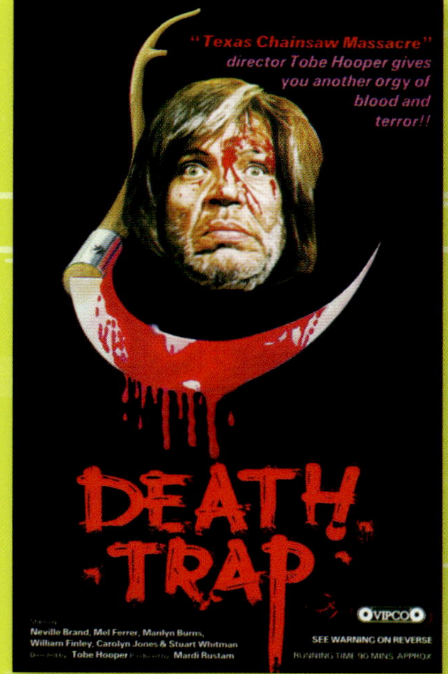

ABOVE LEFT: Although quickly withdrawn by its UK distributor, *Snuff* (Astra Video, 1982) still found itself on the "video nasty" list. It started out as a biker movie called *The Slaughter*, filmed in Argentina in 1971. To capitalize on the urban legend of "snuff" films—in which people are actually murdered on camera—new footage was added and all cast and crew credits removed.

TOP RIGHT: Featuring a number of old Hollywood actors, the uncut version of Tobe Hooper's backwoods horror *Death Trap* (VIPCO, 1982) was unsuccessfully prosecuted as a "nasty" in the UK. Reputedly, police also mistakenly seized copies of Sidney Lumet's murder mystery *Deathtrap* (1982) that starred Michael Caine and Christopher Reeve in an adaptation of a stage play.

BOTTOM RIGHT: Following the horrific torture and murder of two-year-old James Bulger in 1993, British media reports blamed the video of *Child's Play 3* (MCA Universal Home Video, 1991) for motivating his pair of ten-year-old killers. Although a police investigation concluded that there was no link between the movie and murder, it still led to calls for a further clampdown on videos.

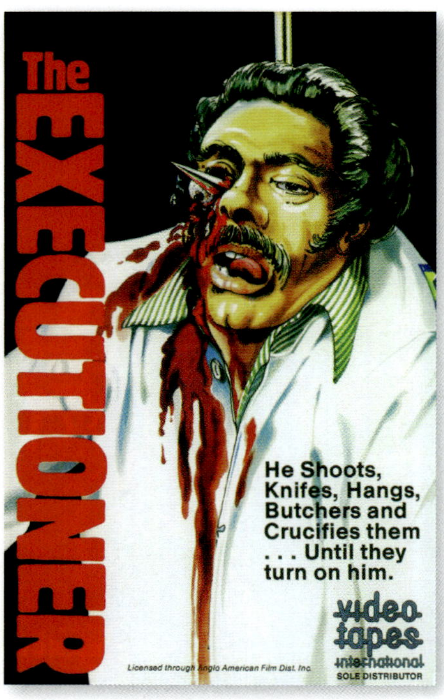

TOP LEFT: Despite its lurid video box cover, *Cataclysm* (Video Unlimited, 1982) was scripted by Oscar winner Philip Yordan and starred veteran heavies Cameron Mitchell and Marc Lawrence. Credited to three directors, it was released under various titles, including *The Nightmare Never Ends*, while an edited-down version of the film turned up in *Night Train to Terror* (1985).

BOTTOM LEFT: Filmed in 1974 as *Like Father, Like Son, The Executioner* (Video Tapes International, 1983) was the only completed directing credit for singer and actor Duke Mitchell (who, with comedy partner Sammy Petrillo, met Bela Lugosi and a Brooklyn Gorilla). Despite the over-the-top UK box art, it was actually a Mafia gangster movie set in Hollywood.

ABOVE RIGHT: Porno star John Holmes was credited with special effects makeup and had a small role in Walt Davis's *Evil Come Evil Go* (Mercury Video, 1983), a sleazy 1972 softcore slasher comedy in which adult film actress Cleo O'Hara played an evangelical traveling preacher who, together with her lesbian partner, murdered various people while they were having sex.

TOP LEFT: Released in the US as *Scum of the Earth* in 1974, low-budget filmmaker S.F. Brownrigg's *Poor White Trash* (Intervision, 1983) starred Norma Moore as a newlywed who found herself menaced by Gene Ross's peculiar backwoods Texas family. Some of the cast had previously worked on Brownrigg's debut feature, *Don't Look in the Basement* (1973).

TOP RIGHT: *The Steel Claw* (Cyclo Video, 1983) was actually a 1961 war film, directed by and starring George Montgomery as a one-handed marine on a mission behind Japanese lines in the Philippines. It was totally misrepresented by this UK video sleeve that made it appear to be a slasher movie and, after complaints from customers, the distributor was forced to reissue the videotape with new cover art.

BOTTOM: Dutch video box for *The Nail Gun Massacre* (VUH Video Holland, 1986), shot in Texas in 1985 and the only directing credit for Terry Lofton. After a young girl (Michelle Meyer) was raped by a gang of construction workers, a mysterious figure in a motorcycle helmet started killing them and plenty of others with the eponymous weapon of choice.

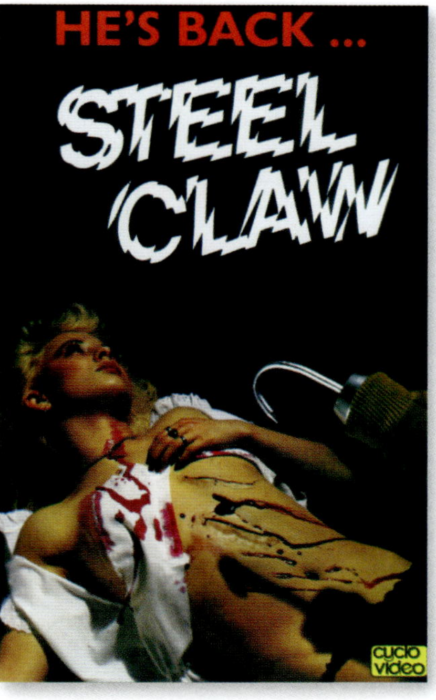

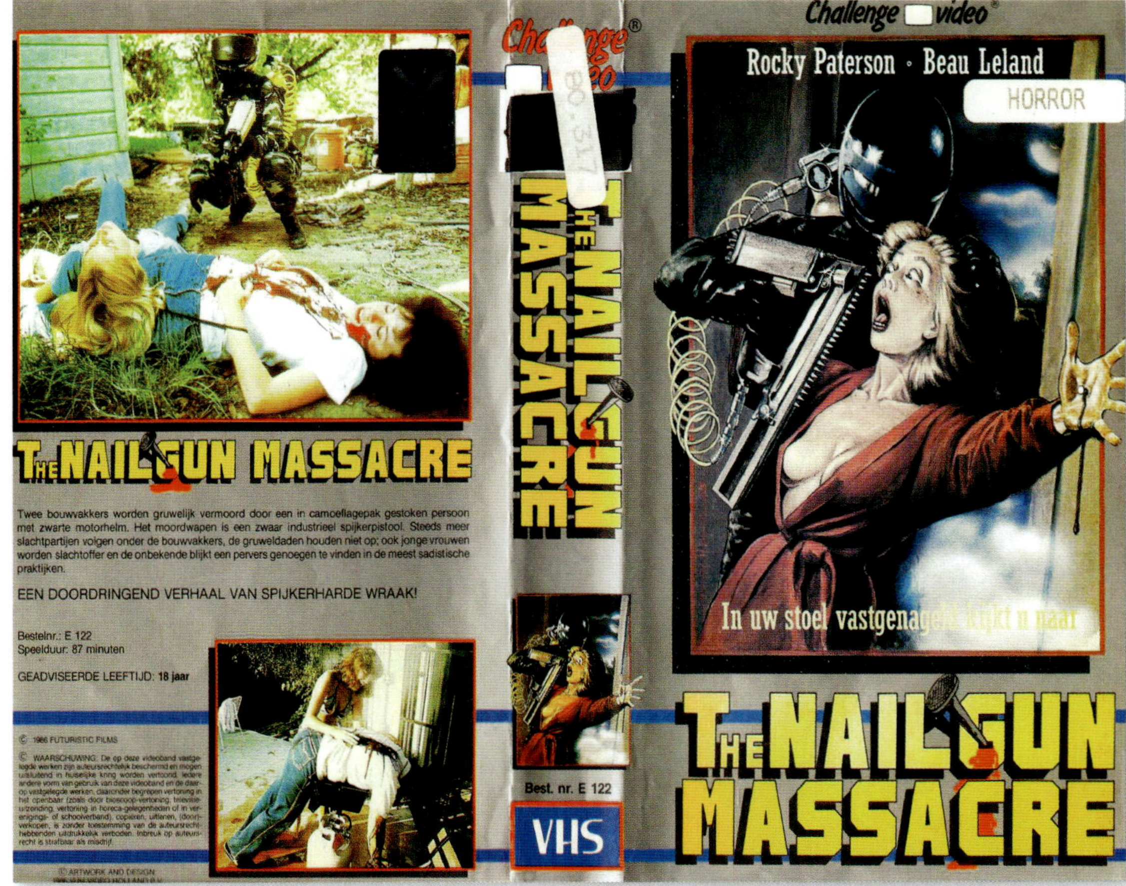

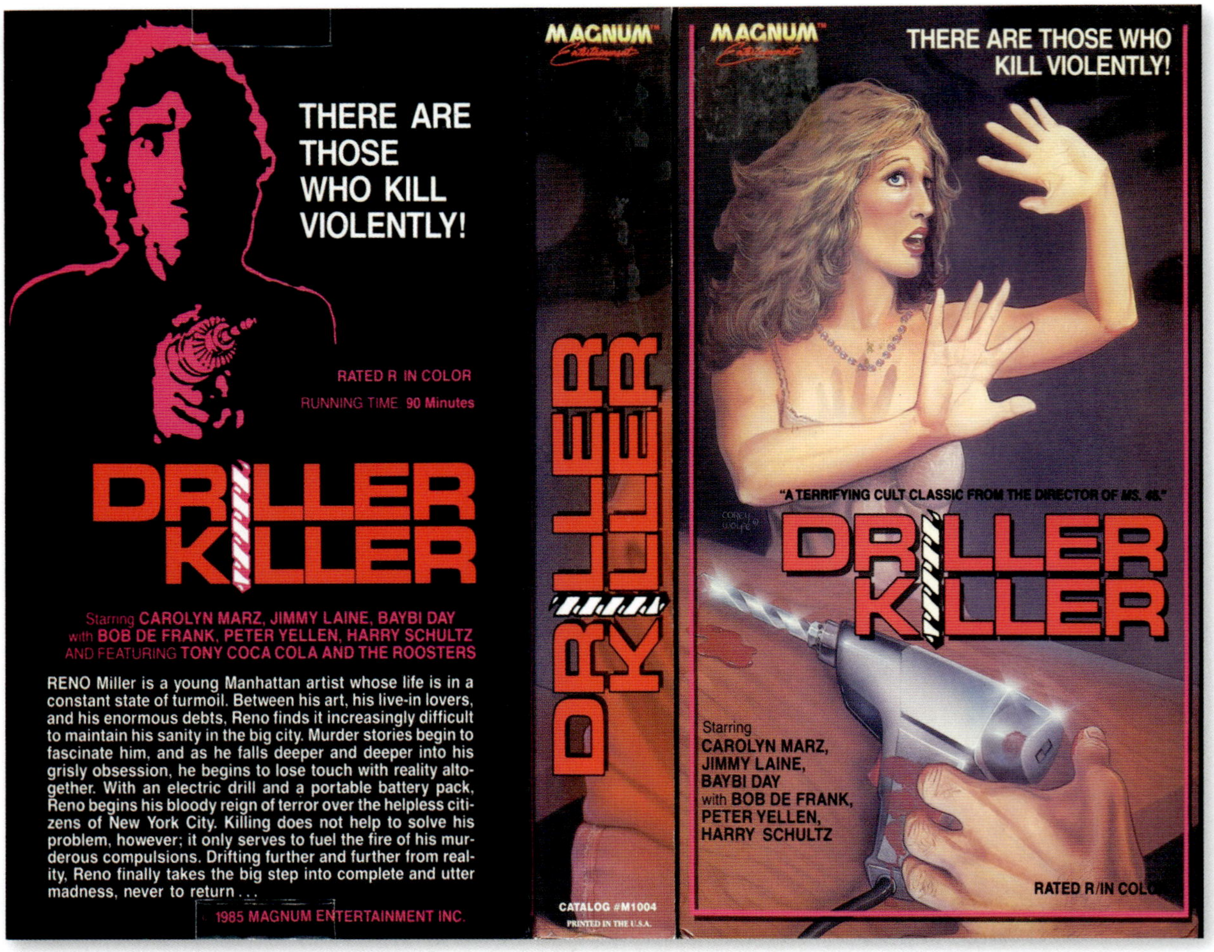

TOP: One of the most notorious titles on the DPP's list of banned films in the UK, *The Driller Killer* (Magnum Entertainment, 1985) was even released on video in the US in this R-rated version missing six minutes. Debuting director Abel Ferrara (as "Jimmy Laine") played the deranged New York City artist who murdered random vagrants after dark with a power drill.

BOTTOM LEFT: Herschell Gordon Lewis's classic gorefest *Blood Feast* (Astra Video, 1982) was made back in 1963 and was the oldest movie to appear on the banned list. Mal Arnold's crazed Egyptian caterer collected body parts from his victims in an attempt to bring an ancient goddess back to life. Stephen King calls it the worst horror movie he ever saw.

BOTTOM RIGHT: Almost as notorious as The *Driller Killer*, Meir Zarchi's *I Spit on Your Grave* (Astra Video, 1982) starred Camille Keaton as an aspiring NYC writer who hunted down the men who sexually assaulted her and left her for dead. It was finally released in the UK in a heavily cut version in 2001 and to this day only remains available in that country in censored form.

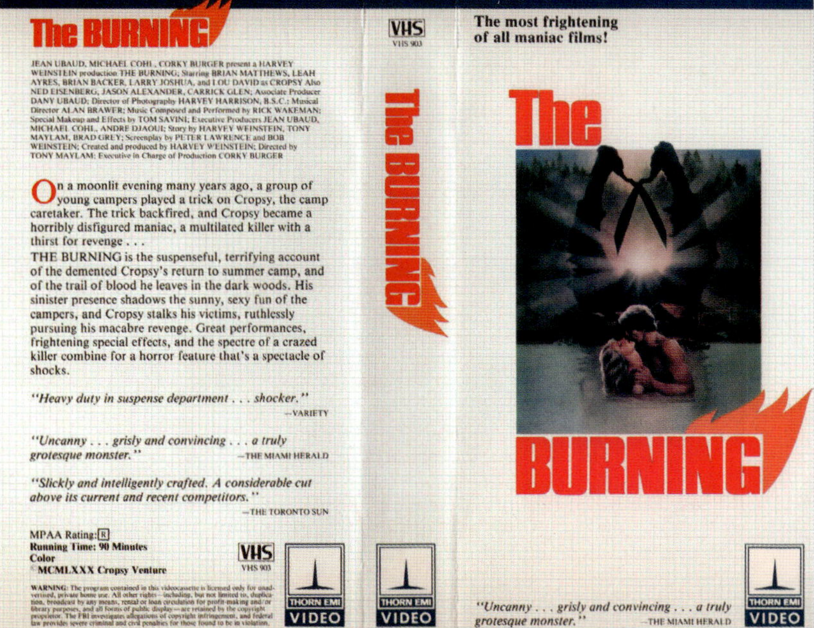

TOP: Dutch video cover for Wes Craven's disturbing directing debut *The Last House on the Left* (Empire Video, n.d.), in which the parents of a teenage girl plotted revenge on the gang of psychopathic thugs who kidnapped and murdered their daughter and her friend. Refused a certificate when submitted for UK theatrical release in 1974, it was only passed uncut in that country in 2008.

BOTTOM: Tony Maylam's *The Burning* (Thorn EMI Video, 1981) was a *Friday the 13th*-style slasher in which the horribly burned janitor at a summer camp returned years later to take revenge on the young campers. Although originally cut for its theatrical release in the UK, an uncensored version was mistakenly released on video, which resulted in it being added to the "video nasty" list.

THE "VIDEO NASTY" LIST

A list of the thirty-nine videos officially prosecuted as being obscene by the Director of Public Prosecutions in the UK (1983–85).

Absurd (Medusa, 1982)
Andy Warhol's Frankenstein (VIPCO, 1982)
Antropophagus: The Beast (Video Film Promotions, 1983)
Axe (Video Releasing Organization, 1982)
The Beast in Heat (JVI, 1982)
Blood Bath (Hokushin, 1983)
Blood Feast (Astra Video, 1982)
Blood Rites (Scorpio Video, 1983)
Bloody Moon (Inter-Light Video, 1981)
The Burning (Thorn EMI Video, 1982)
Cannibal Apocalypse (Replay Video, 1982)
Cannibal Ferox (Replay Video, 1982)
Cannibal Holocaust (Go Video, 1982)
The Cannibal Man (Intervision, 1981)
The Devil Hunter (Cinehollywood, 1981)
Don't Go in the Woods (Video Releasing Organization, 1982)
The Driller Killer (VIPCO, 1982)
Evilspeak (FilmTown, 1983)
Exposé (Intervision, 1979)
Faces of Death (Atlantis Video Productions, 1982)
Fight for Your Life (Vision-On, 1982)
Forest of Fear (Monte 1982)
The Gestapo's Last Orgy (Video Film Promotions, 1983)
The House by the Cemetery (Vampix/Videomedia, 1983)
House on the Edge of the Park (Skyline Video, 1982)
I Spit on Your Grave (Astra Video, 1982)
Island of Death (AVI, 1982)
The Last House on the Left (Replay Video, 1982)
Love Camp 7 (Market Video, 1983)
Madhouse (Medusa, 1983)
Mardi Gras Massacre (Gold Star/Derann, 1982)
Night of the Bloody Apes (Iver Film Services, 1983)
Night of the Demon (Iver Film Services, 1982)
Nightmares in a Damaged Brain (L.U. Productions, 1982)
Snuff (Astra Video, 1982)
SS Experiment Camp (Go Video, 1982)
Tenebrae (Videomedia, 1983)
The Werewolf and the Yeti (Canon Video, 1982)
Zombie Flesh Eaters (VIPCO, 1981)

INDEPENDENTS' DAZE

"Making a film with no money or schedule is ten times harder than it is to make a big-budget show where you're surrounded by a gang of super-talented people."

Fred Olen Ray

"A COOL-CAT RETRO BLOOD-SUCKER FROM A PSYCHEDELIC DIMENSION, A FAUSTIAN PODIATRIST UNABLE TO CURB HIS FETISHISTIC SEXUAL DEPRAVATIONS, AND A GHASTLY LEGION OF LIP-SMACKING LESBIAN VAMPIRES AND GO-GO DANCING GIRL GHOULS . . ."

***CARESS OF THE VAMPIRE 2: TEENAGE GHOUL GIRL A GO-GO* VIDEO BOX BLURB (1997)**

Independent filmmaking has existed since before the birth of commercial cinema. In fact, it could be argued that those movie pioneers of the late nineteenth century—before the introduction of pictorial storytelling and the establishment of a studio system—were all amateurs who were merely experimenting with a new technological innovation.

Just as theatrical movie releases had long been separated into main attractions and B movies or "second features," so the video market ushered in the era of the direct-to-video (DTV) production—a second tier of films specifically made and distributed almost exclusively for home video consumption—and by the mid-1990s it often became difficult to distinguish some DTV productions from their theatrical equivalent.

It was also the case that many feature films that, for one reason or another, could not get a release in movie theaters now had a ready-made distribution network on video at a fraction of the cost. This also encouraged the bigger studios to start churning out multiple DTV sequels to many better-made movies.

As the cost of video cameras and editing systems came down in price, so a new generation of filmmakers—who perhaps had no formal training or previous experience in movie-making—could finally turn their hands to creating the kind of productions they had always dreamed of. More importantly, there was now a ready-made audience that was not only clamoring for new and innovative product, but was also willing to accept almost anything shot on a handheld camcorder in somebody's basement.

When the home video boom swept around the world, numerous independent distribution labels quickly started popping up alongside the major video releasing companies as they decided to take the plunge into the prerecorded video market of the 1980s and '90s.

Many of these productions were cheaply and shoddily produced on low budgets for maximum profit, but over time the standard gradually improved.

What nobody could perhaps have predicted was that the rise of the independents marked a last gasp for the home video boom, as better and more sophisticated data-recording technology was already being developed that would soon sweep away the VHS format forever . . .

PREVIOUS SPREAD: *Hollywood Chainsaw Hookers* (Dir: Fred Olen Ray, 1988).

THIS PAGE: *Caress of the Vampire 2* (Dir: William Hellfire, 1996).

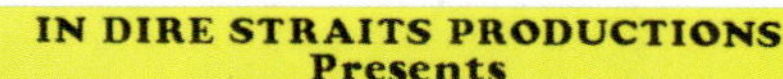

TOP LEFT & RIGHT: Originally filmed in 1958 in Ontario, California, *Teenagers Battle the Thing* (Monument Entertainment, 1997) remained mostly unseen until 1975, when "Don Fields" (Dave Flocker) edited it into his only other directing credit, *Curse of Bigfoot* (Star Classics, 1989), bringing back original costar Bill Simonsen as an older version of his same character. A group of high school students on an archaeological dig of an ancient Native American campsite accidentally released a mummified corpse that turned out to be a Bigfoot monster in the revised version. Both films were subsequently released separately on home video.

BOTTOM LEFT: Perhaps one of the most controversial independent video productions released in the UK was the gore-splattered *Suffer Little Children* (Films Galore, 1985), made by the teenage pupils of the Meg Shanks Theatre School. One of the first British shot-on-video movies to get a video release, although never officially classed as a "video nasty" it still attracted a lot of criticism.

BOTTOM RIGHT: Shot on video in New Jersey, G.W. Lawrence's *The Mummy's Dungeon* (I.D.S. Productions, 1993) was like watching a home-movie remake of Herschell Gordon Lewis's *Blood Feast* (1963), as a crazed photographer set his blood-drinking mummy on various "models." Despite an "Adults Only" tag, it was pretty mild, although the mummy was surprisingly effective.

TOP LEFT: The cover of the 1989 Star Classics video box for *The Alien Dead* cleverly recreated the photographic poster art for *The Evil Dead* (1981). Filmed in 1980 in Florida for $12,000, cowriter/director Fred Olen Ray managed to get former *Flash Gordon* (1936) star Buster Crabbe to star as the sheriff of a town whose inhabitants were turned into zombies by a crashed meteorite.

TOP RIGHT: Although Fred Olen Ray failed to get his remake of Roger Corman's *Attack of the Giant Leeches* (1959) made, he did produce an unofficial version of the director's *The Wasp Woman* (1959) as *Evil Spawn* (Camp Motion Pictures, 1987). He also shot John Carradine's unrelated cameo appearance. The movie was subsequently reedited into *The Alien Within* (1990).

BOTTOM LEFT: Brinke Stevens (who considers this her best movie) graces the video cover of Fred Olen Ray's *Haunting Fear* (Rhino Home Video, 1991), based on Edgar Allan Poe's story "The Premature Burial." Filmed in six days on an estimated budget of $115,000, the supporting cast included genre stalwarts Karen Black, Robert Clarke, Robert Quarry, and Michael Berryman.

BOTTOM RIGHT: Perhaps not quite so high on Brinke Stevens's list of favorites is *Scream Queen Hot Tub Party* (Colourbox, 1992), written and directed by Fred Olen Ray and Jim Wynorski under pseudonyms. Shot in just one day, the other scream queens are Monique Gabrielle, Kelli Maroney, Michelle Bauer, and Roxanne Kernohan, who was killed in a car accident the following year.

FRED'S FORMATIVE FRIGHTFESTS

Independent American producer, screenwriter, and director Fred Olen Ray was born in Ohio and started making his own movies in Florida when he was still a teenager. Following a small role in Ken Wiederhorn's *Shock Waves* (1977) starring Peter Cushing and John Carradine, he made his professional debut as a director with *The Alien Dead,* filmed in 1980 when he was in his mid-twenties. The film was a minor success when released direct-to-video five years later.

Meanwhile, Ray decided to move to Hollywood, where he raised the funds for two low-budget horror movies—*Scalps* (1983), which featured cameos by Carroll Borland and Forrest J Ackerman, the editor of *Famous Monsters of Filmland,* and *The Tomb* (1986), starring old-timers Cameron Mitchell and John Carradine.

From there Ray began to move into other genres, including science fiction, action/adventure, sword and sorcery, crime dramas, comedies, and erotic thrillers, and to date has more than 160 titles to his credit. More recently, he has become a prolific director of made-for-TV "holiday" films.

He is also the head of Retromedia Entertainment Group, which releases Blu-rays and DVDs of his own productions as well as archival films, while his book, *The New Poverty Row: Independent Filmmakers as Distributors,* was first published in 1991.

THIS PAGE: A selection of promotional video flyers: Fred Olen Ray's *The Phantom Empire* (1987) [TOP LEFT] starred Sybil Danning, Jeffrey Combs, Robert Quarry, and Russ Tamblyn and was a homage to the Saturday morning serials of the 1930s and '40s. Linnea Quigley, Michelle Bauer, and the original "Leatherface," Gunnar Hansen, starred in Ray's *Hollywood Chainsaw Hookers* (1988) [TOP RIGHT], about a murderous cult of Los Angeles prostitutes. Fred Olen Ray coproduced Gary Graver's psycho-thriller *Moon in Scorpio* (1987) [ABOVE] featuring Britt Ekland, John Phillip Law, William Smith, and Robert Quarry.

THIS PAGE: Along with releasing obscure domestic and European movies, Charles Band's Wizard Video began issuing its own direct-to-video titles in 1986, including a trio of micro-budget science fiction/horror movies written and directed by Tim Kincaid, better known for his gay porno films. Sometimes movies are so bad they are good; that was not the case with these.

TOP LEFT: The first in Tim Kincaid's loose "mutant sleaze trilogy," sex-starved insectoid aliens living in the sewers tried to impregnate New Yorkers in *Breeders* (1986), which carried the dubious marketing hype "A World Premiere in Your Own Home." Shot in ten days for $80,000, Ed French (who worked with Kincaid on all three movies) created the special effects.

TOP RIGHT: A group of heroes, led by a drifter named Neo (Norris Culf) and his robot sidekick, crossed a postapocalyptic wasteland to rescue a scientist and free the slaves of the sinister Dark One in Tim Kincaid's *Robot Holocaust* (1987). Released theatrically in a slightly different version in Italy, it was also lampooned in an episode of *Mystery Science Theater 3000* in 1990.

BOTTOM: Set in New York in 1992, an evil scientist used a sexual narcotic to turn humanoid "cyborgs" into vicious killing machines in Tim Kincaid's *Mutant Hunt* (1987). Only bounty hunter Matt Riker (Rick Gianasi) and his elite team of mercenaries could stop them. Shot back-to-back with *Breeders*, this was the last film released under the original Wizard Video label.

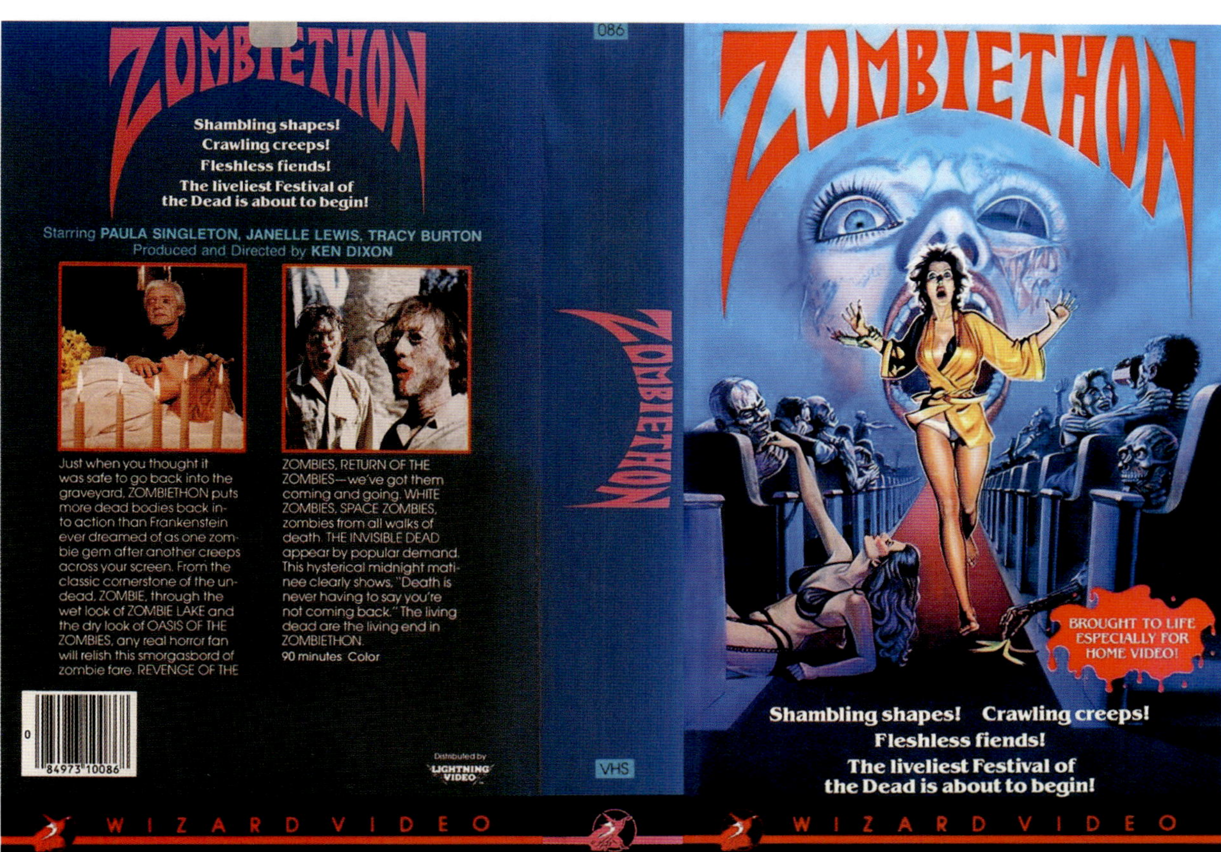

TOP: "Brought to life especially for home video!" *Zombiethon* (1986) was the fourth and final clip compilation assembled by Ken Dixon for producer Charles Band. With a wraparound story about a woman fleeing into a Los Angeles movie theater full of zombies, it included key excerpts from such Wizard releases as *The Astro-Zombies*, *A Virgin Among the Living Dead*, and *Dawn of the Dead*.

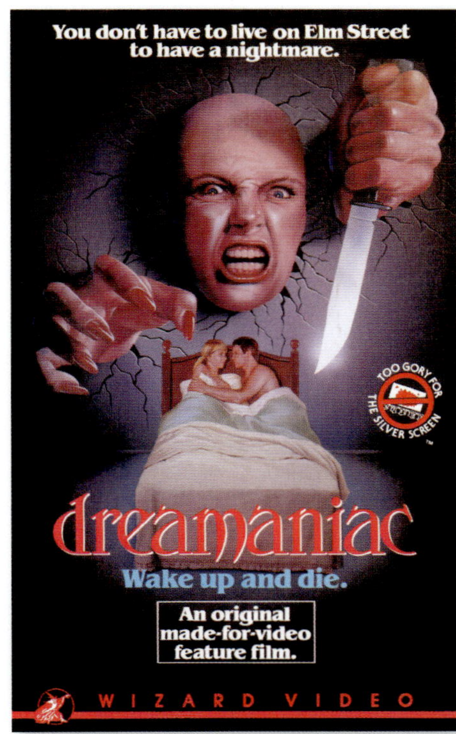

BOTTOM LEFT: David DeCoteau was another director who began his career in the gay porn industry. Made for around $60,000, his mainstream debut, *Dreamaniac* (1986), was shot on 16mm and edited on videotape. The video came with "Too Gory for the Silver Screen" emblazoned on the box and included a bonus *Total Terror Test*, which served as a trailer for other Wizard titles.

BOTTOM RIGHT: Gorman Bechard's horror-comedy *Psychos in Love* (1987) was shot on 16mm in Connecticut for $75,000 and picked up by Charles Band for direct-to-video release through Wizard Video. Carmine Capobianco (who coscripted) and Debi Thibeault played a pair of psychotic serial killers who found themselves being blackmailed by a cannibal plumber.

ABOVE LEFT: The rise in direct-to-video releases led to a mini-boom in vampire movies in the 1990s. One of the earliest entries during this resurgence was Peter Flynn's *Project Vampire* (E.I. Independent Cinema, 1998), which was originally released in 1993. Myron Natwick starred as an undead scientist whose "longevity serum" turned those who used it into throat-ripping bloodsuckers.

TOP RIGHT: At least director "William Hellfire" (William Apprecino) had some fun with the micro-budget *Caress of the Vampire 2* (E.I. Independent Cinema, 1997). A cool retro-vampire, a go-go dancing ghoul and a fetishistic podiatrist teamed up to create a hit record while taking over the world. Although not quite the instant "cult classic" it aspired to be, it dared to be different.

BOTTOM RIGHT: Even cheaper looking was *Sorority House Vampires* (Cinematrix Releasing, 1997), directed by Geoffrey de Valois and Eugene James. A sorority pledge named Buffy (Kathy Presgrave) not only had to contend with all kinds of sexual shenanigans, but also a vampire named Count Vlad (Robert Bucholz). Shot on video in 1990, it wasn't released for several years.

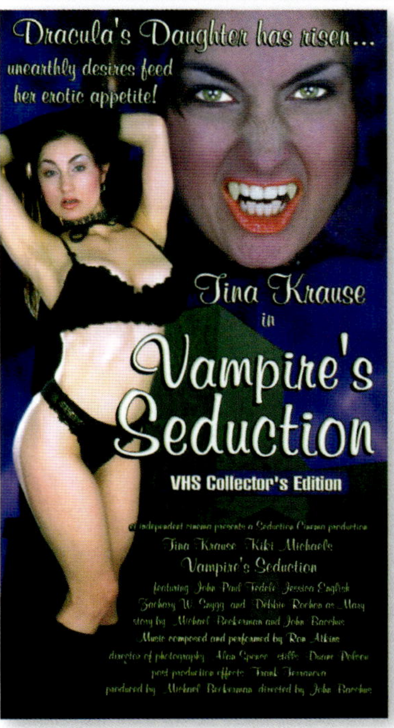

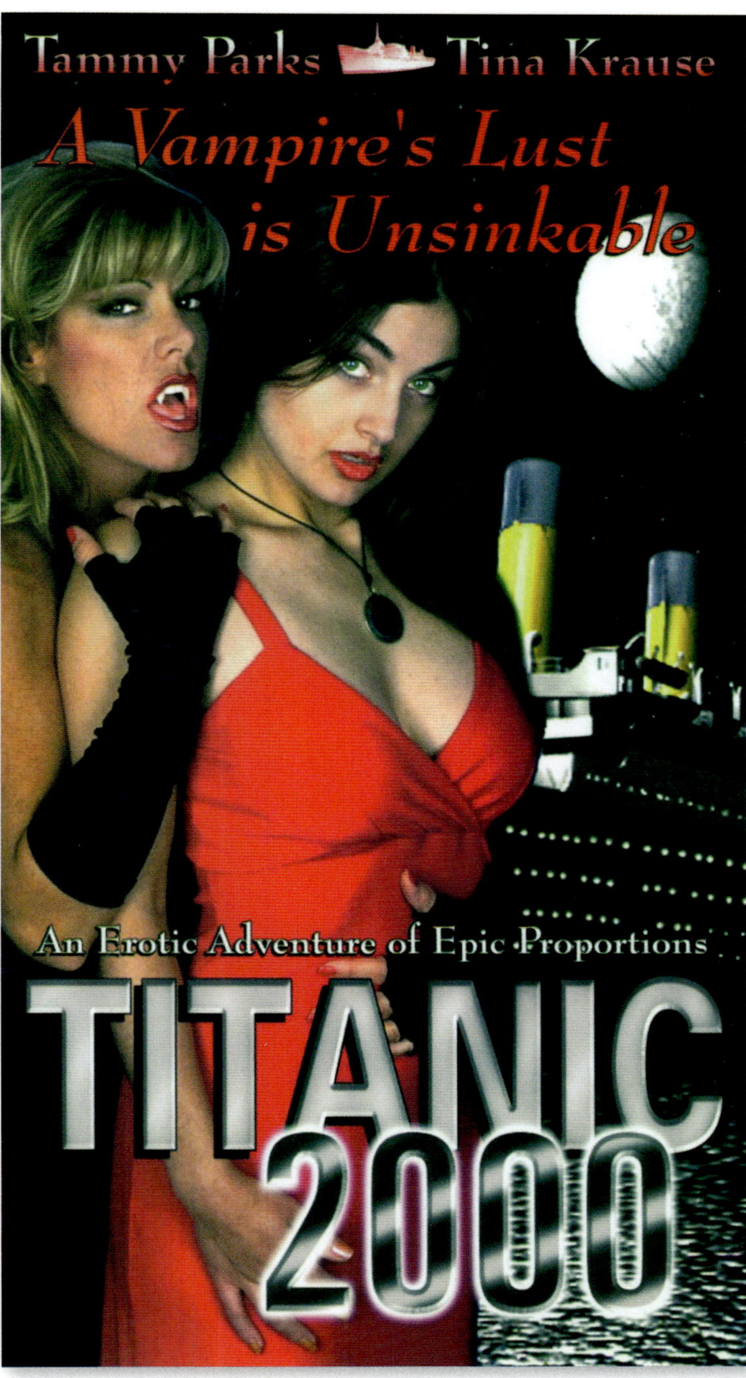

TOP LEFT: Writer/director Everette Hartsoe starred as a comic-book writer who made the mistake of calling up an escort service that specialized in sexy bloodsuckers in the shot-on-video *Vampire Call Girls* (EH! Productions, 1998), which is really nothing more than a series of striptease performances. "Lilith Stabs" (Laurie Wright) made her debut as one of the big-breasted vampires.

BOTTOM LEFT: New Jersey-based distributor E.I. Independent Cinema launched Seduction Cinema in 1998, which specialized in shot-on-video softcore erotic horror movies. Written and directed by "John Bacchus" (Zachary Snygg), *The Vampire's Seduction* (Seduction Cinema, 2000) was the label's first production. It starred Tina Krause as Dracula's undead daughter, Dracoola.

ABOVE RIGHT: Tina Krause also costarred in John P. Fedele's comedy *TITanic 2000: Vampire of the Titanic* (Seduction Cinema, 1999), in which Tammy Parks's big-breasted bloodsucker Vladamina stowed away on a modern version of the steamship. During the late 1990s, Seduction Cinema helped create a whole new subgenre of shot-on-video softcore lesbian vampire films.

TOP LEFT: Apparently the only credit for producer/director David A. Goldberg, *Demon Lust* (Outlaw Video, 2001) was shot on video in Pittsburgh in 1996 as *Eyes Are Upon You*. It featured a fully naked Brinke Stevens as a mysterious woman who had sex with her victims and then transformed into a giant spider-monster. Tom Savini turned up as a ruthless mob enforcer.

TOP RIGHT: The 1988 horror movie *Witchcraft* has, to date, spawned no less than fourteen direct-to-video sequels. Michael Paul Girard's *Witchcraft IX: Bitter Flesh* (Vista Street Entertainment, 1997) was shot in four days and is typical of the series, as a Los Angeles call girl channeled the spirit of regular series character, warlock and lawyer Will Spanner, to stop a demonic serial killer.

BOTTOM LEFT: A "found-footage" erotic parody of *The Blair Witch Project* (1999), Zachary Snygg's *The Erotic Witch Project* (Seduction Cinema, 1999) followed a trio of college girls into the New Jersey woods looking for the legendary Erotic Witch. Their video footage revealed that they had been turned into sex-crazed lesbians. To date it has been followed by three sequels.

BOTTOM RIGHT: Shot in three days under his usual "John Bacchus" alias, Zachary Snygg's *Mistress Frankenstein* (Seduction Cinema, 2000) found the great, great grandson of Dr. Frankenstein bringing back to life his dead wife, Baroness Helena Frankenstein (Darian Caine). Unfortunately her new brain came from a lesbian nymphomaniac, with predictable results.

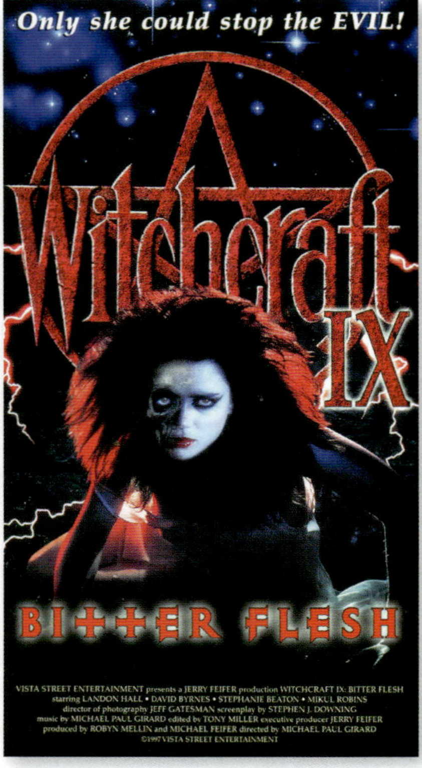

TOP LEFT: Originally shot on 8mm film and released in 1988, Mark Pirro's dated, stereotypical comedy *Curse of the Queerwolf* (EDDE Entertainment, 1994) starred Michael Palazzolo as Larry Smalbut who, after being bitten by a transvestite, inherited the curse of the dickenthrope. Forrest J Ackerman, the editor of *Famous Monsters of Filmland*, had a cameo.

TOP RIGHT: Set in a postapocalyptic New York City of 2010 overrun with werewolves, a pair of traditional lycanthropic brothers battled it out for control of the city, and eventually the world, in *Rage of the Werewolf* (Marotta Pictures, 1999). Nobody could accuse cowriter/director Kevin J. Lindenmuth of not being ambitious! Debbie Rochon turned up as a vampire.

BOTTOM: They don't come much more obscure than *Tales of the Urban Werewolf* (1997)—yes, the title's wrong on the box!—which was released by Brain Escape Pictures, yet another video label from E.I. Entertainment Pictures, specializing in extremely low-budget movies. A drug addict looking for a cure was transformed by a Native American shaman into a silly-looking werewolf.

TOP: The only directing credit for African-American film editor John N. Carter, *Zombie Island Massacre* (Allied Troma, 1996) was filmed in Jamaica and originally released in 1984. After witnessing a voodoo ritual on a Caribbean island, a group of stranded tourists spent the night in an old mansion, where they were killed off one by one.

BOTTOM: *The Video Dead* (Medusa Home Video, 1987) was the only directorial credit for assistant director Robert Scott. A mysterious television set showing a never-ending black-and-white horror movie titled *Zombie Blood Nightmare* was a paranormal gateway for the living dead to cross over into the real world. Filming took more than a year as it was shot mostly on weekends.

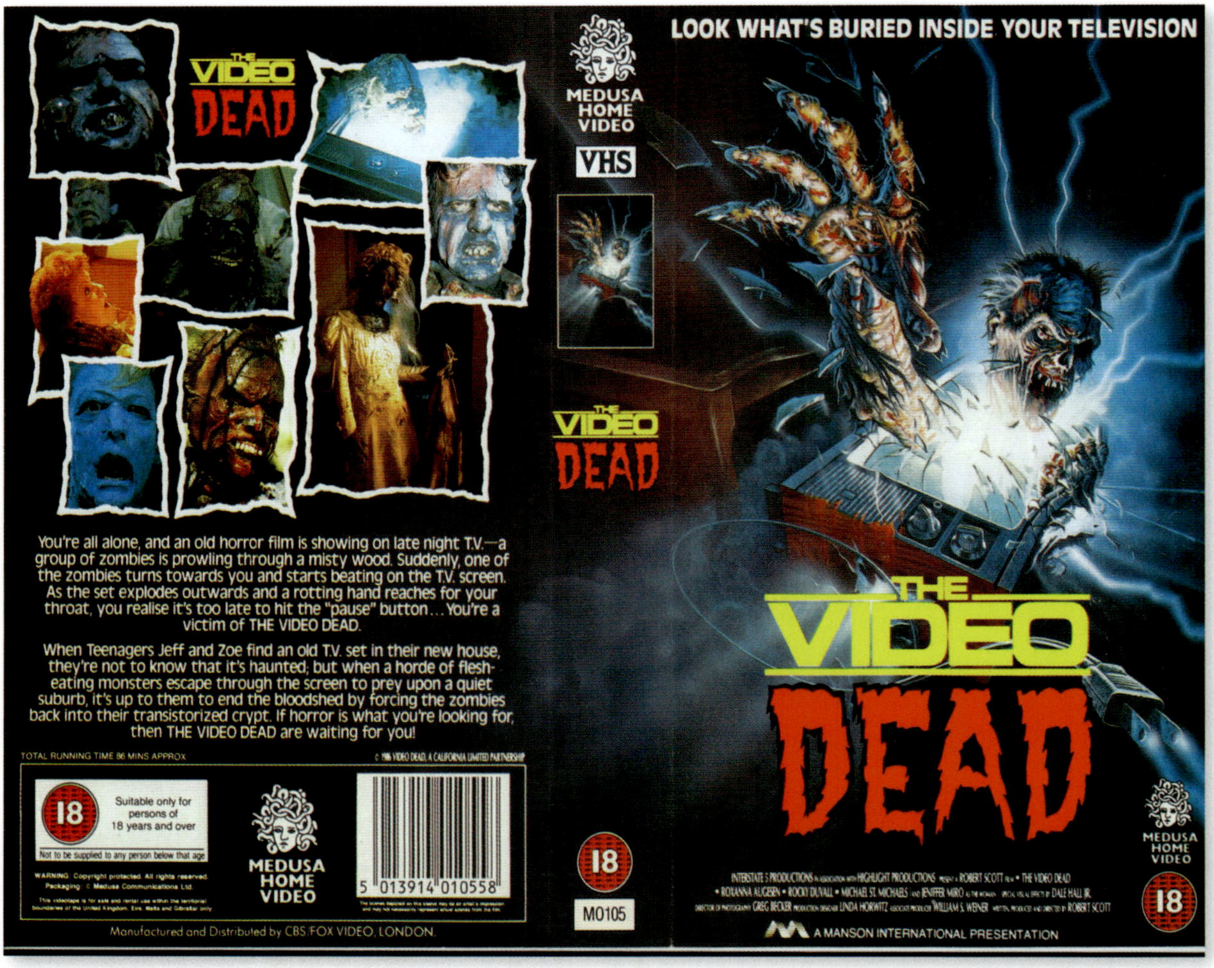

ABOVE LEFT: Released by Entertainment-International Pictures in 1986, Samuel M. Sherman's *Raiders of the Living Dead* (Very Strange Video, 1997) was originally started three years earlier by Brett Piper. A mad doctor revived executed prisoners as zombies on a remote island prison. Veteran screen actress Zita Johann (*The Mummy*, 1932) came out of retirement for this.

TOP RIGHT: Gary Whitson's shot-on-video *Female Mercenaries on Zombie Island* (W.A.V.E. Productions, 1998) was set in a postapocalyptic 2008. Two female mercenaries (Tina Krause and Laura Giglio) set out to stop a mad scientist who was transplanting the brains of the old men in power into new bodies so she could take over the world. It was followed by a sequel in 2008.

BOTTOM RIGHT: Released under yet another of E.I. Independent Cinema's distribution labels, Thomas J. Moose's gross-out comedy *Zombie Toxin* (Shock-O-Rama Pictures, 1998) was shot on video in Manchester, England. A contaminated batch of home-brewed wine turned people (including the director/cowriter, who also starred) into defecating and vomiting cannibal zombies.

TOP LEFT: Edited down from the 1977–78 Japanese TV series *Dinosaur War Aizenborg*, *Attack of the Super Monsters* (Quality Video, 1992) was a combination of live action and animation. Intelligent, mutated dinosaurs emerged from their underground caverns and declared war on mankind. Only the super-powered teens of Gemini Command could defeat them.

TOP RIGHT: Director Ursi Reynolds's only filmmaking credit, the independent shot-on-video comedy *Ganjasaurus Rex* (Rhino Video, 1988) was about a giant dinosaur that terrorized a pair of California marijuana growers and their hippie friends. Made on a micro budget, the monster effects were created using a stop-motion plastic toy and a person in a dinosaur costume.

BOTTOM LEFT: Written, coproduced, directed, and edited by Mark Alan Polonia, who also starred, *Saurians* (Polonia Bros. Entertainment, 1994) was about two dinosaurs released from hibernation by a blasting company. Shot on video, the dinosaur effects were created using puppets. Polonia and his brother Anthony continue to churn out low-budget horror movies, including *Saurians 2* (2023).

BOTTOM RIGHT: New Zealand video cover for Aaron Osbourne's *Zarkorr! The Invader* (Video Unlimited, 1996), which was released by Full Moon Home Video. An "average" postal worker was chosen by a female alien hologram to save the Earth from the city-crushing monster of the title. The scenes of the man-in-a-rubber-suit creature were shot before the script was even written.

TOP LEFT: Australian video cover for the anthology movie *Deadtime Stories* (Premiere Home Entertainment, 1987), which marked the directorial debut of Jeffrey Delman. A babysitting uncle related three scary fairy tales to his nephew about a trio of witches, a werewolf version of "Little Red Riding Hood," and a psychological thriller based on "Goldilocks."

BOTTOM LEFT: Marvel Comics artist Jackson Guice's artwork graced the box cover for *Satan Place: A Soap Opera from Hell* (Thunderhill Entertainment, 1990), a shot-on-video anthology film coscripted and directed by Scott Aschbrenner and Alfred Ramirez. The stories concerned an abusive husband, zombie revenge, and a girl hooked on late-night TV, before a satanic finale.

ABOVE RIGHT: The third and final directing credit for Hollywood screenwriting brothers Jim and Ken Wheat, *After Midnight* (CBS/Fox Video, 1990) featured a psychology professor telling his students three stories about fear. These involved a creepy old house, a group of teen girls getting lost on the wrong side of town, and a telephone stalker. The twist ending revealed it was all a dream.

TOP: Indie Las Vegas filmmaker Ray Dennis Steckler had an eclectic career that ranged from low-budget comedies and horror to softcore and hardcore adult movies. Written and directed under different pseudonyms, Steckler's 1979 film *The Hollywood Strangler Meets the Skid Row Slasher* (Vegas Video, 1988) costarred his wife Carolyn Brandt as one of the psychos of the title.

BOTTOM: One of a handful of movies made by editor/producer/director Donald M. Jones, *Murderlust* (Prism Entertainment, 1987) starred Eli Rich as a Sunday school teacher who, in his spare time, abducted and murdered young women and disposed of their bodies in the Mojave Desert. It was shot over twelve days on weekends to save money on equipment rental costs.

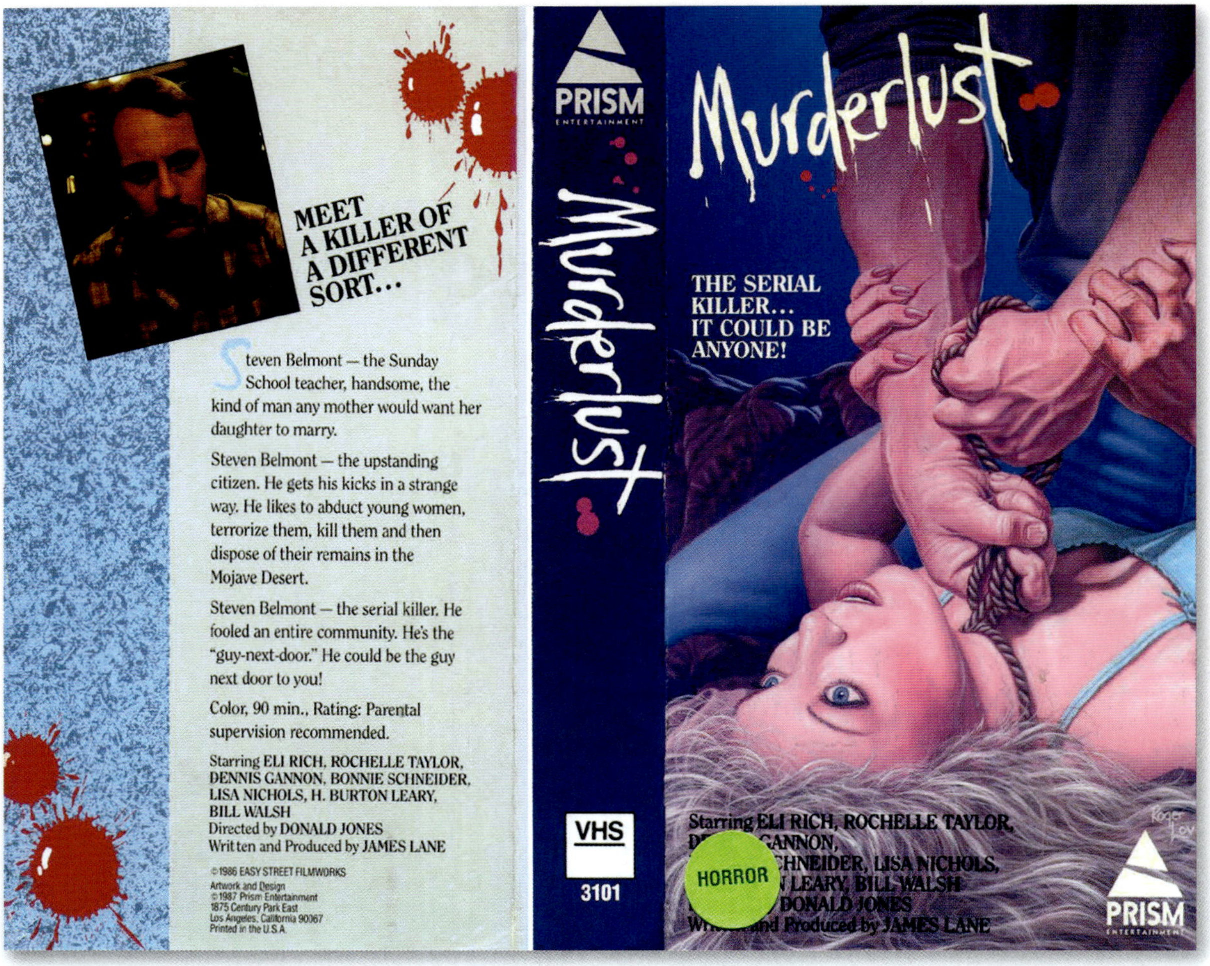

TOP LEFT: Released unrated on video, Tim Ritter's no-budget *Killing Spree* (Twisted Illusions, 1990) starred Asbestos Felt as a paranoid newlywed who believed that his wife was cheating on him. However, when he began murdering her perceived lovers with a ceiling fan, a screwdriver, and a lawnmower, he discovered they wouldn't stay dead. It was shot over twelve days in Florida.

TOP RIGHT: Also released unrated on VHS, *The Scare Game Double Feature* (Tempe Video, 1994) contained two short films written and directed by Eric Stanze. In *The Fine Art*, a woman suspected that her new boyfriend might be the Cedar Hill Slayer, while in Stanze's directorial debut, *The Scare Game*, a demon collected the souls of other dimensional game-players.

BOTTOM LEFT: Following a botched bank robbery attempt, one of the perpetrators took refuge in an abandoned house where he soon discovered he was being haunted by an axe-wielding butcher and his undying horde of mutilated victims in Ronnie Sortor's shot-on-video debut *Singster* (Salt City Home Video, 1998). It was later reissued in a "final cut" as *Sinistre*.

BOTTOM RIGHT: The uncensored "director's cut" of Pete Jacelone's shot-on-video feature debut *Psycho Sisters* (Shock-O-Rama Cinema, 2000) featured never-before-seen deleted material and behind-the-scenes footage. J.J. North and Theresa Lynn starred as sibling serial killers who, upon their release from a psychiatric institute after many years, went on a gruesome murder rampage.

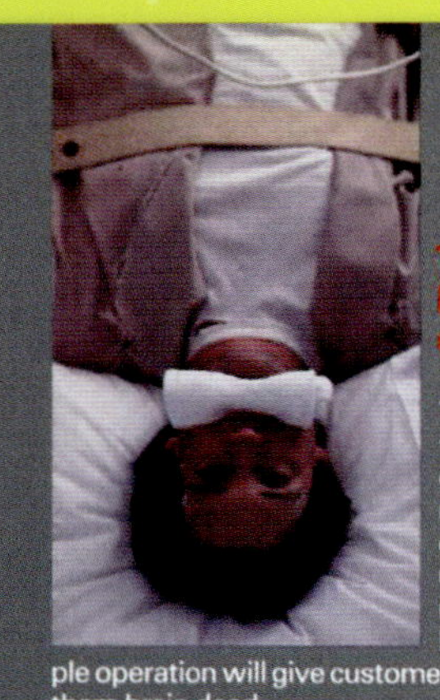

TOP: In the late 1980s, producer Julie Corman asked a number of summer interns at Concorde Pictures/New Horizons to go through hundreds of old scripts. They discovered one written by the late Charles Beaumont for Roger Corman in the 1960s, which Adam Simon liked and updated for his directorial debut as *Brain Dead* (MGM/UA Home Video, 1990), with a nod to H.P. Lovecraft.

BOTTOM: Loosely based on the novel by "Harry Adam Knight" (John Brosnan), Adam Simon's *Carnosaur* (New Horizons Home Video, 1993) was shot in eighteen days on a budget of $850,000. John Carl Buechler used an animatronic puppet and life-sized model to create the dinosaur effects. Released four weeks before *Jurassic Park* (1993), it was followed by two sequels.

When I was growing up in the 1960s and '70s, the very idea that someday movies would be arranged on shelves like books seemed a crazy fantasy. Movies were immaterial dreams even when we managed to see them, and more often we simply dreamed about the unavailable films we longed to see while staring at grainy stills in poorly printed books about them.

The VHS tape and the graphic sleeves they came in were new, magical objects heralding the transformation of films themselves from literally larger-than-life experiences to something you could hold in your hand, and led directly to today's world of more-or-less everything available all of the time. It was a new magic that was also, unbeknownst to us, the beginning of the end of the old magic.

Two memories that encapsulate for me the dark, if tawdry, magic of VHS horrors:

In the 1990s, wandering the overstuffed, labyrinthine aisles of the now long-gone Vidiots in Santa Monica, swooning at the rows of not-exactly-legal VHS copies of gory Italian horror films that I'd only ever dreamed of seeing as a kid in the '70s—Mario Bava, Dario Argento, Lucio Fulci *et al*—and picking out a stack to take home to the literally condemned pile of Gothic California I lived in then, on the crumbling edge of a cliff over the Pacific.

When I see the old VHS art for those films now I can close my eyes and hear the eerie ventriloquism of dubbed dialogue, the postrecorded screams, and the surreal swoon of music by Ennio Morricone, Bruno Nicolai, and others, all blended with the roar of the waves crashing below the house.

Part of the magic of VHS sleeves was what the graphic images of the gaudy sleeves hid: they contained, of course, a minimalist black object—like miniatures of Stanley Kubrick's consciousness-changing black monoliths. And these objects themselves had a kind of creepy aura—for me not separable from the image in David Cronenberg's *Videodrome* (1983) of the fleshy VHS tape inserted into someone's stomach.

My own "videodrome" experience came courtesy of Japan, or rather an early bootlegged and fan-subbed VHS copy of a Japanese film.

While borrowing a friend's flat in London, I found an unlabeled black VHS tape with a note for me saying simply—*Watch this!* Trusting the taste of my host, and his knowledge of my own taste, I inserted the tape into the sucking slot of the VCR and was soon myself sucked into one of the transformative horror films of our time. The *mise en abyme* I fell into, watching an anonymous black videotape about the deadly consequences of watching an anonymous black videotape kept me terrified all night.

There can have been no better way to have first seen Hideo Nakata's *Ringu* (1998).

Sometimes no sleeve is the scariest sleeve of all.

Adam Simon

"IT'S THRILLS AND CHILLS AS BLOOD SPILLS WHEN JIMMY'S GHOST SETS ABOUT ITS FRIGHTFUL REVENGE, HIS KILLERS UNAWARE OF THE GRUESOME FATE THAT AWAITS THEM."

***BONES* VIDEO BOX BLURB (2002)**

ABOVE: Coscripted by Adam Simon and Tim Metcalfe, Ernest Dickerson's *Bones* (New Line Home Entertainment, 2002) starred rapper Snoop Dogg (Calvin Cordozar Broadus, Jr.) as a murdered numbers runner who returned from the dead twenty years later to revenge himself on his killers. The movie costarred "blaxploitation" veteran Pam Grier as Jimmy Bones's former lover.

CONTRIBUTOR BIOS

Peter Atkins was born in Liverpool and now lives in Los Angeles. A founding member of Clive Barker's theater group The Dog Company, he later became an author and screenwriter, with the first three *Hellraiser* sequels (1988–96), *Wishmaster* (1997), and other movies to his credit.

Stephen R. Bissette was a pioneer graduate of the Joe Kubert School (1976–78). His comics work includes DC's *Saga of the Swamp Thing* with writer Alan Moore and inker John Totleben (1983–87), for which he cocreated the character of John Constantine. He now contributes commentary tracks to Blu-rays.

Ramsey Campbell is Britain's most important horror writer and has won multiple awards for his novels and short stories. His early work was influenced by H.P. Lovecraft, but he long ago found his own, unique voice. He has been reviewing movies since the 1960s, and adapted three Universal horror movies into books.

Luigi Cozzi is an Italian film director and screenwriter. A science fiction fan from an early age and a correspondent for *Famous Monsters of Filmland*, his movie credits include *Starcrash* (1978) and *Alien Contamination* (1980). With Dario Argento he co-owns the store Profondo Rosso in Rome.

Joe Dante is another early contributor to *Famous Monsters of Filmland*. After starting out cutting trailers for Roger Corman, he went on to become a major Hollywood screenwriter, producer, and director with *Piranha* (1978), *The Howling* (1981), *Gremlins* (1984), and the sequel *Gremlins 2: The New Batch* (1990).

Barry Forshaw is a leading authority on crime fiction worldwide and writes for various newspapers and magazines. His books include *British Crime Film*, *British Gothic Cinema*, *Italian Cinema*, *Film Noir*, *World Cinema*, and *Sex and Film*. He also contributes booklet essays and commentary tracks to Blu-rays.

Sir Christopher Frayling is former Rector of the Royal College of Art, Chair of Arts Council England, and is currently Professor Emeritus of Cultural History at the RCA. An historian, critic, author, and award-winning broadcaster, he was knighted in 2000 for "services to art and design education."

Mick Garris is a Hollywood director and screenwriter who has frequently collaborated with Stephen King on movies and TV projects. He has also created such shows as *She-Wolf of London* (1990–91), *Masters of Horror* (2005–07), *Fear Itself* (2008–09), and *Post Mortem with Mick Garris* (2010–16).

Graham Humphreys is a British artist and designer who has been creating film posters and video box covers since the early 1980s, best known for his iconic images for *The Evil Dead* and *A Nightmare on Elm Street* series. *Hung, Drawn and Executed: The Horror Art of Graham Humphreys* was published in 2019.

Stephen Jones is an award-winning writer and editor with more than 165 books published. Back in the day he also worked on the first three *Hellraiser* films (1987–92), *Nightbreed* (1990), and such direct-to-video titles as *Night Life* (1989), *Split Second* (1992), *Mind Ripper* (1995), and *Last Gasp* (1995).

C. Courtney Joyner is an award-winning author, scriptwriter, and director, with more than twenty-five screenplays to his credit. Best known for his work for Charles Band's Full Moon Entertainment, he has recorded commentaries, written documentaries, and appeared on more than 200 Blu-ray releases.

Stephen King is the world's most popular and successful horror author. Starting with *Carrie* (1976), many of his novels and short stories have been adapted into movies and TV series, and he has written a number of original screenplays. In 1986 he directed *Maximum Overdrive* for producer Dino De Laurentiis.

Tim Lucas has been writing about films since 1972, and cofounded the critical magazine *Video Watchdog* with his late wife, Donna. His books include the award-winning non-fiction study *Mario Bava: All the Colors of the Dark* and the novels *Throat Sprockets* and *The Man with Kaleidoscope Eyes*.

R.C. Matheson is the son of legendary author and screenwriter Richard Matheson. He has scripted, cocreated, produced, and executive produced numerous movies, TV shows, and miniseries, and is the author of the suspense novel *Created By* and the Hollywood novella *The Ritual of Illusion*.

David McGillivray started out as a UK film journalist and bit-player. His stints working for the magazine *Films and Filming* and the British Film Institute's *Monthly Film Bulletin* led to him writing screenplays for director Pete Walker. His autobiography, *Little Did You Know*, was published in 2019.

Lisa Morton started her career working as a model-maker on *Close Encounters of the Third Kind* (1977) and other movies before going on to write several screenplays and become an award-winning novelist and short story author. Her non-fiction study *The Art of the Zombie Movie* is published by Applause Books.

Kim Newman is a UK author, film critic, and broadcaster. Best known for his series of *Anno Dracula* books, he has written extensively about cinema, including *Nightmare Movies: Horror on Screen Since the 1960s*. He has also recorded commentaries and appeared on hundreds of Blu-ray releases.

David J. Schow is one of the original "Splatterpunk" authors and during the 1990s he wrote a regular column for *Fangoria* magazine. His screenplays include *Leatherface: Texas Chainsaw Massacre III* (1990) and *The Crow* (1994). He contributes essays and commentary tracks to Blu-rays.

Adam Simon began his career with Roger Corman, writing and directing *Brain Dead* (1990) and *Carnosaur* (1993). He also wrote and directed the Samuel Fuller documentary *The Typewriter, the Rifle & the Movie Camera* (1996) and cocreated and executive produced the WGN TV series *Salem* (2014–17).

Brinke Stevens is one of the original "Scream Queens." Her first major screen role was in *The Slumber Party Massacre* (1982), executive produced by Roger Corman. Since then she has been in more than 200 movies. More recently, she directed *Sorority Babes in the Slimeball Bowl-O-Rama 2* (2022).

OPPOSITE: Better than having a second TV set in your home back in 1978 was JVC's top-loading VHS Home TV Recording System, which allowed the user to record up to three hours on a single cassette while watching a different program on another channel.

TITLE INDEX

TV's most entertaining hours. Yours to enjoy time and time again...
JVC
with a JVC VHS
3 hour Colour
TV/Video Recorder...
With JVC/VHS a new dimension is added to your existing colour TV set. Now, with JVC's VHS Home TV Recording System, the whole world of TV entertainment is yours to keep and view, time and again. In the past, you often had to forego programmes you wanted to see – either because of other commitments, or because someone else wanted to watch another channel. Sometimes, two of your favourite programmes were on at the same time on separate channels. Or you were watching something special and friends dropped in, or the phone rang. Now with JVC/VHS you can record the programme of your choice, to view it whenever it suits you. So, no more viewing dilemmas for you and your family.
FEATURING • The versatile VHS system – originated and developed by JVC plays up to full 3 hours on a single cassette (also available 2 hour; 1 hour ; ½ hour cassettes) • Easy connectability to VHS-socket of your existing TV receiver • Records TV programmes as you view them • Records TV programmes as you view a different programme • Records TV programmes when you're absent, with the 24-hour built-in timer • Pause control – prevents recording of unwanted material • Audio dubbing control – permits replacement or addition of sound track on previously recorded tapes • Video in/out jacks to enable recording from one VHS to another • An electronic TV tuner • Digital tape counter – aids in locating any particular tape section • Search control – easy, automatic rewinding of the tape to any pre-determined point • Attractively harmonizing, compact, lightweight design • Low power consumption of only 35 watts • Covered by 12 months' warranty.
Simulated TV Picture.
The recording of television programmes is permissable only where copyright or other rights of third parties are not infringed. This advertisement should not be taken as authorising the recording of copyright material.
It's better than having a second colour TV set in your home... much better!
For further information contact: JVC/VHS Division, P.O. Box 307, North Ryde, N.S.W. 2113
972
JVC VHS
is the right choice!

ART CREDITS

Key: b=bottom; c=center; l=left; r=right; t=top; br=bottom right; bl-bottom left; tr=top right; tl=top left; tc=top center

Cover: Recreation UK poster artwork for *Return of the Living Dead* copyright © Graham Humphreys 2012; Frontispiece: copyright © Graham Humphreys p2; Detail of *Blood Feast* half-sheet (Box Office Spectaculars, 1963) pp4–5; US video box cover for *The Black Castle* (MCA Home Video, 1995) p6; Detail of US *Frankenstein* title lobby card (Universal, 1931) pp18–19; US video box cover for *Dracula's Daughter* (MCA Home Video, 1992) p25; US video box cover for *The Black Cat* (Universal Home Video, 1998) p28; Detail of *Brain of Blood/Vampire People* combo one-sheet by Gray Morrow (Hemisphere Pictures, 1972) pp38–39; US video box cover for *Blood of Ghastly Horror* (Super Video, 1984) p48; Detail of UK *Creepshow* quad by Tom Chantrell (Alpha, 1982) pp58–59; Detail of Belgian *Dracula Has Risen from the Grave* poster (Warner Bros.-Seven Arts, 1969) pp78–79; US video box cover for *Brides of Dracula* (MCA Universal Home Video, 1992) p.84; Spanish video box cover for *Frankenstein and the Monster from Hell* by Rafael Cortiella Juancomarti p.89; Detail of US *Robot Monster* half-sheet (Astor Pictures, 1953) pp98–99; US video box cover for *Tarantula* (MCA Universal Home Video, 1993) p110l; US video box cover for *The Monolith Monsters* (MCA Universal Home Video, 1994) p111r; US video box cover for *Godzilla, King of the Monsters* (Paramount/Gateway, 1992) p114bl; Detail of original art for US *Dollman vs. Demonic Toys* poster (Paramount/Full Moon Entertainment, 1993) pp118–119; US poster art used to promote *Inhuman/Shadow Over Innsmouth* (Empire Pictures, 1986) p136; Detail of US *Black Sunday* half-sheet (American International Pictures, 1961) pp138–139; Preliminary artwork for Spanish video box of *Virgin Among the Living Dead* (Hobby Video, 1987) p154l; Detail of *Yûrei yashiki no kyôfu: Chi wo sû ningyô* (aka The Vampire Doll) poster (Toho, 1970) pp158–159; Ghanaian poster for *Hellraiser* by Heavy J p174tl; Ghanaian poster for *Hellbound: Hellraiser II* by artist Papa Warsti p174tr; Ghanaian poster for *Hellraiser III: Hell on Earth* by Joe Mensah p174br; Detail of Ghanaian poster for *Hellraiser III: Hell on Earth* by Leonardo p175tl; Ghanaian poster for *Fist of the North Star* by Leonardo p175tc; Ghanaian poster for *Wishmaster 2: Evil Never Dies* p175tr; Detail of UK *House by the Cemetery* quad by Enzo Sciotti (Eagle Films, 1981) pp178–179; Detail of US *Hollywood Chainsaw Hookers* poster (Camp Motion Pictures, 1988) pp198–199. Every effort has been made to trace the copyright holders of artworks in this book. Elephant Books would be happy if contacted to correct any errors or omissions in future editions.

COVER: Graham Humphreys was not happy with his original video sleeve painting for Vestron Video International's 1983 release of Dan O'Bannon's *Return of the Living Dead* (see page 69), so in 2012 he recreated the art for a special screening event held at a cinema in London. The artist produced yet another design for the movie's US Blu-ray release in 2016.

SPINE: Graham Humphreys's spine logo for First Independent Films' series of "First Fright" video releases in the UK in 1991.

RIGHT: This Video Game Authority (VGA) slabbed and graded copy of the 1983 CBS/Fox Video drawer box for *Star Wars* is one of only two originally sealed copies known to exist. It sold at auction in February 2023 for $32,500 including buyer's premium.

ENDPAPERS: The VHS spines from the boxed set of Ted Newsom's thirteen-part documentary series *100 Years of Horror* (Passport Video, 1996), which mostly included clips from trailers and was hosted by Christopher Lee.

ACKNOWLEDGMENTS

Thanks to the following, who all helped in the creation of this volume: Adam Newell, Paul Palmer-Edwards, Sharon Gosling, Mandy Slater, Heritage Auctions, Monster Brains, Michael Marshall Smith, Peter Coleborn, VHS Wasteland, and especially to Joe Dante for his terrific Foreword, Graham Humphreys for his artwork, and all those guest contributors who were kind enough to share their "video memories" with us. Special thanks go to Stephen R. Bissette, Randy and Sara Broecker, Amanda Foubister, and Kim Newman for supplying additional images and information for this book.

Numerous sources were consulted during the compilation of this work, too many to list here, but I would like to acknowledge *From Betamax to Blockbuster: Video Stores and the Invention of Movies on Video* by Joshua M. Greenberg (Massachusetts Institute of Technology, 2008); *Shock! Horror!: Astounding Artwork from the Video Nasty Era* (FAB Press, 2005) by Francis Brewster, Harvey Fenton, and Marc Morris; and *Empire of the 'B's: The Mad Movie World of Charles Band* (Hemlock Books, 2013) by Dave Jay, Torsten Dewi, and Nathan Shumate.

Dracula & The Vampires

VS 5401

Frankenstein

VS 5402

Double Demons

VS 5403

The Gruesome Twosome

VS 5404

Ghosts & Phantoms

VS 5405

Witches & Demons

VS 5406